Hiring, Firing and Discipline for Employers

First print.

This publication is available from:
American Chamber of Commerce Resources, LLC
1033 S Claremont Ave
Chicago, IL 60603
(866) 439-2227
hrsimple.com

Price: For information on ordering, including quantity discounts and distribution arrangements, contact American Chamber of Commerce Resources at (866) 439-2227.

RAA

This book and the entire Human Resources Library, is dedicated to Dick Apland, who spoke his piece, shared a piece and was at peace. Thanks Dad.

About FordHarrison LLP

Today organizations must operate in a highly regulated, litigious business climate. However, employers are able to minimize the legal risks involved in making employment decisions without compromising business needs.

Founded in Atlanta in 1978, FordHarrison has built a national practice in all aspects of labor and employment law with offices across the country. More than 200 labor and employment lawyers at the firm strive to provide clients with sound legal advice, practical counseling and excellent client service.

FordHarrison is committed to providing assistance to employers to allow their management teams to successfully deal with increased litigation, government agency investigations, collective bargaining or union organizing drives by helping to provide the necessary knowledge and insight to deal with these issues.

We concentrate our practice on all areas related to labor and employment law – including employment litigation and class actions, business immigration and employee benefits – so our clients gain from in-depth legal experience in all facets of these issues. We provide current, relevant information to our clients through a variety of resources, such as our *SourceBook,* newsletters, seminars and briefings. These resources provide valuable preventive maintenance tools to help clients understand the numerous state and federal labor and employment laws.

About the editors

Frank L. Day is a management side labor and employment attorney in the Memphis office of FordHarrison, LLP. He has more than 10 years of experience helping his clients accomplish their business objectives through employment law counseling and litigation. Frank has successfully represented employers across the country in cases alleging discrimination, wrongful discharge, retaliation, etc. He has extensive litigation experience in many different forums where he has helped clients prevail on summary judgment, at trial and on appeal. Frank frequently serves as a faculty member at employment law seminars and he has published a number of scholarly articles in publications such as the *ABA Employment Law Newsletter*, the *Tennessee Bar Journal*, the *University of Memphis Law Review* and *The Federalist*. Frank is licensed to practice in Tennessee, Arkansas and Kentucky.

Mollie K. Wildmann is licensed in both Tennessee and Arkansas, defending employers against a variety of claims, including discrimination, harassment, and retaliation under Title VII, the Americans with Disabilities Act, and the Family and Medical Leave Act, as well as claims brought under the Fair Labor Standards Act. She also has a focus in the area of traditional labor law, assisting clients in a variety of matters including collective bargaining negotiations, responses to unfair labor practice charges before the National Labor Relations Board, assisting clients responding to union organizing campaigns, and preparing post-arbitration briefs.

Regardless of the problem or issue, Mollie will get to know clients on both a personal and professional level as she believes this helps her focus on their specific needs while working in partnership with them to obtain desired outcomes unique to the client's business goals..

Editors' foreword

Today's marketplace holds few constants. But there is one certainty: every company, no matter the size, possesses only one true advantage over its competition and that is its people.

On any given day, the operations, manufacturing processes, products and distribution methods, even well laid marketing campaigns can be copied with relative ease.

But no amount of imitation can duplicate the workforce. How this unique resource is managed will determine the success or failure of an organization.

Therefore, in order for a company to achieve a competitive advantage it must hire the right people. Once hired, an employer needs to create an environment in which those new hires will be successful. This is not easy. It requires effective management practices, which must also be in compliance with the laws of the United States and applicable state law.

This book will help ensure that employment practices are legal. Frank Day and Mollie Wildmann are management attorneys with FordHarrison, LLP. They represent employers on employment related matters, including wage and hour disputes, discrimination claims, investigations by government agencies, including the Department of Labor (DOL) and Equal Employment Opportunity Commission (EEOC) and their state-agency equivalents and provide counseling on all types of employment practices and policies. Frank and Mollie undertook the task of compiling and editing the federal and state employment laws in this that affect hiring, firing and discipline.

Chapter table of contents

Table of contents

Chapter

01

Snapshot – An HR audit

The following list of questions should serve as an introduction to a number of fundamental employment law concepts and the answers to each question will enable users to determine if "best practices" generally are being followed. Of course, this list of questions will not ensure full compliance with all laws and regulations that govern the employer-employee relationship, but it is a good starting point. If a "no" answer to any of the following questions is provided, use the page number reference to understand why the answer is "no" to assess whether or not there are any violations of the law within the workplace. This page of questions is provided as quick reference and introduction.

Yes	No		Page
❑	❑	Does the company have a regularly updated employee handbook and does it state that employment is not guaranteed?	69
❑	❑	Are hiring managers aware of what questions can and cannot be asked of job applicants?	22
❑	❑	Are medical examinations given to applicants only after the employment offer, and are they given to all applicants in the job category?	47
❑	❑	What should and should not be asked of references?	57
❑	❑	Is there a discipline policy and do supervisors understand it and apply it consistently?	77
❑	❑	Should job descriptions be utilized?	4
❑	❑	Is the company prepared to respond to union-organizing activity?	203
❑	❑	Do supervisors and managers know when a company can be sued for negligent retention or supervision of an employee?	194
❑	❑	What laws protect whistleblowers?	133-137, 193

Chapter 02

Pre-employment issues

Before a hiring decision is made, a position description should be written clearly defining exactly the type of individual who will meet the criteria of the job and the culture of the department and the company.

The content of a job advertisement

Federal law prohibits an employer from using a job advertisement that limits or prefers applicants based upon:

- race
- color
- religion
- sex (which includes gender identity or expression and sexual orientation)
- national origin
- age.

State laws also may contain similar or additional restrictions. For instance, some states, such as New Jersey, have enacted a prohibition against employers excluding individuals who are currently unemployed from consideration for employment.

Under Title VII of the Civil Rights Act (Title VII) and the Age Discrimination in Employment Act (ADEA), an employer may indicate a preference based upon religion, sex, national origin or age if it is a "bona fide occupational qualification" (BFOQ) for employment. This exception is limited.

> **Example**
> In certain situations, a prison may establish a BFOQ and only hire employees that are the same gender as the prison inmates.

There is no BFOQ exception for race or color preferences.

Some employers, including certain federal contractors, may be required to include the notation "equal opportunity employer" on job advertisements.

The Americans with Disabilities Act (ADA) does not require employers to actively recruit individuals with disabilities. However, an employer may not engage in recruitment activities that exclude candidates with disabilities and should make information about job openings available to people with disabilities.

The content of a job description

Managers and employees should be involved in writing job descriptions because they possess the most knowledge. Provide them with a job analysis questionnaire that asks for information such as the following:

- What is the overall purpose of the job? This will provide a job summary.
- What are the essential functions of the job and the percent of time devoted to the tasks? A good definition of "essential functions" should be included.
- Information regarding the physical, visual, mental and audible demands of the job needs to be identified and included in the description in order to comply with the ADA.
- Attached is a sample of a typical job analysis questionnaire and job description.

A sample job description form can be found on the following page.

Legal qualifications for employment

Any required qualification for employment is unlawful if it has an "adverse impact" on any protected group and disproportionately eliminates more applicants in a protected group from consideration than a non-protected group, unless the employer can prove that the requirement is job-related and consistent with business necessity. For instance, a requirement that an applicant have a high school diploma may disproportionately exclude certain racial groups. Similarly, if an employer refuses to consider applicants with extensive prior experience because the employer believes the applicants are overqualified, the employer may be accused of unlawfully screening applicants based on age.

Legal issues may arise if an employer considers the following factors or uses the following requirements when evaluating job applicants:

- arrest record and/or conviction record
- weight-lifting ability
- minimum height and weight requirements
- maximum weight requirements
- garnishment history, credit rating and bankruptcy
- minimum educational requirements
- grooming requirements
- citizenship
- language requirements.

JOB ANALYSIS QUESTIONNAIRE

General Instructions

Please read each question carefully before answering it. Make all your answers as complete and as clear as possible.

Employee's Name: ______________________________

Employee's Job Title: ______________________________

Department: ______________________________

Supervisor's Name: ______________________________

Supervisor's Job Title: ______________________________

JOB DUTIES

BASIC JOB SUMMARY

In a few sentences, summarize the overall purpose of the employee's job. You might begin by saying, "The overall purpose of this job is to ... "

____

____

____

____

____

ESSENTIAL JOB FUNCTIONS – GUIDELINES

In the table beginning below, please list the essential functions of the job. The term "essential functions" means fundamental job duties that are intrinsic to the job. For instance, a job function may be considered essential for any of several reasons, including the following:

1. **Reason the job exists:** For example, if a person is hired as a company driver, the ability to drive would then be an essential function since it is the primary reason the job exists.

2. **Time performing the function:** The amount of time spent performing a particular function may give you a clue as to whether or not it is essential. If an administrative assistant spends 75% of their time typing, then typing is probably an essential function.

Those duties that the employee is responsible for doing during the absence of another employee or those that are only marginal functions of the position should be included under "Other Job Functions."

For the following table of essential functions, number each function and estimate the percent of time each major area takes daily. **Most importantly, please describe the functions in a**

way that will be clear to someone who does not understand this type of work. Please be as specific as possible.

DESCRIPTION OF ESSENTIAL FUNCTIONS	% OF TIME

OTHER JOB FUNCTIONS

Please list below the job duties and responsibilities that are only marginal functions of the job. **Again, describe each function specifically and in a way that will be clear to someone who does not understand this type of work.**

____

____

____

What is the most difficult part of this job? ______________________

____

____

JOB REQUIREMENTS

A. **Formal Training** – How much education is necessary for competent performance in this position?

____

____

B. **Years of Experience** – How much job-related experience is typically needed to perform this job at a competent level?

____

____

C. **Special Skills/Knowledge** – Any skills or special knowledge needed to perform this job?

____

____

D. **Mental Demands** – What does the employee have to concentrate on to perform the job?

____

____

E. **Physical Demands** – What are the physical demands, i.e. walking, lifting (how much), bending, sitting?

____

____

F. **Responsibility for Guidance of Others** – How many employees does this person supervise directly or indirectly? What type of worker is supervised?

____

____

G. **Supervision Received** – What amount of supervision does the job normally require, such as, frequent too little or none? Which task requires most supervision?

____

____

H. **Responsibility for Accuracy** – What are the typical kinds of errors made? Who checks the employee's work? What would be the effect of such errors, if not detected?

____

____

I. **Judgment and Decisions** – What kind of independent decisions does the employee make? What decision can the employee make without referral to the supervisor? Does employee have decision to approve or reject?

____

____

J. **Personal Contacts** – What contacts with other people is the employee required to make other than with co-workers and the immediate superior? Who does the employee talk to **outside** of the company? Who does the employee talk to relative to business inside the company?

____

____

K. **Audible Demands** – Does this job require hearing? If so, give examples:

____

____

L. **Visual Demands** – Does this job require vision? If so, give examples:

____

____

COMPANY USE JOB DESCRIPTION

JOB TITLE: Human Resources Representative

FLSA: Non-exempt

REPORTS TO: Director of Human Resources

DEPARTMENT: Human Resources

JOB PURPOSE: Primarily responsible for assisting the Human Resources Director with departmental activities including administration of benefits plans. Serves as the initial contact for HR concerns company-wide including satellite plants.

ESSENTIAL JOB FUNCTIONS:

1. Maintains and expands knowledge and understanding of existing and proposed federal and state laws/regulations affecting human resources management.
2. Prepares salaries and hourly employee performance evaluation forms and distributes to appropriate supervisors and managers monthly. Upon receipt of completed forms, enters pay increase into payroll system and updates review schedule.
3. Completes and processes payroll change notices for various departmental changes, shift changes, job changes, time off for bereavement, vacation, longevity days and the like. Receives and resolves payroll issues for all company locations.
4. Coordinates with health insurance carrier and medical providers to resolve employee claims issues. Participates in benefit administration to include claims resolution and change reporting.
5. Prepares and generates absentee/turnover and other special reports pertaining to employee personnel information and data for all company locations.
6. Manages annual open enrollment for health and welfare plans, including arrangement of distribution of materials from carriers, communication of changes to employees and on-site representation by providers. Processes changes within deadlines. Processes 401(k) enrollments, loans, rollover and withdrawal requests.
7. Administers, in conjunction with other department members, the company's self-funded Short-Term Disability program. Ensures disabled employees are paid benefits at the correct rate.
8. Assists Human Resources Director in development of personnel policies and procedures. Writes, revises, edits and proofreads company procedures manual and employee handbook.
9. Participates in preparation of annual departmental budget under the direction of Human Resources Manager.
10. Plans and implements special events planning for company functions including, but not limited to the annual picnic, service awards, Employee Appreciation Day, holiday meals,

etc. Administers other special programs including company scholarship program, education program and employee morale programs.

11. Maintains knowledge of and compliance to, all Company rules and Code of Ethics.

12. Attendance at work, including presence at work during regular work hours or other schedule as may be assigned by the department manager, is essential. Acceptance of overtime assignments may also be required in order to meet department goals and objectives.

OTHER JOB FUNCTIONS:

1. Performs other various assignments including, but not limited to: verification of employment, administration of safety shoe and safety glasses reimbursement program, coordination of selection of Employee of the Month, creation of time cards for new employees ordering flowers as needed, creation and distribution of monthly [Company] calendar and administration of the uniform rental program.

2. Performs other various duties as may be assigned.

REQUIREMENTS:

Knowledge - Should possess excellent oral/written communication skills for internal/external relations with others, including good listening skills and willingness to work directly with office and plant employees on a daily basis; must possess the ability to treat employees with respect while dealing with them in a firm, fair and consistent manner without personal bias; understand general arithmetic; understand data processing applications including Microsoft Word and Excel; basic knowledge of business and accounting practices (knowledge usually acquired through two years of college or combination of course study and two to four years Human Resources experience).

Mental - Requires a relatively high degree of concentration intermittently to compile reports and analyze data approximately 50% of time; periods of mental effort and concentration followed by other aspects of the job with lesser concentration and attention requirements.

Physical - Requires walking/standing approximately 20%, sitting approximately 80% and lifting up to 15 lbs. approximately 1% of time; involves repetitive stooping, forward bending and crouching approximately 10% of time.

Manual Dexterity - Requires use of hands, arms and feet for repetitive lifting; use of hands and arms to operate computers, typewriters, time clocks, adding machines, copy machines and other general office equipment and to record written information.

Audible Demands - Requires ability to hear verbal instructions and to communicate with internal departments and outside sources in person and via telephone.

Visual Demands - Requires ability to read written instructions, correspondence and other documentation as well as operate office equipment such as computers and printers. Color and depth perception not necessary.

Environmental - Requires capability of performing essential job functions in an established office environment under lighting and climate control tolerances, with some exposure to plant environments with the presence of dust, fumes, noise and fluctuating temperatures due to lack of climate control.

NOTE: SUPERCEDES ALL PRECEDING JOB DESCRIPTIONS

The previous job description is intended to describe the general content, identify the essential job functions and set forth the requirements for the performance of this job. It is not to be construed as an exhaustive statement of job functions or requirements.

APPROVALS:

______________________________ ______________
Supervisor/Manager Date

______________________________ ______________
Second Level Supervisor/Manager Date

______________________________ ______________
Staff Member Date

______________________________ ______________
Human Resources Representative Date

This job description has been reviewed, accepted and/or changed by the following person:

REVIEWED BY: ______________________________ DATE: __________

REVIEWED BY: ______________________________ DATE: __________

Arrest and conviction records

Increasingly, employers are facing the dilemma of how extensively they should prescreen an applicant's criminal background. On the one hand, they wish to avoid negligent hiring suits for an employee's violent or harassing behavior. On the other hand, they fear accusations of discrimination.

The EEOC and many courts have taken the position that policies precluding the hiring of applicants with arrest records result in discrimination against minorities, because a greater percentage of minorities tend to have arrest records than do non-minorities. Additionally, a majority of states, as well as cities and counties have enacted laws, referred to as "ban-the box laws," requiring that public entities refrain from asking about conviction records on job applications. Many states, including California, Colorado, Connecticut, Delaware, Georgia, Hawaii, Illinois, Maryland, Massachusetts, Minnesota, Nebraska, New Jersey, New Mexico, Oregon, Rhode Island and Vermont, have laws requiring private employers to remove criminal history questions from job applications. These laws differ as to when in the hiring process an employer may seek information regarding an applicant's conviction records.

In November of 2018, the EEOC issued Enforcement Guidance regarding the use of arrest and conviction records. This guidance provides that "in some instances," use of an applicant's criminal history may violate federal law prohibiting employment discrimination.

The EEOC, echoing previous guidance regarding an employer's use of criminal history, continues to assert that arrest records are not proof of criminal conduct (although the existence of an arrest may "trigger an inquiry into whether the conduct underlying the arrest justifies an adverse employment action"). On that basis, if it appears that the applicant or employee actually engaged in the conduct for which he or she was arrested, the conduct is job-related and the conduct occurred relatively recently, then the employer may be justified in excluding the applicant/employee. However, the EEOC continues to assert that an employer's exclusion of an applicant based solely on an arrest record is not job-related and is inconsistent with business necessity.

To the contrary, the guidance states that an employer may consider a conviction (as opposed to an arrest) as conclusive evidence that a person has committed the crime alleged. After considering all of the circumstances, if the employer reasonably concludes that the applicant's or employee's conduct is evidence that he or she is not suitable to perform the duties of the position in question, the employer may reject or terminate that person. In all cases, a "criminal conduct exclusion" must be job-related and consistent with business necessity. Thus, employers who refuse to hire an applicant because of an applicant's criminal history records may later be required to show in a discrimination suit that the criminal conduct directly diminished the applicant's suitability to perform the job.

Because an applicant might not truthfully reveal his or her arrest or conviction record and depending on the position and the employer's needs, it may be prudent to check outside sources. The three most common methods are:

1. contacting the applicant's references (past employers)

2. contacting law enforcement agencies or reviewing court records in locations where the applicant has spent time, such as places where he or she went to school, had other jobs and the like, as disclosed on the employment application

3. hiring a private investigator or agency to perform a background check.

Because some of these investigative methods may be unlawful or require certain disclosures to the applicant under federal law, counsel should be consulted before adopting any investigative method other than job reference checks. For instance, as stated previously, an employer's inquiries into or access to criminal or arrest record information may be unlawful or severely restricted. Criminal, credit and other types of background checks performed by third parties are usually subject to the requirements of the Fair Credit Reporting Act (FCRA). Further, some state laws may limit or restrict an employer's ability to make such inquiries.

Under the EEOC Enforcement Guidance discussed previously, when an arrest or conviction record is revealed the issue of "job-relatedness and business necessity" arises – that is, whether the conduct underlying the arrest makes the applicant unfit for the position. An employer can establish this in two ways:

1. by being formally validated under the Uniform Guidelines on Employee Selection Procedures

2. by performing "targeted screens" such as an individualized assessment of the applicant's criminal history using the following three considerations:

    - the nature and gravity of the offense

    - the time that has passed since the arrest

    - the nature of the position sought.

Employers utilizing "targeted screens" should carefully consider these elements to determine whether a business justification exists to exclude the applicant from employment based on the arrest or conviction. The EEOC's policy guidance also provides that any individualized assessment will consist of a notice to the individual and an opportunity to demonstrate that the exclusion should not be applied, as well as consideration by the employer as to whether the additional information provided by the individual warrants an exception to the exclusion.

Weight-lifting ability requirements

Designating a job as "male only" because it requires lifting heavy weights or similar strenuous activity violates Title VII. A requirement that an employee be able to lift a certain minimum weight may also be unlawful because it may have an adverse impact on women. If the requirement does have an adverse impact, the employer must show that the requirement is job-related and consistent with business necessity. In some cases, the employer must also show that less restrictive alternatives are not acceptable. Weight-lifting requirements may also create issues under the ADA. Employers may need to accommodate applicants who cannot meet the weight-lifting requirements because of a disability.

Height and weight requirements

A requirement that employees be a certain height or weight may have an adverse impact on women, since women are statistically shorter and lighter than men. Such requirements may also have an adverse impact on certain nationalities or other protected groups and could be determined to be unlawful unless the employer can prove that the minimum height or weight is job-related and consistent with business necessity. In some cases, the employer must also show that less restrictive alternatives are not acceptable.

Employers sometimes utilize policies excluding obese individuals from employment due to asserted health or insurance risks. Such policies may be unlawful. In some cases, individuals who are obese may be protected by the ADA. Additionally, an employer may not explicitly apply different indicators of physical attractiveness to burden one gender disproportionately.

Garnishment, credit rating and bankruptcy

Most states have enacted laws restricting an employer's ability to make employment decisions based upon garnishment of an employee's wages. Additionally, individuals with one or more garnishments of one debt are protected from discharge under Title III of the Consumer Credit Protection Act. Under Title VII, employers may be found to have discriminated if they refuse to hire a person solely due to bad credit references because racial minorities may not be accorded the same advantageous credit status that is often given to non-minorities. Unless a potential employer is prepared to demonstrate the job-relatedness of credit inquiries, credit standing alone should not be the basis for denying employment. If the applicant is applying for a position in which serious credit problems would adversely affect job performance, such as an accounting position, an employer might be able to demonstrate the job-related necessity of such a requirement. Federal law also prohibits employment discrimination "solely because" an individual has:

- sought protection under the Bankruptcy Act
- been insolvent before seeking protection under the act
- not paid a debt that is dischargeable under the act.

Educational requirements

The EEOC and most federal courts do not favorably view employer attempts to require a high school diploma or college degree from a job applicant unless doing so is job-related and consistent with business necessity. Due to historical discrimination and limited educational opportunities for some minority groups and older persons, statistics may show that a greater percentage of these persons lack formal educational achievement. Again, the employer must be prepared to show that the requirement is job-related and consistent with business necessity. In some cases, the employer must also show that a less restrictive alternative is not acceptable. The EEOC and the courts have required employers to show that a degree or diploma accurately demonstrates a suitability to perform the task in question and that all - or substantially all - of the applicants who do not have this diploma or degree are unable to perform the task.

Grooming requirements

Grooming requirements are generally lawful. However, depending upon the circumstances, the law may require an employer to modify them for certain individuals. Some grooming requirements have been challenged on the grounds that they discriminate against individuals based on sex, religion or disability. If an employee sincerely holds a religious belief that conflicts with an employer's grooming requirements, the employer will be required to "reasonably accommodate" the employee's religious belief unless such accommodation would impose an "undue hardship" on the employer. Examples of "reasonable accommodation" in this context might include allowing employees with long hair to work with masks or hairnets or assigning such employees to jobs in which a grooming requirement is not necessary for safety reasons.

Employers should also be aware that some states, including California, Illinois, Kentucky, Maryland (Montgomery County), Michigan, New Jersey, New York, Ohio (Akron, Cincinnati and Toledo), Wisconsin, Virginia, are moving toward an interpretation of racial discrimination laws by which they encompass discrimination based upon hair. Thus, to the extent an employer has a provision in its employee manual or elsewhere that sets forth restrictions as to grooming hair, including restrictions as to length or style or volume, it should consider removing such provision, or, at a minimum, revising it, to ensure that it is not applied in a discriminatory manner.

Citizenship requirements

The Immigration Reform and Control Act (IRCA) prohibits discrimination against citizens and "intending" citizens. While the IRCA makes it unlawful to hire an illegal immigrant or anyone else who is not authorized to work and cannot produce proof of identity and work authorization, it specifically prohibits discrimination on the basis of citizenship status. Therefore, a job requirement of U.S. citizenship is unlawful. Furthermore, while adoption of a citizenship requirement is not prohibited under Title VII, having such a requirement could violate the act's prohibition of race, color or national origin discrimination under a disparate impact theory.

Language requirements

In many localities, requiring employees to be fluent in spoken or written English could have an "adverse impact" on protected groups. In such situations, requiring employees to speak and write English may be unlawful unless the employer can show that fluency in English is job-related and consistent with business necessity. In some cases, the employer must also show that a less restrictive alternative is not acceptable for the job in question. The EEOC takes the position English-only rules applied at all times violate Title VII. Some courts have followed the EEOC guidelines, although others have not.

The content of an employment application

Employment applications and interviews are the starting point for gathering information about prospective employees. In designing a job application form, employers should strive for questions that will result in securing complete, accurate and useful information about the applicant and his or her qualifications for the position.

Format

First, the employer should consider whether the question is one that is prohibited by law, such as one that discriminates against or adversely impacts a protected group. Second, the employer should determine whether the information requested is necessary for the hiring decision. An employer should keep in mind it may be required to justify the inquiry at some time in the future. Third, if an employer must ask questions that might be viewed as discriminatory, such as medical questions, it should obtain this data after a conditional offer of employment has been made or after the person has been hired. All medical information, including drug-testing information, should always be kept in a separate file from the employee's personnel information.

Nondiscrimination statement

Many employment application forms contain language asserting that the employer is an equal employment opportunity employer and does not discriminate. Some employers may be under an affirmative action obligation that requires a statement of nondiscrimination. Because the employment discrimination laws vary from state to state and because state legislatures frequently enact new laws that prohibit additional categories of discrimination, the employer's form should be reviewed so that any nondiscrimination statement refers to all prohibited forms of discrimination.

Disabled applicants

When providing a candidate with an employment application, an employer should ensure that applicants with disabilities have an opportunity to fill out the application. This may involve making a reasonable accommodation, such as helping an individual with a visual impairment complete the application form.

"Active" status

To reduce the likelihood of legal claims when a position is filled long after an application was received from an unsuccessful applicant, it may be beneficial for the application form to include a statement that forms are only considered active for a specified period of time, such as 30 days.

> **Note:**
> Federal laws may require the employer to retain applications for a specific period of time. Even those applications that are no longer active must be retained for the legally mandated timeframe.

Reference authorization

The application should include authorization to obtain information from all former employers, educational institutions and other references mentioned on the form. A general indemnification for and release of liability arising out of such inquiries should also be included in the authorization. It is also possible to have applicants sign specific releases for each of their former employers, which may increase the likelihood of obtaining accurate and detailed references.

Dishonesty

The application form should prominently state that misstatements or omissions on the application may result in a failure to hire or in immediate discharge when discovered by the employer. An employer should consider including the following statement in bold letters: "I understand that any misstatements or omissions in this application will result in a decision not to hire me or to discharge me if discovered after I am hired."

After-acquired evidence of dishonesty on a job application

In a 1995 case, the U.S. Supreme Court held that evidence of employee misconduct discovered after a discriminatory and unlawful discharge is not a complete restriction to recovering damages. The after-acquired evidence must be considered, however, when determining the appropriate remedy for the discriminatory discharge. As a general rule, when an employer belatedly discovers that an employee engaged in misconduct of such severity that the employee could have been lawfully discharged for the misconduct, the employee may only recover back pay from the date of the unlawful discharge to the date the employer discovered the misconduct. Additionally, such an employee is not entitled to reinstatement.

Employment at-will disclaimer

Employers should consider stating in the application that the employment is at-will (in those states that recognize employment at-will) and may be terminated for any reason. The application should also state that any change in the at-will nature of the employment is not valid unless it is in writing and signed by the president or certain other officers of the company. However, complete reliance should not be placed on clauses expressly noting the at-will nature of employment, as some courts have held that such disclaimers can be set aside if there is evidence of supplemental oral and/or written assurances of continued employment.

Arbitration provision

Employers should also consider including a mandatory employment dispute arbitration provision in the employment application or utilizing a separate arbitration agreement as part of the application process. (Specific requirements in this regard depend upon the jurisdiction at issue. Local, federal and state law should be consulted before attempting to implement mandatory arbitration. Notably, employers such as Facebook and Google recently ended forced arbitration for certain claims.) These agreements increasingly include waivers of the employee's right to a collective or class action. Courts have generally found these waivers to be enforceable. These agreements also may prevent employees from litigating their claims to a jury and reduce the cost of defending lawsuits. Arbitration may, however, increase the number of claims because it is less expensive for the employee than litigation. It may also reduce available procedures to the employer, such as an appeal of an adverse decision.

Jury waiver provision

Employers who have not been satisfied with arbitration agreements may want to consider implementing a jury waiver agreement as an alternative dispute resolution tool.

Used as an alternative dispute resolution tool, the employer requires employees to sign a jury waiver agreement as a condition of employment. The agreement could be included in the employment application. Under a jury waiver agreement, employees retain all substantive and procedural rights to sue their employers, except the right to request a jury. Instead, they agree to have their claims tried before a judge, who is the ultimate decision maker. The judge decides all motions as if the case were ultimately being tried to a jury. All possible remedies remain available to the employee; the only difference is that the risk of one juror running amok and convincing the rest to go along is eliminated if the waiver is enforced. If the judge errs in making a judgment, appeals are subject to full review – just as in jury cases. This is a key difference between decisions under jury waiver agreements and arbitration decisions; the latter are subject to a very limited standard of review.

Class/collective action waiver

Employers may also want to consider including a class/collective action waiver provision in their employment agreements and applications. By signing a class/collective action waiver, an employee agrees not to proceed in a lawsuit as part of a class or collective action. Over the last few years, the number of employment related class/collective action lawsuits has increased significantly, particularly with respect to lawsuits alleging violations of the Fair Labor Standards Act (FLSA). A class action waiver decreases employers' exposure to potentially enormous class/collective action liability and litigation costs.

Abbreviated statute of limitations for employment related claims

Employers may want to consider including a provision that shortens the statutory limitations period for filing employment discrimination lawsuits.

> **Note:**
> Some states, like Florida, have enacted laws prohibiting the shortening of statutes of limitation. For instance, Florida law state: "Any provision in a contract fixing the period of time within which an action arising out of the contract may be begun at a time less than that provided by the applicable statute of limitations is void." Furthermore, in 2019, 12 states extended the statute of limitations for sex abuse lawsuits; and five additional states passed bills, which if approved will do so. Employers should thus check local, federal and state laws for any state in which they have operations to ensure that any contractual shortening of a limitations period is enforceable under state law.

Inquiries that cause problems

Employers should be cautious about making certain inquiries, such as:

- **Maiden name –** Inquiring into an applicant's maiden name may be evidence of sex discrimination. The EEOC has indicated that a permissible variation of this question is: "If you have used another name or names during the past five years, please list those names."
- **Relationship of person to be notified in emergency** – If an application form asks an employee to identify the employee's relationship to "the person to

be notified in case of an emergency," the form should not require the person to be a relative nor ask whether the person is a spouse. This is also a good example of a question that does not need to be asked at the pre-hire stage. It should be included only in the paperwork for a new employee, such as in a post-hire form.

- **Age or date of birth** – The ADEA prohibits discriminating against persons 40 years of age and older. For this reason, inquiring as to the applicant's age or date of birth could be used as evidence in a future age discrimination suit. Certain age inquiries may be justifiable due to other considerations, such as compliance with child labor laws. A statement such as, "if you are under age 18, you will need to provide the company with evidence that you are legally able to work" is permissible.

- **Citizenship** – Discrimination based on national origin or citizenship is unlawful, but proof of identity and work authorization is required by the IRCA for all new employees. Hence, citizenship questions on an application should be omitted. The application should simply note: "All applicants will be required to furnish proof of identity and legal work authorization within three business days of hire."

- **Language fluency** – A question regarding an applicant's fluency in foreign languages may be used as evidence of illegal national origin discrimination, because it might identify the applicant's national origin. Certain questions regarding language fluency may be justified, however, if language fluency is necessary for the job. For instance, if the employer serves a substantial Spanish speaking population, the employer may be able to show that it needs to hire employees who are capable of communicating with Spanish speaking customers or clients. If foreign language fluency is not necessary for the job position, the employer should request this information only after the person is hired and it should be kept separate from the files used for promotions and other personnel decisions.

- **Place of birth** – Another question potentially giving rise to a claim of national origin discrimination is one requesting the applicant to state his or her place of birth. The employer should avoid asking this question.

- **Gender** – Because Title VII of the Civil Rights Act (Title VII) and several state-specific laws prohibit sex discrimination in employment, a question regarding an applicant's gender should not appear on an application form. Again, if needed for recordkeeping, ask for this information only after hire.

- **Existence and identification of children/dependents** – Questions asking whether the applicant has any children or dependents may be used as evidence of gender or marital status discrimination. Questions or requests such as: "Have you made arrangements to care for children?" "List children and their ages;" and "List family living in local area," should not be used on an application. A legitimate inquiry as to the applicant's availability and dependability can be addressed with an alternative inquiry, such as stating the regular hours of work and asking: "Can you work these hours?" Any such questions must be asked of all applicants.

- **Marital status** – Although federal law does not prohibit discrimination based on marital status, some states forbid marital status discrimination. Should such information be needed, it should be obtained after hire.

- **Name and/or occupation of spouse** – Objections have been raised regarding inquiries into the name or occupation of an applicant's spouse, both on marital status grounds and on the grounds that disclosure of this information may identify the applicant's religion or national origin. This information should be obtained only after hire.

- **Homeowner or renter** – In some regions, statistics show that a greater percentage of minorities and females do not own homes as compared to white males. Therefore, any preference given to applicants who own their homes might be found to be discriminatory. For residence information, simply ask for the applicant's current address, prior addresses and length of time at each address.

- **U.S. Armed Forces record** – Questions that inquire into the existence, nature and extent of the applicant's service in the U.S. Armed Forces may also pose problems. Title VII specifically permits preferences for veterans under federal, state and local veterans' preference laws, despite arguments that this type of preference discriminates against females. An employer is most likely not covered by veterans' preference laws, however, unless it is a federal contractor supplying goods or services in excess of the required statutory amount. If the employer is not subject to a veterans' preference law, its inquiry into an applicant's service in the U.S. Armed Forces is unnecessary, unless it pertains to job-related military experience, training or supervision. Further, questions regarding a "general," "undesirable," or "dishonorable" discharge from the U.S. Armed Forces may be similar to questions about arrest and/or conviction records, which pose risks of discrimination claims, as discussed herein.

- **Criminal records** – As discussed previously, refusing to employ an individual based solely on an arrest or conviction record may constitute unlawful discrimination. Further, certain states may require that an employer not ask about an applicant's criminal history on the job application. Where such an inquiry on a job application is permitted, the EEOC suggests that the following language appear near the inquiry: "Conviction of a crime will not necessarily be a barrier to employment. Factors such as age at the time of the offense, type of offense, remoteness of the offense in time and rehabilitation will be taken into account in determining effect on suitability for employment."

- **Surety bond rejection or forfeiture** – A policy of rejecting all applicants who have been subject to refusal or forfeiture of a surety bond may also be discriminatory. If this information is reasonably necessary for pre-hire evaluation of employees who need to be bonded, such a question should only be asked of those applicants.

- **Availability for weekend, overtime or other work –** A question regarding whether the applicant is willing to work Saturdays, Sundays and holidays may improperly inquire into an applicant's religious beliefs. If such a question must be asked, include a statement advising the applicant that they need not disclose any religious basis for the inability to work these hours and that reasonable efforts will be made to accommodate the needs of employees. The same concern exists as to inquiries about whether an applicant is willing to work overtime.

- **Workers' compensation history and/or health characteristics** – The ADA prohibits making any medical inquiries about an applicant's disability before an offer of employment is extended. In light of this fact, federal regulations prohibit inquiries into an applicant's workers' compensation history because they might reveal the existence of a disability. Accordingly, no questions regarding workers' compensation or health or medical information should be included on the application.

- **Pregnancy** – The Pregnancy Discrimination Act (PDA) prohibits employers from refusing to hire a female applicant because she is pregnant, might become pregnant or was recently pregnant, unless the BFOQ defense to discrimination applies. Accordingly, no questions regarding a female applicant's pregnancy status or family plans should be included in the application.

- **Religion** – Title VII prohibits discrimination in hiring based on religion, among other factors. Employers should check the laws of the state in which they have operations to determine whether questions regarding the applicant's religion are permissible. As a matter of best practices, employers should avoid questioning an applicant regarding his or her religion.

- **Credit history** – Some states, including California, Colorado, Connecticut, Delaware, Hawaii, Illinois, Maryland, Nevada, New York, Oregon, Vermont, Washington State and Washington D.C., limit employers' use of credit information in employment decisions.

- **Unemployed status** – If an employer considers unemployment status in rejecting applicants, it must do so consistently, without regard to race, color, national origin, religion, sex, disability, age or genetic information. Employers also must not screen out applicants based on unemployed status if it does not help accurately identify responsible and reliable employees. Additionally, employers may have to make exceptions to a policy of rejecting applicants based on unemployed status if the status was caused by a disability. Employers should check the laws of the state in which they have operations to determine whether questions regarding unemployment status are permissible.

- **Social Security number** – While federal law does not prohibit employers from asking for a Social Security number on employment applications, it is not considered a best practice because of the threat of identity theft and/or other privacy concerns. Further, some states have enacted laws with specific requirements for protecting individuals' privacy.

- **Salary history** – With equal pay under the regulatory spotlight, a growing number of states are prohibiting employers from asking job applicants about salary history. Based on the premise that wage discrimination follows the market value of women at hire, this legislation aims to create equal footing at the point of job offer. Maine and Alabama are the most recent states to enact this legislation, joining Delaware, Hawaii, Maryland, Massachusetts, New Jersey, New York, Oregon and Pennsylvania.

State laws should also be consulted to determine whether the applicable state places further restrictions on pre-employment inquiries.

State-specific limits on pre-employment inquiries

State	Limits to pre-employment inquiries
Alabama	Cannot make inquiries based on: • salary history
Alaska	Cannot make inquiries based on: • sex • physical or mental disability • marital status • changes in marital status • pregnancy • parenthood • age • race • creed • color • national origin.
Arizona	Cannot make any non-job-related inquiry related to: • race • color • religion • sex • age • mental or physical disability • national origin • genetic test results • association with individual with disability. Ban the Box policy: Cannot make inquiry into criminal history until an applicant has submitted an application and received an initial interview.
Arkansas	Not prohibited, but as matter of best practices, employers should not make any non-job-related inquiry related to: • race • ancestry • religion • gender

State	Limits to pre-employment inquiries
Arkansas (continued)	• pregnancy, childbirth and related medical conditions • mental or physical disability • national origin.
California	Cannot make any non-job-related inquiry related to: • race or color • religion • national origin • ancestry • physical or mental disability • medical condition • marital status • sex or sexual orientation • gender identity or expression • genetic information • military or veteran status • age • arrests • credit history • salary history • reproductive health decision making. Ban the Box policy: Cannot inquire into criminal history until an employer makes a conditional offer of employment to an applicant.
Colorado	Cannot make any non-job-related inquiry related to: • disability • race or color • creed • sex • sexual orientation • age • national origin • ancestry • salary history.

State	Limits to pre-employment inquiries
Colorado (continued)	Other possible discriminatory topics may include: • political affiliation (if public employer) • veteran's status (if public employer) • organizational membership (if public employer) • home ownership or rental • arrests • criminal history (if a public employer) • convictions not substantially related to job • credit rating • military service unrelated to job • sealed records. Ban the Box policy: May not inquire into an applicant's criminal history on an initial employment application or advertise for employment stating that individuals with criminal histories may not apply. Applies to all employers regardless of size as of September 2021.
Connecticut	Should not make any non-job-related inquiries related to: • age • race • color • national origin • ancestry • religion • sex • pregnancy • sexual orientation • marital status • disability • potential to be a parent • gender identity or expression • civil union status • genetic information • criminal history • credit history • salary history.

State	Limits to pre-employment inquiries
Connecticut (continued)	No background checks are permissible until after an offer of employment has been made.
Delaware	Cannot make inquiries related to: • age • race • color • national origin • religion • sexual orientation • marital status • physical or mental disability • genetic information • criminal history • credit history • gender identity • salary history.
District of Columbia	Unless the inquiry is job-related, cannot make inquiries related to: • race • color • national origin • religion • sex • pregnancy, childbirth, related medical conditions or breastfeeding • sexual orientation • age • marital status • disability • personal appearance • gender identity or expression • genetic information • matriculation • credit information • political orientation • salary history (applies to government agencies).

State	Limits to pre-employment inquiries
District of Columbia (continued)	Ban the Box policy: Employers with 11+ employees cannot make an inquiry into criminal history until a conditional offer has been extended.
Florida	No specific prohibitions, but should avoid questions related to: • race • color • religion • national origin • ancestry • sex • pregnancy • age • marital status • disability. Employers should not inquire about an applicant's HIV status, whether the applicant has been tested for HIV or illicit information about a related medical condition. Employers should check their city and county ordinances for specific Ban the Box legislation.
Georgia	Georgia has no comprehensive anti-discrimination law, but there are separate state laws that employers should be aware of when making age or disability related inquiries. Ban the Box policy: Cannot make an inquiry into criminal history until after the initial stage of the application process. Salary history ban for all city employers in Atlanta.
Hawaii	Cannot inquire regarding: • race • sex • sexual orientation • gender identity/expression • pregnancy, childbirth or related medical conditions • age • religion • color • ancestry

State	Limits to pre-employment inquiries
Hawaii (continued)	• disability (including association with an individual with a disability) • marital status • breastfeeding • National Guard obligations • genetic information • domestic or sexual violence victim status • whether individual has been tested for HIV • salary history • credit history (including record of garnishments, bankruptcy, assignment of income for child support purposes or work injury). Ban the Box policy: Cannot make an inquiry into criminal history until a conditional offer has been extended. May only inquire about felony convictions within the past seven years and misdemeanors within the past five years, excluding periods of incarceration.
Idaho	No specific prohibitions, but inquiries related to the following are extremely disfavored: • race • color • religion • sex • national origin • age • disability. Questions that elicit information about an applicant's medical conditions are specifically prohibited.
Illinois	Cannot inquire into arrest records or criminal records that have been expunged or sealed. Cannot inquire regarding: • workers' compensation or Occupational Disease Act claims • disability • race • color • religion • age • marital status • order of protection status • military status

State	Limits to pre-employment inquiries
Illinois (continued)	• unfavorable discharge from military service (except dishonorable discharge) • sexual orientation • pregnancy • sex • national origin • citizenship • credit history • salary history. Ban the Box policy: Employers with 15+ employees cannot make an inquiry into criminal history on applications or during the early part of the selection and recruiting process. No criminal background checks before a job interview, or until a job offer for all employers in Chicago or Cook County.
Indiana	Cannot inquire into the following unless it is job related and there is no less intrusive way to ensure the applicant will be able to fulfill the essential functions of the job: • disability • race • color • religion • age • sex • national origin • ancestry • status as a veteran • use of tobacco products outside course of employment • criminal history (applies only to contractors doing business in Indianapolis).
Iowa	Employers should avoid questions related to: • age • race or color • national origin • religion/creed • sex

State	Limits to pre-employment inquiries
Iowa (continued)	• pregnancy • sexual orientation • gender identity • qualified disability (including AIDS). **Note:** Certain cities, including Waterloo, in Iowa have implemented ordinances restricting employers from inquiring about candidates' criminal record information.
Kansas	Employers should avoid questions related to: • race or color • national origin or ancestry • ancestry • religion • sex • disability. The Kansas Human Rights Commission has also compiled a chart of Acceptable and Inadvisable Inquiries for guidance. Ban the Box policy: State agencies cannot inquire into criminal history during the initial application process.
Kentucky	Employers should avoid questions related to: • age • race or color • national origin • religion • sex • disability • whether the individual is a smoker • AIDS or HIV status. City agencies cannot ask for applicants' salary histories, nor can employers in the Louisville Metro area. Ban the Box policy: Applications for all jobs within the Kentucky executive branch may not include questions about criminal history. In Louisville, the city may cancel contracts with companies that do not ban the box.
Louisiana	Inquiries into the following may be used as evidence of discrimination: • age • race or color

State	Limits to pre-employment inquiries
Louisiana (continued)	• national origin • religion • gender. Cannot make inquiries regarding disability or genetic information. City agencies may not ask for applicants' salary histories, nor may employers in New Orleans. Ban the Box policy: No criminal history questions on job applications for contractors doing business in New Orleans.
Maine	Cannot inquire about: • race or color • sex • physical or mental disability • religion • age • ancestry • national origin • sexual orientation • workers' compensation claims • protected activity under whistleblower's statute • salary history. Ban the Box policy: Employers are prohibited from including criminal history inquiries on application forms, but can engage in such inquiries during the interview process once it has been determined that the applicant is otherwise qualified for the position. Maine also has restrictions related to AIDS testing, workplace smoking policies and social media access of applicants.
Maryland	Cannot inquire about: • illness or disability • genetic information • credit history • salary history • criminal charges or convictions that have been expunged. Employers in Montgomery County may not inquire into an applicant's salary history.

State	Limits to pre-employment inquiries
Maryland (continued)	If a public employer, cannot inquire into criminal history until the applicant has been provided an opportunity for an interview. Ban the Box policy: Effective January 30, 2021, Maryland passed a law prohibiting employers with 15 or more full-time employees from inquiring about an applicant's criminal history before the first in-person interview is conducted. Employers must also abide by the more restrictive ordinances enacted by Montgomery County, Prince George's County and the city of Baltimore, if applicable. Employers in Baltimore with 10+ employees may not perform any background checks until after a job offer has been extended. No criminal history questions or checks can be initiated until after the first interview by employers with 15+ employees in Montgomery County or by employers with 25+ full-time employees in Prince George's County.
Massachusetts	Employers prohibited from asking questions related to: • race or color • religion • national origin • sex • gender identity • sexual orientation • genetic information • pregnancy/conditions related to pregnancy • age • ancestry • status as a veteran • maternity • disability/handicap • salary history. Cannot ask about: • arrest, detention or disposition (if no conviction) • first convictions for certain misdemeanors • any misdemeanor conviction that occurred five or more years ago. Ban the Box policy: Cannot use a written employment application to ask about criminal history.
Michigan	Cannot make inquiries related to: • religion

State	Limits to pre-employment inquiries
Michigan (continued)	• race • color • national origin • sex • height • weight • disability • marital status • genetic testing and information Public employers are also prohibited from making inquiries related to: • sexual orientation • gender identity or expression • political affiliation • salary history (until after an offer of employment has been made). Ban the Box Policy: Public employers cannot conduct background checks until a conditional offer of employment is made. Detroit and Kalamazoo also have ordinances for contractors doing business within those cities. Additionally, Grand Rapids, Michigan, passed an ordinance stating that employers are not allowed to consider arrests not leading to a conviction, nor to refuse to hire an applicant based on his or her criminal record without determining whether the crime would pose a risk to the "health, safety or welfare of other employees or persons or to property." The ordinance also allows individuals to report unlawful discrimination to the City Office of Diversity and Inclusion (ODI) within 180 days of an incident.
Minnesota	Cannot make inquiries related to: • race • color • creed • religion • national origin • sex • sexual orientation and gender identity • marital status • familial status • status regarding public assistance

State	Limits to pre-employment inquiries
Minnesota (continued)	• membership in National Guard or Army Reserves • membership or activity in local commission • disability • age • genetic information. Ban the Box policy: Cannot inquire into an applicant's criminal history until after the applicant has been selected for an interview or before a conditional offer of employment.
Mississippi	Jackson city government cannot ask for salary history
Missouri	Should not make inquiries related to the following on an application or in an interview: • race • religion • color • national origin • age • sex, including sex stereotyping • ancestry • disability • salary history (employers with six or more employees). Employers in Kansas City and St. Louis may not inquire into an applicant's salary history. Ban the Box policy: The following cities prohibit criminal history checks until after the job interview and/or making a conditional job offer: Columbia (all employers), Kansas City (employers with 6+ employees) and St. Louis (employers with 10+ employees).
Montana	Cannot make inquiries related to: • age • race or color • religion/creed • sex • national origin • religion • marital status • pregnancy/maternity

State	Limits to pre-employment inquiries
	• physical or mental disability.
Nebraska	Should avoid inquiries related to: • race or color • religion • national origin • age • marital status • sex • disability. Ban the Box policy: If a public employer, cannot inquire into a job applicant's criminal history until after the employer has determined that the applicant meets the minimum job requirements.
Nevada	Employers should be cautious of making inquiries related to: • race or color • religion • national origin • age • sex • sexual orientation/gender identity or expression • disability • credit history • salary history. Ban the Box policy: Public employers cannot make inquiries into criminal history until the earliest of: • the final interview conducted in person • the appointing authority has made a conditional offer of employment to the applicant • if applicable, the applicant has been certified by the Administrator of Human Resources. Nevada's Equal Rights Commission has prepared a Guide to Pre-Employment Inquiries, which contains a discussion of state law requirements on preemployment inquiries, together with a listing of impermissible inquiries and acceptable alternatives.
New Hampshire	Cannot make inquiries related to: • age • sex

State	Limits to pre-employment inquiries
New Hampshire (continued)	• sexual orientation • race • color • marital status • disability • religion • national origin.
New Jersey	Should not make inquiries related to: • race • creed • color • national origin • ancestry • age • marital status • civil union status • domestic partnership status • sex • pregnancy • affectional or sexual orientation • genetic information • gender identity or expression • disability (including HIV) • nationality • obligation to serve in the U.S. Armed Forces • salary history. Ban the Box policy: Cannot inquire into a candidate's criminal history until the employer has conducted the first interview with the candidate.
New Mexico	Should avoid inquiries related to: • age • race or color • national origin or ancestry • religion • sex

State	Limits to pre-employment inquiries
New Mexico (continued)	• sexual orientation or gender identity • serious medical condition • disability. Ban the Box policy: Cannot inquire into an applicant's conviction history on an initial employment application until an applicant has been "selected as a finalist."
New York	Cannot make inquiries related to: • age • race, including hairstyle • creed • color • national origin • sex (including gender identity and transgender) • sexual orientation • military status • marital status • domestic violence victim status • disability • genetic information • salary history. Ban the Box policy: Employers should become familiar with the policy as New York's is one of the nation's most comprehensive "ban-the-box" laws restricting employers' use of criminal history in the employment process. City ordinances also apply in Buffalo, New York City, Rochester and Syracuse.
North Carolina	Should avoid inquiries related to: • race • color • national origin • religion • sex • salary history (all public employers). Employers in Wake County and Charlotte also should avoid inquiries related to gender identity, gender expression, sexual orientation and hairstyles. Employers in Winston-Salem also should avoid inquiries ethnicity, creed, sexual orientation, gender identity, gender expression, protected

State	Limits to pre-employment inquiries
North Carolina (continued)	hairstyles, pregnancy, disability, age, veteran status, marital status, familial status or political affiliation. Cannot require applicants to identify themselves as disabled. Employers should check their city and county ordinances for specific ban the box legislation.
North Dakota	Cannot make inquiries related to: • age • race or color • national origin • genetic information • religion • sex • participation in lawful activity off work premises during nonworking hours • marital status • public assistance status • disability.
Ohio	Cannot inquire about: • race or color • religion • sex (including pregnancy, childbirth or related medical conditions) • national origin or ancestry • disability • age • military status. Salary history ban for all employers with at least 15 employees in the cities of Cincinnati and Toledo. Cincinnati prohibits employment discrimination on the basis of gender identity and expression, sex, breastfeeding status, military status and familial status. Applies to employers with four or more employees. Ban the Box policy: Public employers cannot inquire about an applicant's felony convictions at the time the application is submitted to the public employer.
Oklahoma	Cannot make inquiries related to: • race • color

State	Limits to pre-employment inquiries
Oklahoma (continued)	• religion • sex • national origin • age • genetic test results (states are immune to this prohibition) • applicants' use of tobacco • disability or extent of disability. Ban the Box policy: Employers should not inquire as to felony convictions on employment applications.
Oregon	Cannot make inquiries related to: • race (including hairstyle) • religion • color • sex • sexual orientation • national origin • marital status • age • disability • association with member of protected group • unemployment status • credit history • salary history • driver's license (unless driving is required by the position). Ban the Box policy: Cannot inquire about a job applicant's criminal history during the initial stages of the application process (i.e., before a job interview). Employers in Portland may not conduct criminal background checks prior to making a conditional job offer.
Pennsylvania	Cannot make inquiries related to: • race • color • religion • ancestry • age • sex

State	Limits to pre-employment inquiries
Pennsylvania (continued)	• national origin • genetic information • disability or nature or severity of disability • use of guide dog for disability • salary history (public employers statewide, city employers in Pittsburg and ALL covered employers in Philadelphia). Ban the Box policy: Employers with at least one employee in Philadelphia and contractors/vendors doing business in Pittsburgh are prohibited from conducing criminal background checks prior to making a conditional job offer.
Rhode Island	Cannot inquire related to: • race or color • religion • sex or sexual orientation • gender identity or expression • disability • age • ancestry • arrest records • prior convictions (prior to offer of employment) • salary history. Ban the Box policy: Employers are prohibited from asking criminal history on an application or at any time prior to the first interview.
South Carolina	Should not make inquiries regarding: • age • race • sex • color • national origin • religion • existence, nature or severity of disability. Columbia city agencies and county offices in Richland County cannot request salary history information. Cannot make inquiries related to use of tobacco products or genetic information.

State	Limits to pre-employment inquiries
South Dakota	Generally, cannot ask about: • age • race • color • ancestry • religion • sex • genetic information • disability.
Tennessee	Employers should be cautious when making inquiries related to: • age • race • color • religion/creed • sex • national origin. Ban the Box policy: State employers cannot inquire about an applicant's criminal history on the initial job application. **Note:** As of 2021, in Tennessee, individuals who have committed nonviolent or low-level assault offenses can have their record expunged in very limited circumstances. Similarly, an additional new law makes a simple assault committed after July 1, 2000, eligible for consideration of expungement. The law does not apply to those convicted of domestic abuse.
Texas	Employers should be cautious when making inquiries related to: • age • race • color • religion • sex • sexual orientation • gender identity • national origin.

<table>
<tr><th>State</th><th>Limits to pre-employment inquiries</th></tr>
<tr><td>Texas (continued)</td><td>Employers cannot inquire about an applicant's disability or about the extent of an applicant's disability until after the employer has extended a conditional offer of employment to the applicant.

Ban the Box policy: Employers with 15+ employees in Austin my not inquire into criminal background history prior to extending a conditional job offer. The DeSoto Fair Chance Ordinance prohibits inquiries about an applicant's criminal history on an initial job application.</td></tr>
<tr><td>Utah</td><td>Cannot ask questions related to:
• age
• race
• color
• ancestry
• religion
• sex
• sexual orientation
• gender identity
• national origin
• pregnancy, childbirth and pregnancy-related conditions
• disability.
Employers cannot request the following information before an applicant is offered a job: Social security number, Date of birth or Driver's license number.

Salt Lake City prohibits asking about salary history of applicants for city government positions.

Ban the Box policy: Public employers cannot inquire as to criminal history during recruiting process.</td></tr>
<tr><td>Vermont</td><td>Should avoid inquiries related to:
• race or color
• age
• national origin
• ancestry
• religion
• sex
• sexual orientation
• gender identity</td></tr>
</table>

State	Limits to pre-employment inquiries
Vermont (continued)	• place of birth • salary history • credit history • disability • salary history. Ban the Box policy: Cannot inquire as to applicants' criminal history on an initial employment application.
Virginia	Generally, should not inquire about: • race • color • age • national origin • ancestry • religion • sex • marital status • pregnancy and related medical conditions • disability. Cannot request a genetic test. Ban the Box policy: Public employers cannot inquire into criminal history at the initial application stage.
Washington	Cannot make inquiries related to: • age • race • color • national origin • ancestry/genetic information • religion • sex • sexual orientation • marital status • credit history • honorably discharged veteran or military status

State	Limits to pre-employment inquiries
Washington (continued)	• disability or the use of a trained guide dog or service animal by a person with a disability • salary history. Ban the Box policy: Cannot inquire about applicants' criminal history during the initial stages of the application process. Employers in Seattle must have a legitimate business reason to automatically exclude applicants with arrest or conviction records.
West Virginia	Cannot make inquiries related to: • race • religion • color • national origin • ancestry • sex • blindness • physical or mental impairment • age.
Wisconsin	Cannot make inquiries related to: • age • race • creed • color • disability • marital status • sex • sexual orientation • national origin • ancestry • military service • use or non-use of lawful products off duty and off premises • arrest or conviction records • salary history.

State	Limits to pre-employment inquiries
Wyoming	Should not make inquiries related to: • age • race • color • national origin • ancestry • religion • sex • pregnancy • disability.

Employer comments on forms

Employers should avoid designating areas on the application form as "For Office Use Only" or otherwise inviting stray comments or impressions to the application form. Applications are a permanent record of hired employees and such comments could later prove embarrassing or result in a lawsuit. Indeed, an employment application may be subpoenaed from an employer as evidence in an EEOC investigation or lawsuit. A post-hire form for eliciting information that is only needed after the applicant is hired is recommended.

Retention of applications

Title VII and the ADEA require certain records to be kept for one year from the date of the record (including application) or personnel action involved, whichever is later. Some states require such records to be retained for a longer period of time. Additionally, if a charge of discrimination or a lawsuit is filed, records must be kept through final disposition of the charge or lawsuit.

Working with employment agencies

Employers often use employment agencies to recruit, screen and refer potential employees. Employment and referral agencies are required to abide by the federal anti-discrimination laws, including Title VII, the ADEA and the ADA, as are other entities, such as labor unions and organizations providing training programs.

At the same time, an employer may be liable for the discriminatory conduct of any employment agency that it utilizes to assist in hiring employees. As a result, it is important that employers ensure that the agencies they utilize are aware of and abide by anti-discrimination laws. This same caution should be exercised with regard to search firms.

Use of artificial intelligence

On May 12, 2022, the U.S. Equal Employment Opportunity Commission (EEOC) issued a "Technical Assistance" (TA) document addressing compliance with ADA requirements and agency policy when using artificial intelligence (AI) and other software to hire and assess employees. The agency also published a short "Tips for Workers" summary of this guidance. Neither of these documents has the force or effect of law, nor are they binding on employers. The guidance is meant to be educational, "so that people with disabilities know their rights and employers can take action to avoid discrimination." There are several take-aways regarding the Commission's likely expectations and areas of focus when regulating the use of such tools in hiring or assessing employees:

- **Accessibility**
  Employers should account for the fact that on-line/interactive tools may not be easily accessed or used by those with visual, auditory or other impairment.

- **Accommodation**
  Barring undue hardship, employers should provide alternatives to the use or application of these tools if an individual's disability renders the use of the tool more difficult or the accuracy of the tool's assessment less reliable.

- **Accommodation, II**
  Beyond providing reasonable accommodations in accessing/using these tools, employers should ensure that the tools assess an individual in the context of any reasonable accommodation they are likely to be given when performing their job.

- **ADA vs. Title VII**
  The EEOC stresses that disability bias requires different design and testing criteria than does Title VII discrimination, such as access considerations and the potential for inadvertent disability-related inquiries or medical examinations.

- **Promising practices**
  Noting that employers are responsible for ADA-violating outcomes even when a software tool is created or used by a third-party vendor or agent, the Commission provides examples of so-called "Promising Practices" that employers can engage in to demonstrate good-faith efforts to meet ADA requirements.

The TA document uses various illustrative examples of the tools the EEOC aims to regulate. These range from résumé scanners and virtual assistants/chatbots to video-interviewing software and software that tests an individual's personality, aptitude, skills and "perceived 'cultural fit.'" Employers using any of these tools in their recruiting, hiring and review of applicants and employees (which, by some estimates, is up to 83% of employers) should take careful note of the EEOC's position as to where these tools may run afoul of the ADA.

The TA document focuses broadly on three themes, specifically, how the use of algorithmic decision-making may violate the ADA with respect to:

- reasonable accommodation for applicants and employees
- where AI decision-making tools may "screen out" individuals with disabilities
- where an AI-based tool may violate ADA restrictions on disability-related inquiries.

You can access the document online in its entirety at:

- https://www.eeoc.gov/laws/guidance/americans-disabilities-act-and-use-software-algorithms-and-artificial-intelligence

Chapter

Pre-employment testing 03

Steve Jobs, the former CEO and chairman of Apple Inc., believed that his most important responsibility was hiring the best employees. Jobs understood that a company's employees are its single greatest investment. Before a company invests in an expensive new piece of equipment, management will typically research the product, secure information from vendors and test the product before making a final decision. Businesses should at least devote the same time and effort to hiring decisions, but federal and state laws make it unlawful for employers to use certain forms of testing when make hiring decisions. This chapter will discuss how employers can lawfully use pre-employment testing to identify the "right employee."

Employers may wish to use pre-employment tests to screen applicants. It is important for any such business that uses pre-employment testing as part of the hiring process to ensure that any such test does not violate the Americans with Disabilities Act (ADA). Any such business should ensure that the qualification standards or selection criteria do not tend to screen out persons who qualify as disabled under the ADA unless the standard or criteria being measured is both job-related and consistent with business necessity.

Medical examinations

According to the Americans with Disabilities Act (ADA), employers may not require pre-employment medical examinations until a conditional offer of employment has been extended to the applicant. The test would also violate the ADA unless the employer requires all applicants who fall within that same job category to complete the medical examination.

Alcohol tests

An alcohol test would qualify as a medical examination under the ADA. It is noteworthy that alcoholism could qualify as a disability under the ADA and an employer is restricted as to when tests may be given. An employer should wait until after making an initial offer of employment before requiring an alcohol test and the employer should ensure that it could justify the use of this test as job-related and consistent with business necessity.

Drug tests

The Americans with Disabilities Act (ADA) does not prohibit pre-employment drug testing. In fact, tests for illegal drug usage do not qualify as a medical examination under the ADA. Nevertheless, employers should ensure that they do not receive information about an applicant's lawful use of prescription drugs. A number of states have recently legalized the use of marijuana. Employers that receive federal funding are still required to consider marijuana an illegal drug, but employers that operate in such states should consult with counsel. Furthermore, some state statutes prohibit or restrict the use of drug testing. Any business that intends on adopting a drug testing policy should consult with counsel to ensure that its policy does not violate any federal or state statutes or regulations.

Job-related performance tests

At the pre-offer stage, employers may ask about an applicant's ability to perform specific job-related functions and may ask an applicant to describe or demonstrate that he or she can perform essential job functions either with or without a reasonable accommodation. Pre-employment tests designed to measure an applicant's ability to perform essential job duties are permissible under the ADA. Nonetheless, an employer would be required to accommodate disabled applicants during testing under certain circumstances.

Physical agility and fitness tests

A physical agility or fitness test, in which an applicant demonstrates the ability to perform job-related tasks, is not a medical examination, but the employer may be required to make a reasonable accommodation for the applicant. If the test tends to screen out applicants with a disability, the employer must show that the test is job-related for the position in question and consistent with business necessity.

Genetic testing

The federal Genetic Information Nondiscrimination Act (GINA) applies to all employers covered by Title VII of the Civil Rights Act (Title VII) and prohibits discrimination by employers and insurers based on genetic information. The ADA does not specifically address the issue of genetic testing. Executive Order 13145 prohibits discrimination by federal agencies on the basis of protected genetic information. Many states now prohibit genetic testing. Accordingly, employers should be cautious and seek counsel before requesting this of employees.

Written exams

Written tests may tend to screen out persons who fall within a protected category and the use of written tests could be unlawful. The Equal Employment Opportunity Commission (EEOC) set forth its position on the subject in a document entitled "Uniform Guidelines on Employee Selection Procedures." The EEOC insists that any written test that has an adverse impact on persons within a protected category is unlawful unless it has been "validated" by psychologists or other qualified experts according to the complicated standards set forth in its guidelines. The validation process is expensive and the courts that have addressed the issue have split. Some courts have followed the EEOC validation approach and others have criticized it.

Polygraph testing

Under the Employee Polygraph Protection Act (EPPA), most types of employers are prohibited from directly or indirectly requiring, requesting, suggesting or otherwise causing a job applicant to submit to polygraph testing. Federal, state and local governments are exempt from this act. Other exemptions include entities that manufacture, distribute or dispense controlled substances. Some states also place limits on polygraph testing. Employers should consult with counsel before adopting any polygraph testing policy to ensure compliance with both federal and state law.

State	Limits to polygraph testing
Alabama	Testing prohibited for continued employment for public employees.
Alaska	Testing is prohibited except for police officers and applicants to become police officers.
Arizona	No laws
Arkansas	No laws
California	Cannot require polygraph for applicants or employees as a condition of employment or continued employment and must provide a notice of rights.
Colorado	No laws
Connecticut	Cannot request or require, except for non-civilian police department and Department of Corrections positions.
Delaware	Cannot require as a condition of employment or continued employment, except for background investigations for police officer applicants.
District of Columbia	Cannot require or use results in hiring or employment. Certain exceptions for specified government employees are provided.
Florida	No laws
Georgia	No laws
Hawaii	Cannot require as conditions of employment or continued employment; but employer may request test if current or prospective employee is told, orally and in writing, that refusing to take the test will not result in being fired or hurt chances of getting a job. However, state law does not have an exception allowing polygraphs as part of ongoing investigation involving economic loss or injury to a business.
Idaho	Cannot require as conditions of employment or continued employment. Certain exceptions for specified government employees are provided.
Illinois	Polygraph testing is prohibited about the following matters unless directly related to employment: • political, religious or labor-related beliefs, affiliations or lawful activities • beliefs about racial issues • issues regarding unions • sexual preferences or activity.
Indiana	No laws

State	Limits to polygraph testing
Iowa	Cannot require as a condition for employment for virtually any reason. Certain exceptions apply for specified government employees.
Kansas	No laws
Kentucky	No laws
Louisiana	No laws
Maine	Cannot use as a condition of employment.
Maryland	Cannot require and must include a notice of the prohibition in bold type on employment applications. Exceptions are made for certain corrections and law enforcement applicants.
Massachusetts	Cannot require for applicants or employees and notice must be provided on application.
Michigan	Cannot require of applicants or employees, threaten to administer or require applicants or employees to waive rights.
Minnesota	Cannot request or require any form of honesty test.
Mississippi	No laws
Missouri	No laws
Montana	Cannot require as condition of employment/continued employment.
Nebraska	Cannot require employee or applicant to take a polygraph test. Cannot discharge employees for refusing to take a polygraph. Can request that test be taken, but only if these conditions are met: • no questions asked about sexual practices; marital relationship or political, religious or labor or union affiliations • examinee is given written and oral notice that test is voluntary and may be discontinued at any time • examinee signs form stating that test is being taken voluntarily • employee requested to take test only in connection with a specific investigation • results of test are not the sole reason for terminating employment • all questions and responses are kept on file by the employer for at least one year. Cannot discharge employees for refusing to take a polygraph. Can request that test be taken, but only if these conditions are met: • no questions asked about sexual practices; marital relationship or political, religious or labor or union affiliations

State	Limits to polygraph testing
Nebraska (continued)	• examinee is given written and oral notice that test is voluntary and may be discontinued at any time • examinee signs form stating that test is being taken voluntarily • employee requested to take test only in connection with a specific investigation • results of test are not the sole reason for terminating employment • all questions and responses are kept on file by the employer for at least one year.
Nevada	Similar to federal law, but provides fewer exceptions allowing testing for manufacturers or distributors of controlled substances; providers or designers of security systems and other security personnel; ongoing investigation.
New Hampshire	No laws
New Jersey	Cannot request or require as condition of employment or continued employment, with certain specified exceptions for employers who deal with controlled, dangerous substances.
New Mexico	Only applicable law applies to peace officers.
New York	Cannot require, request, suggest or permit for applicant or employee and cannot use test results.
North Carolina	No laws
North Dakota	No laws
Ohio	No laws
Oklahoma	No laws
Oregon	Generally prohibited for applicants and employees.
Pennsylvania	Cannot require as condition of employment or continued employment except for employees who dispense or have access to narcotics or other dangerous drugs or public law enforcement.
Rhode Island	Cannot require as condition of employment or continued employment.
South Carolina	No laws
South Dakota	No laws
Tennessee	Similar to federal law
Texas	Certain restriction applicable to specified government employees.
Utah	No laws
Vermont	Cannot require as condition of employment, except for certain specified limited exceptions.

State	Limits to polygraph testing
Virginia	Cannot use to inquire into applicants' sexual activities, unless they are criminal. Certain other restrictions also apply to law enforcement agencies and jails.
Washington	Generally, cannot require as condition of employment or continued employment except for applicants or employees of a company that manufactures, distributes or dispenses controlled substances or works in a sensitive position directly involving national security.
West Virginia	Cannot require or request for applicants or employees and cannot use results from such tests conducted outside the state. Certain exceptions apply.
Wisconsin	Similar to federal law, with limited exceptions and additional penalties.
Wyoming	No laws

Honesty tests

A written psychological test that is designed to measure an applicant's honesty may violate the Americans with Disabilities Act (ADA) and state laws. Some states restrict employers from performing tests to measure honesty whether by written examination, polygraph, voice-stress analysis or the like. Again, employers should consult with counsel before adopting any policy to test for honesty.

Psychological tests

Screening applicants by use of psychological tests may raise Americans with Disabilities Act (ADA) issues if the tests are used to detect mental impairments. Such screening may also raise discrimination issues, depending on the types of questions asked in the test. If lawful, a psychological test should only be required after the employer makes a conditional offer of employment because such a test could qualify as a medical examination under the ADA. Any employer who believes it is necessary to rely on psychological testing should consult with counsel before implementing any such policy.

Interviews

Chapter

04

The employment interview is the most used and often the least valid selection device used by management. Too often interviewers are ill prepared and may be influenced by irrelevant personality factors to determine who is best for the job. That is why we suggest having more than one-person interview each of the candidates. Of course, each interviewer should be trained on the "hows" of conducting an interview.

Preparing for an interview

When interviewing candidates, it is helpful to remember the following four points:

1. **Carefully review the job description prior to the interview**
   Having a detailed job description that accurately sets forth both the requirements of the position and the skills, education and background required to do the job is essential to finding the right person for a position. Additionally, it is important that the person interviewing the applicant understands what the position requires, especially if someone in a department other than the one in which the job opening is located conducts the initial interview.

2. **Carefully review the application form prior to interviewing**
   Prior to conducting an interview, employers should review the completed application. Employers should look for unexplained lapses of employment but avoid inquiring into periods of disability. Make certain that all questions asked on the employment application have been answered (resumes should not be accepted in lieu of completed employment applications) and that the application has been signed.

3. **Ensure the interview setting is appropriate**
   Ideally, an interview should be located in a comfortable location, preferably one that assures privacy (e.g., an office where the door can be closed). The interviewer should take no calls be put through during the interview and should mute the computer. Interviewers should adhere to the time set in the interview schedule, especially if interviewing more than one applicant. Additionally, the interviewee should be made as comfortable as possible and should be given the interviewer's business card so that he or she has ready access to the interviewer's name and position.

4. **Interview questions**
   Interview questions are subject to the same cautions that accompany application questions. If it is not permissible to ask a question on an application, it is not permissible

to ask it in the interview. It is important for an employer to inform interviewers about the requirements of Title VII of the Civil Rights Act (Title VII), the Age Discrimination in Employment Act (ADEA), the Americans with Disabilities Act (ADA) and applicable state laws that specifically detail what questions an interviewer may and may not ask. For more information, please see:

Equal Employment Opportunity Commission (EEOC) Enforcement Guidance on Pre-employment Disability-Related Questions and Medical Examinations:

- https://www.eeoc.gov/laws/guidance/enforcement-guidance-preemployment-disability-related-questions-and-medical

EEOC Enforcement Guidance on Workers' Compensation and the ADA:

- https://www.eeoc.gov/laws/guidance/enforcement-guidance-workers-compensation-and-ada

Remote interviews

Remote hiring and interviewing have become increasingly common. Some special considerations when conducting remote interviews include:

- Do all potential candidates have access to the technology being used to conduct the interview?
- Is the web platform ADA-compliant?
- What accommodations need to be offered to prospects with disabilities?
- Is the interviewer prepared to handle technology issues during the interview?
- Is the interviewer set up in a professional work environment free from individual distractions such as spouses, children, dogs, etc.?
- Will interviews be recorded? If so:
  - Are all interviews being recorded or only those for select candidates? If only select candidates, ensure that no selections are made that could lead to claims of discrimination.
  - Has permission been granted from the candidates to record the interview?
  - How will the recording be retained to satisfy EEO recordkeeping requirements?

Sample interview questions

While all employers need to develop interview questions specific to the position being filled, the following general questions may help the interviewer gain insight into the applicant's personality.

- What motivates you to put forth your greatest effort?
- What criteria do you use to evaluate the organization for which you hope to work?
- What do you see as your greatest success story or accomplishment in your life so far?

- What frustrates you the most?
- Tell me about the best job you ever had and what it was that made it such a good job.
- Describe the characteristics of your best supervisor.
- What were the weaknesses of your previous supervisor?
- Give me an example of a specific problem you have faced on the job and how you solved it.
- Do you see yourself as an idea person?
- What are some ideas you have had that helped improve your job environment?
- Where do you see yourself professionally in five years?
- What do you see as the best qualities you bring to a job?
- What do you see as your weaknesses?
- Tell me about a situation in which you had to deal with a very upset customer or co-worker. What was the problem? What was the outcome?
- Give me an example of a task you have accomplished that was extremely difficult. How did you complete the task?
- When have you had to display leadership qualities?
- Do you prefer working alone or in a group?
- How would someone who knows you well describe you?

ADA concerns

Employers are required to provide reasonable accommodations to applicants with disabilities. An employer should not engage in recruitment activities that exclude candidates with disabilities, such as participating in a job fair at a location that is not wheelchair accessible.

Union questions

It is unlawful for employers to inquire about union membership, union activity, or feelings about unions in general.

Promises

Interviewers should not make statements about job security or continued employment, because the applicant may construe these statements as promises that are enforceable contracts of employment. Employers may face lawsuits where they fail to provide the kind of work experience that was described in the hiring process or they misrepresent the nature or length of employment. Interviewers should avoid predicting, promising or guaranteeing anything about the position or the employer and use words such as "possible," "potential" and "maybe" when describing career opportunities.

Chapter

Background checks 05

Most employers understand that it is very important to hire the right employees. To make good hiring decisions, many employers consider information about the applicant that comes from various sources. This pre-employment due diligence helps companies make informed choices and it also helps them limit their possible exposure for negligent hiring claims. Liability can arise in this context where an employer hires an applicant without conducting a reasonable background investigation. Many services are available that can help employers conduct background investigations, but employers must account for laws such as the federal Fair Credit Reporting Act (FCRA), which regulates certain types of investigations and/or requires employers to make disclosures about such investigations.

- **Credit checks**
  As mentioned, California, Colorado, Connecticut, Delaware, Hawaii, Illinois, Maryland, Nevada, New York, Oregon, Vermont, Washington and Washington D.C., limit employers' use of credit history as part of a pre-employment background check. Further, any such inquiry must also comply with the requirements of the FCRA.

- **Criminal history checks**
  Inquiries about an applicant's criminal history may be justified when the individual will be working with weapons, will have access to people's homes or private lives or will hold a position requiring trust and responsibility. For restrictions on obtaining and/or using information regarding criminal history, see the prior discussion regarding arrest and conviction records.

- **Educational verification**
  An employer should consider verifying all of the schools or institutions listed by an applicant.

- **Department of Motor Vehicles search**
  When an employee will be driving in the course and scope of his or her employment, an employer may want to review the employee's driving record. If the employer secures information about the applicant's driving record from public records, the requirements of the FCRA do not apply. On the other hand, if the employer secures this same information from a consumer-reporting agency, the employer must ensure compliance with the FCRA.

Reference checks

An employer should contact all previous employers to check the applicant's job titles and duties, work performance and reason for leaving. Former employers should be asked whether they would hire the applicant again. Former employers may also be asked whether there is anything else in the applicant's background that would otherwise affect the applicant's suitability for employment, including whether the applicant is honest, reliable or has ever engaged in any improper conduct.

Many employers are reluctant to provide detailed information about former employees because of privacy concerns and the potential costs associated with defending a defamation lawsuit. Employers should ensure that they only provide accurate information and for the proper reasons. An employer should not ask an applicant's references any questions that the employer would not directly ask of the applicant; of course, every question asked should seek information about the applicant's ability to perform the job duties associated with the position. The most common questions to ask are as follows:

- **Verify the employment dates.** Employed from _______ to _______.
- **Verify the positions held.** Beginning ______________ Ending ____________.
- **How was his or her attendance record?**
  Absences per month ______ Tardies per month _________
- **Why did he or she leave your company?**
  ☐ Voluntary ☐ Involuntary
  Reason ____
  Eligible for rehire? ☐ Yes ☐ No If no, explain:____________________________________
- **Information furnished by:** ___________Title___________ Date: ______

The Americans with Disabilities Act

If a reference or a background check is a necessary part of an employer's application process, the employer should ensure that it conducts these inquiries in compliance with the Americans with Disabilities Act (ADA), which makes it unlawful to use qualification standards, employment tests or other selection criteria that screen out or tend to screen out disabled individuals, unless the standards, tests or other selection criteria are shown to be job-related for the position in question and consistent with business necessity.

Fair Credit Reporting Act compliance

The federal Fair Credit Reporting Act (FCRA) governs an employer's request for or use of a "consumer report" or "investigative consumer report" prepared or collected by a "consumer reporting agency." The FCRA's requirements do not apply if the employer uses its own employees to search any state records depository for background information, such as sending an employee to the county courthouse to check the public records for any lawsuits filed by or against an applicant or employee (compilations of publicly available background information by a third party may still constitute a "consumer report" subject to the FCRA).

Definitions

A "consumer report" includes a written or oral summary of a person's credit-worthiness, credit standing, credit capacity, character, general reputation, personal characteristics or mode of living.

An "investigative consumer report" is a consumer report containing information about a person's character, general reputation, personal characteristics or mode of living that was obtained through personal interviews with neighbors, friends, associates or others who have knowledge of such information about the consumer.

A "consumer reporting agency" includes any person who, for money or on a non-profit basis, regularly compiles or evaluates consumer credit information or other information on consumers for the purpose of providing consumer reports to third parties. If a consumer reporting agency verifies an applicant's job references by merely checking the facts on the application, such as dates worked, job title and final rate of pay and provides this information to the employer, the consumer reporting agency has provided a consumer report. On the other hand, if the consumer-reporting agency essentially conducts an interview by asking about job performance or whether the former employee was discharged for cause, a report to the prospective employer about this information constitutes an investigative consumer report.

In December 2003, President Bush signed legislation reauthorizing the FCRA, which included a provision to exempt third party investigations of employee wrongdoing from the reporting and disclosure provisions of the FCRA. The provision amended the act's definition of "consumer report" to exclude communications made by a third party to an employer in connection with the investigation of suspected misconduct relating to employment or compliance with federal, state or local laws and regulations, the rules of a self-regulatory organization or any pre-existing written policies of the employer. To be excluded, the communication must not be made for the purpose of investigating a consumer's credit worthiness, credit standing or credit capacity. Additionally, to be excluded, the communication can only be made to certain entities including the employer, federal, state or local officers or agencies or a self-regulatory organization with authority over the employer or employee.

After taking an adverse action based on such a communication, the employer must disclose to the consumer a summary containing the nature and substance of the communication; the employer is not required to disclose the sources of the communication. The provision was included to counteract a Federal Trade Commission (FTC) interpretation of the FCRA that impedes the use of third party investigations of harassment and other workplace misconduct (known as the "Vail Letter").

Acceptable and prohibited uses of consumer reports

A credit-reporting agency may furnish a consumer report to an employer for employment purposes. The term "employment purposes" includes an employer using the consumer report to evaluate the consumer for employment, promotion, reassignment or retention. A consumer-reporting agency may not include any medical information in a report unless it has the consent of the consumer. A consumer-reporting agency also may not report obsolete information regarding bankruptcies, civil suits or judgments, criminal arrests or any other adverse information. This prohibition regarding obsolete information is not applicable to a consumer report "to be used in connection with ... the employment of any individual" that is reasonably expected to make an annual salary of $75,000 or more.

Requirements prior to seeking a consumer report

- Employer's required disclosure to consumer/job applicant/current employee. Before an employer (other than in the trucking industry) obtains a consumer report, the employer must:

    - provide the consumer with "clear and conspicuous disclosure" that the consumer report may be obtained for employment purposes

    - ensure that the disclosure is written in a document that consists only of the disclosure

  if it takes any adverse action against a consumer based in whole or part on the credit report, it will provide the consumer with a copy of the report and a summary of the consumer's rights in accordance with the FCRA's requirements. The FTC has also issued a revised "Summary of Your Rights Under the Fair Credit Reporting Act," effective January 1, 2013, which is available on the agency's website.

    - https://www.consumer.ftc.gov/articles/0070-credit-and-your-consumer-rights

- Employer's required disclosure to consumer reporting agency.

- Additionally, prior to receiving a consumer report from a consumer reporting agency, an employer must certify to the reporting agency that:

    - it has made the required disclosures to the consumer in the proper form

    - it will not use the information in the consumer report in violation of any federal or state equal employment opportunity law or regulation

    - if it takes any adverse action against a consumer based in whole or part on the credit report, it will provide the consumer with a copy of the report and a summary of the consumer's rights in accordance with the FCRA's requirements.

Taking adverse action based on a consumer report

An employer can base an adverse decision regarding a consumer report in whole or part upon information included in a consumer report. An "adverse action" by an employer broadly includes denying employment or "any other decision for employment purposes that adversely affects any current or prospective employee." As described herein, the FCRA requires employers that make adverse decisions based on said information to make certain disclosures to the applicant or employee both before and after the action.

The disclosure requirements for job applicants vary slightly from the requirements for employees.

- **Required disclosure prior to taking adverse action**
  Before engaging in an adverse employment action based on a consumer report, the employer must provide the consumer with both:
  - a copy of the consumer report
  - a written summary of the consumer's rights as prescribed by the FTC (the employer should receive this summary from the consumer reporting agency). A revised Summary of Your Rights under the Fair Credit Reporting Act is available on the FTC's website at:
    - https://www.consumer.ftc.gov/articles/0070-credit-and-your-consumer-rights

  See also the FTC's advice for businesses regarding the use of background checks that is published on its website at the following address:
  - https://www.ftc.gov/news-events/blogs/business-blog/2017/04/background-checks-prospective-employees-keep-required
- **Required disclosure after taking adverse action**
  If the employer engages in an adverse action against the consumer, the employer must notify the consumer. The notification may be done in writing, verbally or by electronic means. It must include the following:
  - a notice of the adverse action
  - the name, address and phone number of the consumer reporting agency that provided the report to the employer
  - a statement that the consumer reporting agency did not make the decision to take the adverse action and thus cannot tell the consumer the specific reasons for the adverse action
  - a statement setting forth the consumer's right to obtain a free disclosure of the consumer's file from the CRA if the consumer makes a request within 60 days
  - a statement of the consumer's right to dispute directly with the consumer reporting agency the accuracy or completeness of any information provided by the agency.
- **Employment in the trucking industry**
  The trucking industry is exempt from the requirement that both the disclosure and authorization to secure the report be in writing. The law allows the required disclosure and authorization to be provided orally or by electronic means for positions "over which the secretary of transportation has the power to establish qualifications and maximum hours of service pursuant to the provisions of section 31502 of title 49 or a position subject to safety regulation by a state transportation agency," but this exemption only applies if the driver does not apply for the job in person.

- **Adverse action based on information obtained from affiliates**
  If a person takes an adverse action involving insurance, employment or a credit transaction initiated by the consumer based on information of the type covered by the FCRA and this information was obtained from an entity affiliated with the user of the information by common ownership or control, the FCRA requires the user to notify the consumer of the adverse action. The notice must inform the consumer that he or she may obtain a disclosure of the nature of the information relied upon by making a written request within 60 days of receiving the adverse action notice. If the consumer makes such a request, the user must disclose the nature of the information not later than 30 days after receiving the request. If consumer report information is shared among affiliates and then used for an adverse action, the user must make an adverse action disclosure as set forth previously.

Use of investigative consumer reports

If an employer wants to obtain an investigative consumer report about an applicant or employee, it must comply with the following requirements:

- The user must disclose to the consumer that an investigative consumer report may be obtained. This must be done in a written disclosure that is mailed or otherwise delivered, to the consumer at some time before or no later than three days after the date on which the report was first requested. The disclosure must include a statement informing the consumer of his or her right to request additional disclosures of the nature and scope of the investigation as described herein and the summary of consumer rights required by the FCRA. (The summary of consumer rights will be provided by the credit-reporting agency that conducts the investigation.)
- The user must certify to the credit-reporting agency that the disclosures set forth herein have been made and that the user will make the disclosure described as follows:

  > Upon the written request of a consumer made within a reasonable period of time after the disclosures required previously, the user must make a complete disclosure of the nature and scope of the investigation. This must be made in a written statement that is mailed or otherwise delivered, to the consumer no later than five days after the date on which the request was received from the consumer or the report was first requested, whichever is later in time.

Penalties

An employee or applicant may receive actual damages, punitive damages and attorneys' fees in a civil suit against an employer or prospective employer for noncompliance with the FCRA. An employer may also be liable for monetary damages to a consumer-reporting agency for obtaining a consumer report under false pretenses or knowingly securing the report without a permissible purpose. Moreover, any person who obtains information from a consumer-reporting agency under false pretenses may be fined and/or imprisoned for up to two years.

Drug tests

Drug test reports may be covered by the FCRA. The Fifth Circuit Court of Appeals ruled that drug test results may be covered by the FCRA because the "results of these drug tests are communications bearing on ... personal characteristics that were used to determine ... eligibility for employment." The FCRA does not apply to any report prepared by a drug-testing lab, which the lab submits directly to the employer after performing a drug test pursuant to the employer's policies. The FRCA applies when a report includes information about the results from prior drug tests.

Document destruction requirements

The FTC's document disposal rule requires employers to properly dispose of consumer information derived from "consumer reports" by taking reasonable measures to protect against unauthorized access to or use of the information in connection with its disposal. The "disposal rule" was issued pursuant to the requirements of the federal Fair and Accurate Credit Transactions Act (FACT), which amended the FCRA. The rule is designed to reduce the risk of consumer fraud, including identity theft created by improper disposal of consumer information.

The disposal rule applies to any person or entity over which the FTC has jurisdiction and who, for a business purpose, maintains or otherwise possesses consumer information. Employers who obtain consumer reports for any of the permissible purposes listed in the FCRA are covered by the disposal rule. While the disposal rule does not specify how employers should dispose of consumer information, it does state in the preamble that the FTC expects covered entities to consider the sensitivity of the information, the nature and size of the entity's operations, the costs and benefits of different disposal methods and relevant technological changes. The preamble also explains that the "reasonable measures" requirement likely requires employers to adopt policies and procedures to ensure that the policy behind these rules is achieved.

Other considerations

State laws

Many states have enacted prohibitions on access and use of consumer reports that are more restrictive on employers than the FCRA. Be sure to consult state and local law before conducting any background checks.

Adverse impact considerations

Poor credit ratings and other information found through consumer reporting agencies may have a disparate impact on a protected group. The employer must then show that this information is job-related and consistent with business necessity.

Workers' compensation

The EEOC Technical Assistance Manual issued under the Americans with Disabilities Act (ADA) states that an employer may not make an inquiry of a third party that the employer could not make of the applicant. An employer should not check an applicant's workers' compensation history from any source until after making the applicant a conditional offer of employment.

Privacy concerns

Background checks also raise privacy concerns and possibly defamation claims. The employer should always give the applicant notice and obtain a release for all information to be obtained.

Chapter

06

The employment relationship

At-will employment

The employee-employer relationship is contractual in nature and is the product of an agreement or series of agreements, including the nature of work, the duration of employment and the conditions of employment. The most common type of employment relationship is employment "at-will." An at-will employment relationship:

- is one for an indefinite term
- may be terminated by either party at any time.

Except where modified by law or contract, an employer may dismiss an employee at-will for good cause, no cause or even for morally wrong cause without being guilty of a legal wrong. At least one state, Montana, does not recognize at-will employment.

Contractual limitations

The at-will contract will be modified by express written agreements between the employer and employee. One form of contractual limitation may be an employee handbook. The courts of some states have held that certain provisions of employee handbooks, such as disciplinary proceedings and statements of company benefits, are binding on employers as part of the enforceable contract. However, if the employer properly and conspicuously states in its applications or handbook that the employment relationship is "at-will," such language will generally hold up in the courts.

Statutory limitations

Federal and state statutes limit an employer's discretion to terminate an at-will employee. Some of the statutes include:

- **Child Support Act**
  Prohibits discipline or discharge of an employee for assignment of wages for child support.
- **Education Professional Negotiations Act**
  Prohibits discharge of teachers for exercising their collective bargaining rights under the act.

- **The Occupational Safety and Health Act**
  Prohibits employment discrimination for exercising rights under the act.

Exceptions to employment at-will

Both state and federal courts have recognized several important public policy exceptions to the ability of an employer to terminate an employee at-will. For instance, based on workers' compensation law, some state courts have recognized a cause of action against an employer for "retaliatory discharge" where the discharge is in "retaliation" for the employee's pursuit of workers' compensation benefits. Other state courts have determined that an employer cannot terminate an employee for whistleblowing, such as where an employee reports a health or safety violation or criminal activity.

Chapter 07

New hire reporting

All employers must report specific information about newly hired employees to a designated agency in their state. The new hire report must contain certain information, including the employee's name, address and Social Security number and the employer's name, address and Federal Employer Identification Number (FEIN). If an employer has employees in more than one state, it has two reporting options:

it may report new hires to the state in which the work is being performed, following the requirements of that particular state

it may select one of the states in which it has employees and report all employees to that state electronically or magnetically.

If the employer chooses the latter option, it must notify the U.S. Department of Health and Human Services (HHS).

Timeframes

According to federal law, employers must submit information regarding every new hire within 20 days of the date of hire unless the submission is made electronically or magnetically. If an employer decides to report electronically or by magnetic medium, it must submit two transmissions each month (if necessary, based on new hiring), but the reports should not be submitted in the time period of fewer than 12 days apart and no more than 17 days apart. For a link to the specific requirements see the following URL:

- https://www.acf.hhs.gov/css/outreach-material/new-hire-reporting-employers

Reporting agency

Once the employer reports the information to the appropriate state agency, the state transmits the data to the National Directory of New Hires (NDNH). This information is used by child support enforcement agencies.

The location of the reporting agencies in all 50 states can be found at:

- https://www.acf.hhs.gov/css/contact-information/state-new-hire-reporting-websites

Reporting returns from layoffs, rehires and leaves of absence

If an employee returns to work and another W-4 form is completed, the employer is required to submit another new hire report. If the employee has not been formally discharged or has not been removed from payroll records, it is not necessary to report the returning individual as a new hire.

Requirements for reporting new hires

1. **Temporary employment agencies and independent contractors**
   Temporary employment agencies must submit a new hire report if they are paying wages to an individual. In contrast, independent contractors and subcontractors are required to make their own reporting and the hiring entity is not. As with most of the information, each state's requirements should be examined.

2. **Labor organizations and hiring halls**
   These organizations must report the employees who work directly for them. If they merely refer individuals to outside employment, they do not have to submit a new hire report for these individuals.

Chapter 08

Policy manuals and employee handbooks

A policy manual and employee handbook should reflect the company's employee relations philosophy. Therefore, it should be viewed by everyone in the organization as being more than a document that gets pulled off the shelf whenever an employment issue arises. Rather, it is a reflection of how an organization will treat each employee and what each employee needs to do to be successful within the company.

Distinctions between a policy manual and an employee handbook

Employers should have separate supervisory policy manuals and employee handbooks. Supervisory policy manuals and employee handbooks serve separate purposes. Employers should develop both and keep them current. Certain information needed by managers should not be included in handbooks distributed to non-management employees. For instance, information such as steps to follow before terminating employees should never be included in employee handbooks. Such information is only appropriate for a supervisory policy manual. However, it is also important to have an employee handbook to apprise employees of company policy. Accordingly, employers should develop and maintain two distinct documents.

Language choices

Supervisor's manuals and employee handbooks should be carefully drafted to ensure that the wording of the manual does not create an enforceable employment contract. Supervisory manuals that are instructive but leave the employer room for discretion are less likely to be deemed to have created an employment contract. As a general rule, words such as "must" and "should" need to be avoided because their use may create an employment contract.

Reviewing the manual and handbook

Supervisory policy manuals and employee handbooks should be carefully reviewed on a periodic basis. The review should include the following considerations:

- Is the current policy up to date?
- Does the organization operate the same way that it did when the policy was adopted?
- Has the policy interfered with operations?

- Has the policy adversely affected employee morale or productivity?
- Has the policy caused complaints?
- Are there charges or lawsuits associated with this policy?
- Has the policy been uniformly and consistently enforced?
- Is there an important standard operating procedure that has not been recorded in the policy?
- Is the policy necessary to:
    - implement an employee benefit or service?
    - inform employees of their responsibilities?
    - help reach sound management decisions on difficult issues?
    - increase consistency in decisions?
    - delegate effectively?
    - reduce legal exposure in personnel matters?
    - implement an organizational objective?

These questions can help in deciding if any of these policies are actually needed. If the policy is not necessary, do not write it. Err on the side of brevity, because employees may construe any included policies as "promises" or "contracts." Consider involving an anti-bias policy taskforce, including female and minority representation, in the review process. When satisfied with the document, have a professional experienced in writing policy manuals audit the document for legal and human resource problems.

Consider distributing all handbooks and guides in binders with the date at the bottom of each page. Future revisions can then be made on a page-by-page basis, reducing reprinting costs. The final step is non-supervisory employee orientation and establishment of a handbook orientation program for new employees.

Include an acknowledgment of receipt

Additionally, employers should establish a supervisory policy manual orientation for all new managers. Employees should always be required to sign an acknowledgment of receipt of an employee handbook, including a statement that the employee agrees to become familiar with the contents of the handbook. This acknowledgment becomes important in event of a lawsuit because employees cannot credibly claim they were unaware of the policies listed in the acknowledgment.

Features to consider during drafting

- **Positive tone**
  The tone of the handbook should be positive. The handbook should give the employee a feeling of pride in the company.

- **User friendly language**
  The handbook should be made user friendly by including a table of contents, question and answer sections and an index. Limit each sentence to a single idea and do not use obscure language.
- **Avoiding language conveying permanency**
  Do not use the word "permanent" to describe employment. Instead, use the word "regular." Avoid using mandatory language such as "shall" or "will."
- **Avoid duration terminology**
  Do not use language that suggests a specific duration of employment. Avoid statements such as "this handbook is an agreement on how we will operate our business. Read through it. Then it will become more than a handbook ... it will become an understanding" or "you will be provided year-round employment to the greatest practical extent." If the employment is at-will, a clear statement that either the employer or the employee may terminate the employment arrangement at any time for any reason should be included.
- **Avoid language indicating a specific work location**
  Do not include any language that implies that the company promises to employ the employees only in a certain location because this may be interpreted as an implied promise not to transfer.
- **New handbooks**
  Any newly issued handbook should indicate that it supersedes any previous handbook.
- **Disclaimers**
  Appropriate employment at-will disclaimers should be included on the application for employment, in letters offering employment, in employee policies and handbooks and in the statement of employee receipt of employee handbook or policies. At-will disclaimers are often placed at the beginning or end of a handbook. To ensure the effectiveness of disclaimers, the language should be carefully drafted, reviewed and clearly and conspicuously displayed.
- **No oral modification clause**
  The handbook should provide that the company can change it unilaterally at any time but that no manager has the authority to make any oral modification of the handbook.
- **Employer instituted rules**
  In most cases, the provisions in the employee handbook are not bargained for and are instituted by the employer under its own authority. In some jurisdictions, it may be necessary to have this clearly noted in the handbook.
- **Avoid statements regarding job security**
  Avoid statements that guarantee employment such as "an employee will be discharged only if he or she fails to properly perform the job assigned" or "good performance is your best guarantee of job security."
- **Consistency**
  Make sure documents are consistent. In other words, the policy manual, the application and the employee handbook acknowledgment of an at-will employee should all note the at-will nature of the employment.

- **Confidentiality provisions**
  A vaguely worded confidentiality provision could be deemed to violate the National Labor Relations Act (NLRA). For instance, an employer's confidentiality provision stated: "We recognize and protect the confidentiality of any information concerning the company, its business plans, its partners, new business efforts, customers, accounting and financial matters." The term "partners" refers to employees. The National Labor Relations Board (NLRB) ruled that the unqualified prohibition of the release of "any information" regarding the employer's "partners" (that is, employees) could reasonably be construed by employees to restrict discussion of wages and other terms and conditions of employment with their fellow employees and with the union. Thus, since the provision violated the NLRA.

- **Nondiscrimination language**
  Employers should assure employees that illegal discrimination is prohibited and that it will not be tolerated in the workplace.

Maintaining the resource

A loose-leaf employee handbook and policy book, as well as a series decimal system and a date on each page are useful because a policy change can be made without replacing the entire book. Also, handbooks and policy books, which should be returned on termination, can be recycled. Copies of all replaced pages should be retained. This is especially useful if the employer becomes involved in litigation in which the wording of the policy or handbook is disputed and the handbook has been changed since the date the plaintiff was employed. A good communication program will greatly improve the ability to keep employees informed of changes to the handbook. Bulletin boards, newsletters and paycheck inserts can be used to inform employees of policy changes. When notifying the employees of new policies, remind them that the change can be found in the employee handbook(s) and make sure the change is reflected in the handbooks.

Essential aspects of the handbook

Initial employment periods

In states that recognize "employment at-will" employees are considered to be terminable at-will unless a union contract, a civil service law or other law or a poorly worded provision in an employee handbook gives them job protection. Setting up a formal "probationary period" of limited duration, followed by "permanent" employment or a guarantee of employment without "just cause" for termination, may lead courts to find that employees have a contractual right to employment following completion of the probationary period. The contractual right may then lead to litigation over whether the employee could only be terminated for just cause and what constitutes just cause, if the employer discharges the employee.

Additionally, establishment of a probationary period can cause new employees to conceal latent performance problems and can mislead supervisors into retaining poor employees. Once the probation period is completed, a supervisor may be under the mistaken impression that the employee cannot be disciplined or discharged without there being serious misconduct. Because benefits and evaluations can come into play after a 60- or 90- day "initial employment period" as easily as they can after a 60- or 90-

day "probationary period," the employer may want to use the term "initial employment period" to define this timeframe and avoid the potential problems discussed previously.

Complaint or problem-solving procedure

Solid complaint procedures enable management to eliminate employee problems, point out employer errors and provide a valuable tool for diagnosing and resolving organizational ills. The term "complaint procedure" is preferable to the union term "grievance procedure." Supervisors should be properly trained to administer a problem-solving procedure and cultivate an atmosphere in which employees feel comfortable discussing a complaint. Often, the mere existence of the complaint procedure can alleviate employee problems before they become bigger problems or lead to unionization.

Suggested problem-solving procedure

1. **First step – Immediate supervisor**
   Have the employee discuss the complaint with the immediate supervisor, who should have the authority to settle most complaints. The supervisor should investigate the problem and, if it appears to exceed the supervisor's authority, he or she should instruct the employee to refer the problem to the next level of authority. If the problem is within the supervisor's authority, he or she should analyze the facts, perhaps confer with a superior, make a decision and inform the employee of the decision. If the employee is not satisfied with the supervisor's solution, the supervisor should inform the employee that he or she may take the problem to the next higher authority without fear of retribution. The employee needs to know that management is concerned about the problem and is willing to do what it can to resolve the issue. If the employee's supervisor is the source of the complaint, the complaint procedure should clearly state that the employee may approach the supervisor's immediate superior without first complaining to the supervisor.

2. **Second step – Next higher level**
   If the complaint was not settled in the first step, the complaint should be put in writing at the second level to clearly identify and preserve the facts and allegations. The employee may present the complaint at the second step orally, but the second step supervisor should report every complaint fully and in writing to upper management. If the employee is encouraged to submit the complaint in writing at the second step, the second step supervisor may assist the employee in writing the complaint unless the employee does not want assistance, or it involves this supervisor. If the second step supervisor feels that the first supervisor has erred, he or she should discuss the facts of the case with that supervisor and explain why a different decision will be reached. The first supervisor should be given an opportunity to revise the decision and thereby preserve his or her standing with the employees. It is important to uphold the original decision if the first level supervisor made a correct determination; but management should not undermine the employee's confidence in the employer by upholding a bad decision.

3. **Third step – Top local business executive, department head or plant manager**
   If the problem remains unresolved, the next higher authority must make a decision. If the employee initiated the complaint procedure at this level or the complaint has not otherwise been written, it should be committed to writing at this point. The resolution should also be in writing. Before the department head or plant manager communicates the resolution to the employee, he or she should contact the lower level supervisors involved and review the complaint with them. Wherever possible, allow the immediate supervisor to make the correction or decision and get full credit for it. Management should follow up on the situation at a later date to see if employer policy has gone into effect and to ensure that no retribution has occurred.

4. **Fourth step (optional) – Appeal to president of the employer**
   Depending on the size of the employer, appeals to the president may be impractical. However, when possible, take the final step in the complaint procedure and notify the president of the organization. A simple internal procedure could be constructed by which the president appoints an officer of the company (such as the vice president or personnel director/human resources manager) to fully investigate the complaint and report to the president in writing. This officer should assist the employee in presentation of the complaint at each level of appeal, if the employee is dissatisfied with the decision.

Other considerations

Binding arbitration

Some employers may wish to establish a complaint or problem-solving procedure that ends in binding arbitration. Employers should be aware that while the U.S. Supreme Court has found employment arbitration agreements to be enforceable, the lower courts charged with determining the enforceability of such agreements may scrutinize them closely to ensure they are fair before requiring an employee to arbitrate employment related claims. Such agreements can contain a jury waiver or a class action and collective action waiver.

Separate procedure for discrimination complaints

An employer may wish to implement a separate procedure for complaints of discrimination based on some prohibited basis, such as sex, national origin, race and the like.

Employee acknowledgment of complaint procedure

An employer should consider distributing an acknowledgment that reiterates the employer's anti-harassment complaint procedure to employees annually. This acknowledgment should indicate that the employee has read it and understands that he or she can complain to someone other than the direct supervisor if the employee feels he or she has been subjected to illegal discrimination or harassment.

Marital status/anti-nepotism policies

Anti-nepotism policies prevent related individuals from working in the same company or department. There are a number of sound reasons for anti-nepotism rules and "no fraternization" policies, including avoiding:

- involvement in emotional problems at the home
- supervisory conflicts between spouses and relatives
- hiring decisions based on favoritism or the appearance of favoritism
- vacation and day off scheduling problems
- family influence regarding grievances and work conflicts.

Employers should be cautious in implementing an anti-nepotism policy if the policy has a disparate impact on a certain protected category under Title VII of the Civil Rights Act (Title VII) and there are alternative means of achieving the same business considerations that led to the policy's implementation.

Title VII does not prohibit discrimination on the basis of marital status. Many state laws, however, prohibit employers from discriminating based on marital status. Generally, a court will not find gender discrimination if the allegedly discriminatory action is based on the identity of the plaintiff's spouse and not on the plaintiff's status as married.

When taking employment actions with respect to employees who have a familial relationship with other employees, employers should be aware that the U.S. Supreme Court has held that Title VII prohibits an employer from retaliating against a third party who has a close associate who files a discrimination claim.

Seniority/longevity policies

Because the term "seniority" often implies legal entitlement, an employer who incorporates concepts of seniority in an employee handbook must exercise caution to avoid the unwitting creation of legally enforceable rights and remedies. In some situations, there may be an advantage to recognizing seniority. For instance, recognizing seniority may help instill a sense of job security that could avoid unionization efforts or help to attract highly qualified candidates for employment. It may also relieve the employer of making difficult decisions based on other factors and thereby avoid accusations of favoritism and can be a good defense in response to a charge of discrimination in layoff or discharge situations. However, seniority can result in the retention and advancement of "borderline" employees, which could discourage more qualified but less senior employees from remaining with the employer long enough to accumulate seniority/longevity.

In weighing the advantages and disadvantages of a seniority/longevity system, an employer should distinguish between giving an employee recognition based on seniority/longevity and granting an employee legally enforceable rights based on seniority/longevity. Assuming some recognition of "seniority" is determined to be in the employer's interest, statements in an employee handbook regarding seniority should use "longevity" or "length of service" rather than "seniority" since it is a "union" word and should be narrowly limited to apply to specific circumstances.

Benefits

Most employers should include a benefits section that explains the benefits to which employees are entitled, such as:

- vacations
- holidays
- sick leave
- leaves of absence
- insurance coverage
- pension plans
- any other benefits to which employees are entitled.

Note:
Several states have begun a push for increased paid family and medical leave. Employers should therefore check their local and state laws to ensure compliance with these benefits. This section should also discuss the eligibility requirements and conditions for receipt of benefits. Employers may want to include a brief description of benefits mandated by federal or state law, such as social security, workers' compensation insurance and unemployment insurance. Employers should clearly classify employees for the purposes of determining entitlement to benefits and should follow these criteria. Failure to do so may result in a finding that contingent or temporary workers have been misclassified and are entitled to benefits.

Family and Medical Leave Act

Regulations issued under the Family and Medical Leave Act (FMLA) require employers to set forth their FMLA policy in any applicable handbook.

Behavioral rules

Employers should include a statement of work safety and conduct rules, identifying the type of conduct the employer expects from employees. These provisions should not refer to disciplinary action that may result from a violation of workplace rules, as this may lead to an argument that the employee can only be discharged for cause. Consider adding the following statement to an employee handbook and policies:

> ABC Company does not violate the law and does not tolerate those who do. If an employee believes that anyone in or associated with the ABC Company has requested or directed him or her to do anything that violates the law or has prohibited the employee from doing anything that the law requires him or her to do, the employee must report this immediately to the Company president or [add title of one other person].

Smoking

Employers may be required to act on complaints by non-smokers that they are adversely affected by smoke in the workplace, depending on the nature of the complaint. For instance, an employer's failure to accommodate a non-smoker's medical need to work in an environment free from second hand smoke may give rise to a claim under the Americans with Disabilities Act (ADA). However, some states have laws that prohibit employers from terminating employees for smoking while not at work or for smoking while at work but in compliance with the employer's policies regarding smoking in the workplace. For comprehensive information regarding workplace smoking, see:

- https://www.tobacco.org

Smokers' claims have met with somewhat less success than non-smokers' claims.

For the most part, employers are free to set rules regarding tobacco use on their premises. However, a minority of states prohibit an employer from taking an adverse employment action based on an employee's lawful or off duty use of tobacco products. Be sure to consult state and local laws. Specifically, an employer who wishes to prohibit smoking on its premises, be sure to consult recent posting requirements.

Progressive discipline

If the handbook or policy establishes a system of progressive discipline, the employer may be challenged as having an obligation to use these procedures. Employers should avoid statements that may later limit their right to discipline or terminate employment such as:

- "Employees shall be discharged for just and sufficient cause only."
- "Employees will only be fired for illegal, immoral or unethical conduct."

Employers should also avoid using any statement that suggests that specific steps of progressive discipline will always be followed. The handbook should provide that the reasons for discharge presented in the handbook are not exclusive and that other circumstances may result in discharge in management's discretion.

Hours of work

Employers may wish to include an hours of work section, if applicable, that describes employees' work schedules, breaks, meal periods, the workweek and the workday established for overtime pay calculations and recordkeeping requirements. Employers who use such a section should clearly state that the overtime provisions only apply to the categories of employees eligible for overtime pay.

Use of cellphones

In light of concerns regarding the safety of the use of cellphones while driving, employers may want to include a policy regarding this. In addition to adopting a cellphone usage policy, employers may want to consider conducting safety training, periodically checking the motor vehicle records of employees who are required to drive a vehicle in the normal course of employment, requiring employees to regularly report moving violations and purchasing appropriate equipment (such as hands free car kits and headsets, speakerphones, one digit dialing features and voice activated dialing) for use by employees that may minimize the risk of accidents. The Cellular Telecommunications Industry Association and the American Automobile Association (AAA), recommend a number of safety tips for using a wireless phone while driving. These include the following:

- ensuring that employees know the features available on their wireless phones and how to use them, such as speed dialing and redialing
- using hands free devices, as well as one button or memory or voice activated dialing
- ensuring that the wireless phone is within easy reach of the driver
- advising employees that they should inform all persons with whom they speak that they are driving
- avoiding the use of the phone in hazardous weather and traffic conditions (this includes placing or answering calls)
- ensuring that employees do not take notes while driving or look up phone numbers (employees should be instructed to pull off the road if note taking or researching a number is necessary)
- asking passengers (if present) to dial the number for the employee
- placing calls when the employee is not moving or before pulling into traffic
- avoiding stressful or emotional conversations while driving
- while driving, only using the wireless phone for emergencies, such as dialing 911 or other local emergency numbers, to call roadside assistance or to help others in an emergency.

Employers may want to incorporate these safety suggestions in any cellphone usage policy. Employers should also consult federal and state law, which may ban certain commercial drivers from using cellphones while operating a vehicle.

Additionally, these cameras could be used to harass other employees by taking photographs in private situations such as locker rooms or restrooms. Accordingly, employers may want to consider including provisions in employee handbooks prohibiting the use of camera phones in private areas, such as restrooms, locker rooms, changing rooms and the like, as well as areas in which research and development is conducted or areas containing proprietary or confidential business information or personnel or medical files.

Other issues to be considered

In addition to the provisions discussed previously, employers may want to consider addressing some or all of the following issues in employee handbooks or supervisory manuals:

- alcohol and drug use prohibition/testing
- appearance/dress codes
- arrest records

- confidentiality/trade secrets/noncompete agreements/conflicts of interest
- emergency/procedures for dealing with workplace violence/threats
- lactation policy in accordance with the Patient Protection and Affordable Care Act
- mission statement
- performance appraisals (company expectations, schedule and process of appraisal, right to comment)
- security issues (including identification procedures, badges and guards)
- solicitation
- transfers
- travel procedures/allowance/reservations
- workplace violence policies, including the possibility of a weapons ban, if allowed by state law.

Potential problem areas of a handbook

Payment of wages

The Fair Labor Standards Act (FLSA) sets the minimum wage and overtime rates. An employer must ensure that any policies for deductions from employee wages comply with the FLSA. State laws frequently set minimum wage rates higher than the federal minimum wage or have overtime provisions that are more favorable to employees. Where state law is more beneficial, most employers will be required to follow the state minimum wage/overtime provisions. State laws also often define when and how often, employees must be paid.

Voting time

Under the laws of many states, employees are entitled to be excused from work for a period of time to vote. The states vary as to whether employers must pay employees for the time spent voting. Several states allow employers to require employees to provide advance notice or proof of participation in the voting process.

State	Voting time
Alabama	Up to one-hour unpaid time off is allowed if the employee starts work less than two hours after the polls open and finishes less than one hour before the polls close.
Alaska	If employee does not have two consecutive hours off while polls are open, employees must give as much paid time as necessary to enable employees to vote.
Arizona	If employees do not have three consecutive hours to vote before or after work, employer must give employees sufficient paid time off work so that they do have three consecutive hours.

State	Voting time
Arkansas	Employees must schedule work hours so that employees have time to vote. The time off is unpaid.
California	Employees must be given sufficient time off to vote when added to voting time available outside of work hours. Up to two hours of time off must be paid. An employee who has sufficient non-working time in which to vote is excluded.
Colorado	Employees must be given up to two hours off with pay, unless they have three consecutive hours to vote outside of work.
Connecticut	As long as employees provide notice within 48 hours of election day, employers are required to provide employees with two hours of unpaid time off between the hours of 6:00 a.m. and 8:00 p.m. to vote on election day.
Delaware	No law
District of Columbia	The District of Columbia requires employers to provide for up to two hours of paid leave for voting. The D.C. law further requires employers to post a "Time Off to Vote" notice in a conspicuous location in the workplace.
Florida	No law
Georgia	Up to two hours off, unpaid, unless the employee has two hours before or after work to vote.
Hawaii	No law. (Prior law providing for up to two consecutive hours of paid time off to vote was repealed effective July 1, 2019).
Idaho	No requirement for private employers.
Illinois	Two hours of paid leave, unless the employee has two hours before or after work to vote.
Indiana	No law
Iowa	If employee does not have three consecutive hours before or after work to vote, the employer must give enough time off work so that employee does have three consecutive hours. Leave must be paid.
Kansas	Sufficient time off so that the employee has two consecutive hours to vote. Leave must be paid.
Kentucky	Employee must be given up to four hours of unpaid time off to vote.
Louisiana	No law. Employers with 20 or more employees cannot fire employee for political opinions or attempt to control whether the employee votes.
Maine	No law
Maryland	Two hours, unless employee has two consecutive hours before or after work. Leave must be paid, with proof of voting.

State	Voting time
Massachusetts	Mercantile, manufacturing and mechanical establishments must give employees unpaid time off during the first two hours after polls open.
Michigan	No law
Minnesota	Sufficient paid time off to vote the morning of an election.
Mississippi	No law. However, it is recommended that employers provide time off to vote to ensure they do not run afoul of the state's non-coercion law.
Missouri	Three hours with pay, unless employee has three consecutive hours away from work to vote.
Montana	No law.
Nebraska	If employee does not have two consecutive hours to vote outside of working hours, employers must give employees sufficient time off so that employee does have two consecutive hours. Leave must be paid, if employee gives notice.
Nevada	Sufficient paid time off between one and three hours (determined by the distance between the place of employment and the polling place) if it is impracticable for employee to vote before or after work.
New Hampshire	No law. Employers are prohibited from influencing or intimidating employees to vote for or against a particular candidate.
New Jersey	No law.
New Mexico	Two hours paid leave, unless polls open more than two hours before a workday or stay open more than three hours after the workday ends.
New York	Sufficient time to vote, unless employee has four consecutive hours outside work time to vote. Employee must be paid for up to two hours.
North Carolina	No law. Employers are prohibited from discharging or threatening workers based on how they did or did not vote.
North Dakota	No law, but employers are encouraged to give time off to vote.
Ohio	Reasonable time off to vote is required.
Oklahoma	Two hours or more under certain circumstances, unless the employee has three consecutive hours before or after work in which to vote. Leave must be paid.
Oregon	No law as Oregon is a vote-by-mail state, with the option to vote in person.

State	Voting time
Pennsylvania	No law. Employers are prohibited from threatening or intimidating employees to influence their political opinions or actions.
Rhode Island	No law. Employers are prohibited from putting information in pay envelopes or positing information designed to influence employees' political actions.
South Carolina	No law. Employers are prohibited from discharging workers because of political opinions or the exercise of political rights and privileges.
South Dakota	Two hours, unless the employee has two consecutive hours before or after work to vote. Leave must be paid.
Tennessee	Reasonable time, up to three hours, unless the employee has three consecutive hours away from work while the polls are open. Leave must be paid.
Texas	Sufficient time to vote, unless the employee has two consecutive hours outside of work to vote. Leave must be paid.
Utah	Two hours at the beginning or end of shift, unless the employee has three hours away from work to vote. Leave must be paid.
Vermont	No law.
Virginia	No law.
Washington	No time off is necessary, as the entire state is vote-by-mail.
West Virginia	Up to three hours, unless the employee has three hours away from work to vote. Leave must be paid.
Wisconsin	Three hours unpaid leave.
Wyoming	Employees are entitled to one hour leave with pay (excluding meal hour), unless the employee has at least three consecutive non-work hours available while polls are open.

Responding to investigations

Employers should consider establishing an "immediate reaction" procedure for use in the event of surprise visits by government agents. Supervisors should be instructed to refer any government investigator to a person designated to work with government inquiries. Any governmental agents should be referred to this person before being allowed onto the premises.

Any policy designed to handle government inquiries should include contacting the company's labor and employment counsel immediately. Contacting counsel early may limit the scope of the governmental inquiry and save the company money.

Garnishments

Federal law prohibits an employer from discharging an employee because his or her earnings have been garnished for "one indebtedness." This statute provides for its violation.

Note:
Under the garnishment law, an employee whose wage is being garnished for more than one indebtedness may be discharged, but such a discharge may raise discrimination concerns under Title VII.

Calculation of the amount to be withheld

Federal law provides that the maximum amount that may be garnished each week may not exceed 25% of the employee's disposable earnings (gross earnings minus any amounts required by law to be withheld) for that week or the amount by which the disposable earnings for the week exceed 30 times the federal minimum hourly wage, whichever is less. The amount of disposable earnings not withheld must be paid to the employee on the regular payday for the pay period in which the wages were earned. The employer should retain the money withheld until the court directs the employer to turn the money over to the plaintiff-creditor or its representative.

Example
If an employee's wages total $400 per week and the deductions for social security and federal income tax total $75, the employee's disposable earnings equal $325 for the week. The amount to be withheld is $81.25 and the amount that can be turned over to the employee is $243.75.

Exceptions to calculations of amount to be withheld

Federal law provides that the previous calculations do not apply in the case of:

- any order for the support of any person issued by a court of competent jurisdiction or in accordance with an administrative procedure, which is established by state law, affords substantial due process and is subject to judicial review
- any order of any court of the United States having jurisdiction over cases under Chapter 13 of Title II
- any debt due for any state or federal tax.

In the case of garnishment to enforce any order for the support of any person, the maximum part of the aggregate disposable earnings of an individual for any workweek subject to the garnishment shall not exceed:

- when such individual is supporting his or her spouse or dependent child (other than a spouse or child with respect to whose support such order is issued), 50% of such individual's disposable earnings for that week
- when such individual is not supporting such a spouse or dependent child as described, 60% of such individual's disposable earnings for that week.

With respect to the disposable earnings of any individual for any workweek, the 50% specified previously shall be deemed to be 55% and the 60% specified shall be deemed to be 65%, if and to the extent that such earnings are subject to garnishment to enforce a support order with respect to a period that is prior to the 12-week period that ends with the beginning of such workweek. Issues can arise regarding conflicting priorities as between garnishments and support orders.

Note:
Most states also have laws regulating garnishments.

Student loans

The rules regarding student loans do not come from a state or federal court, but are issued by the Secretary of Education against an individual who has defaulted on any student loan that is offered by, insured or guaranteed by the federal government. The amount deducted may not exceed 15% of the employee's disposable pay (without the written consent of the employee). An employer who fails to pay the Secretary or the guaranty agency, as directed in the withholding order, is liable for the amount that should have been withheld, plus attorneys' fees, costs and, in the court's discretion, punitive damages. An employer is prohibited from discharging, refusing to employ or taking disciplinary action against an individual because of a garnishment and can be liable to a prevailing employee for attorney fees, back pay, reinstatement and punitive damages.

Chapter 09

Personnel files

Many employers fail to make employee recordkeeping a priority and frequently pay the price when they are required to produce personnel file materials in discovery or when requested by subpoena. In the long run, all businesses will save time and money by taking a proactive approach to properly maintaining and preserving employee records. When a business has reliable policies and procedures in place to ensure that relevant employee documentation is maintained, the business will be better protected from liability and management will be in a position to make more informed employment decisions.

Required and recommended information

This chapter will refer to five different categories of employee records, which are as follows:

1. **Employee history records**
   Employee history documents include those that relate to job performance, including employee performance, promotions and corrective action write ups. Generally speaking, managers need access to employee history records to make appropriate employment decisions.

2. **Medical history and other documents unrelated to an employee's job performance**
   Employers should ensure that medical documents and other information that managers should not consider in making employment decisions are maintained in a confidential file to which managers do not have access. These files will typically contain pre-employment reference checks, candidate interview evaluations, credit reports, employee photos and equal employment opportunity (EEO) data.

   The Americans with Disabilities Act (ADA) and the Family and Medical Leave Act (FMLA) require medical records to be kept confidential. Accordingly, all medical information, including benefits claims forms, reimbursement requests for medical expenses, forms relating to workers' compensation claims, drug testing results, post-offer physical examinations, information voluntarily disclosed by an employee regarding a "disability" under the ADA or the Rehabilitation Act and all records and documents relating to medical certifications, re-certification and/or the medical history of an employee or the employee's family should be maintained in separate and secure file that can only be accessed by appropriate persons.

3. **Immigration Act forms**
The Immigration Reform and Control Act (IRCA) requires employers to verify that employees are authorized to work in the United States. Employees are required to complete Form I-9 at the time of hire to verify that he or she is authorized to work. In the event that the employee presents a work authorization document that has an expiration date, the employer is also required to reverify the employee's work status at an appropriate time. Employers must keep Form I-9 for each employee during the period of employment and for three years after the date of hire or for one year after the employment relationship ends, whichever of these two periods is longer. All businesses must make this form available to the government in the event of an investigation.

   It is a good idea for employers to keep and maintain the I-9 in a separate file for each employee so that managers who are charged with making employment decisions do not have an opportunity to consider the national origin of the employee. By keeping this information in a separate file, an employer helps protect itself against charges of discrimination based on national origin.

4. **Documents related to investigations**
When an employer receives an Equal Employment Opportunity Commission (EEOC) charge, it should keep and maintain all documents relating to any investigation and/or that could potentially be relevant to the subject matter of the charge. If such information is not kept and maintained, the employer could face penalties and/or find itself in a position where it cannot properly defend against certain allegations. Employers should protect the identity of any employees who provide information during the course of any investigation to limit the likelihood of additional claims of retaliation.

5. **Departmental files**
Employers should not permit managers and/or departments to keep and maintain their own employee files. The Human Resources Department should maintain all employee files. When separate files are kept and maintained, inconsistencies that may exist between the respective files could raise questions that could lead to employer liability in the event of a lawsuit.

Information disposal

Sarbanes-Oxley Act requirements

The Sarbanes-Oxley Act (SOX) contains criminal statutes that forbid the destruction, alteration or falsification of records in federal investigations and bankruptcy cases. Those who violate this act may be fined, sent to prison for up to 20 years or both. This is not limited to corporate securities fraud – it applies to all federal investigations, including those conducted by the EEOC, the Occupational Safety and Health Administration (OSHA), the National Labor Relations Board (NLRB), the Wage and Hour Division of the Department of Labor and the Immigration and Naturalization Service (INS), among others.

The Act also amends the obstruction of justice statute to prohibit the corrupt alteration, destruction, mutilation or concealment of documents and other objects or the attempt to do so, with the intent to impair the object's integrity or availability for use in an official proceeding. It also makes it a criminal act to corruptly obstruct, influence or impede an official proceeding or attempt to do so. The "attempt" wording is added to ensure that the failure to destroy documents or influence a proceeding is not a defense to the crime.

Other federal laws

Many federal laws contain recordkeeping requirements mandating that employers retain employment related documents for a specified period of time. For instance, the Fair Labor Standards Act (FLSA) requires employers to retain payroll records for a minimum of three years. Other statutes, such as the Occupational Safety and Health Act (OSH Act), require employers to retain records for even longer periods of time. Before developing and implementing any document disposal policies and procedures, an employer should review all relevant federal and state statutes that relate to document retention.

Employee access to personnel files

Employers often gather and retain personal information about applicants and employees such as:

- resumes
- interview reports
- pre-employment investigations
- pension information
- medical records
- results from psychological tests
- conviction records
- credit reports
- drug test results
- performance appraisals
- salary data.

An employer can face liability if it does not take adequate steps to ensure that such information is protected from disclosure, but employers are also required to give employees access to some records that it keeps and maintains. For instance, records relating to drug testing performed pursuant to regulations adopted by the U.S. Department of Transportation (DOT) must be made available to the employee. Employees must also have access to any records that indicate that he or she has been exposed to toxic chemicals or harmful physical agents. Nonetheless, it is a general rule that employees do not have a right to review the contents of their personnel files unless state law or a collective bargaining agreement provide otherwise.

State	Employee access to personnel files
Alabama	When a disciplinary document is placed in employee's personnel file, public employers must supply a copy of the documentation to employee no later than 10 days after its inclusion in the file.

State	Employee access to personnel files
Alaska	Employers should allow current and former employees to inspect and copy the contents of the personnel file. Employers are permitted to charge a reasonable copying fee. State employees have the right to examine their own personnel files and/or authorize others to do so.
Arizona	Employers must allow an employee or his or her designated representative to inspect and copy payroll records pertaining to that employee.
Arkansas	Public employers only. Personnel records must be made available to the employee and/or his or her representative.
California	Employees are allowed to inspect all documents related to qualifications for employment, promotion, additional compensation, termination or discipline. They are not permitted access to records relating to possible criminal offenses, letters of reference or ratings, reports or records that were obtained prior to the employee's employment.
Colorado	Public employees only. Employees may inspect their files (former state and public employees can do so as well).
Connecticut	Employers are required to permit employees to inspect and, if requested, copy their personnel file not more than seven business days (not more than 10 business days for former employees), after the receipt of a written request from an employee.
Delaware	Employees may be limited to inspection once per year and must show reasonable cause.
District of Columbia	None for private employers. District government employees may inspect, subject to restrictions.
Florida	Employees and former employees or their representatives have the right to access medical records concerning the employee's exposure to toxic substances.
Georgia	Public employees only.
Hawaii	State employees may have access, subject to certain restrictions. It is unclear for former state employees.
Idaho	Government employees can inspect and obtain copies, subject to certain exceptions.
Illinois	Subject to restrictions, current and former private and public employees may make written requests to view their personnel files and copy.
Indiana	Current and former public employees may inspect.
Iowa	Current private and public employees may examine and copy files, with certain restrictions (former employee access is unclear).
Kansas	Public employers only, but limited to the names, positions, salaries and lengths of service.
Kentucky	Current and former state government employees may inspect and copy, subject to certain exclusions.

State	Employee access to personnel files
Louisiana	Only current school employees must be allowed to inspect. Other employees have right to inspect certain documents.
Maine	Current and former public and private employees may inspect and copy. Employers may charge a reasonable copying fees.
Maryland	Certain access must be granted to state government employees and "persons in interest."
Massachusetts	Current and former employees may review file at place of employment during normal business hours and, under certain circumstances, obtain a copy of the file. Employers may limit inspection to twice per year.
Michigan	Upon written request, current and former private and public employees may inspect and obtain copies, subject to limitations and reasonable copying fees.
Minnesota	Current and former employees may inspect upon good-faith request, subject to certain limitations and reasonable copying fees.
Mississippi	None
Missouri	None
Montana	State employees are required to have access to their personnel records and may file written response to information contained in file.
Nebraska	Employees of public-school districts may inspect.
Nevada	Current and former employees may inspect and obtain copies, subject to certain restrictions and reasonable copying fees.
New Hampshire	Most current and former private and public employees may inspect or copy, subject to exceptions, as well as reasonable copying fees.
New Jersey	None
New Mexico	None
New York	Public employers only.
North Carolina	Current and former private sector employees have a right to access personnel records indicating their exposure to toxic materials or harmful physical agents. Current and former state, county and municipal employees may inspect, subject to certain exceptions.
North Dakota	Current state employees may inspect and copy during normal business hours and employers may charge reasonable copying fees.
Ohio	Medical records only.
Oklahoma	None for private employees. Unless the records are made confidential by law, an employee of a public body has the right to access his or her own personnel files.

State	Employee access to personnel files
Oregon	Current and former private and public employees (subject to some limitations) may inspect certain records in their personnel files and employers may charge a reasonable copying fee.
Pennsylvania	Current private and public employees may inspect certain documents within their personnel files.
Rhode Island	Current and former employees may inspect and copy, subject to certain limitations. Employers may charge a reasonable copying fee.
South Carolina	Limited to access to records concerning employee exposure to potentially toxic materials or harmful physical agents.
South Dakota	Certain state employees may inspect.
Tennessee	Current state and local government employees may inspect and copy at any reasonable time.
Texas	Current government employees may inspect as personnel records of government employees are public records under statutory law.
Utah	Current state employees and employees of political subdivisions may inspect and copy, subject to reasonable copying fees. The law is unclear about former state employees.
Vermont	It appears that information in personnel files must be made available to employees of a public agency.
Virginia	Personnel records containing information concerning identifiable individuals are exempt from inspection and copying under the state's Freedom of Information Act, but access may not be denied to public employees who are the subject of such records.
Washington	Subject to exceptions, private and public employees may inspect.
West Virginia	None
Wisconsin	Employees may inspect and obtain copies, subject to certain exceptions and limitations. Employers may charge reasonable copying fees.
Wyoming	Employees may have access to their personnel files, including application information, performance ratings and scholastic achievement. Employers may charge a reasonable copying fee.

Note:
The above chart merely provides an overview of the general approach adopted in each state and the District of Columbia. It does not attempt to set forth the specific requirements of the law that applies in each jurisdiction. Employers should consult the state law of each jurisdiction to confirm its obligations.

Medical records storage

As a general rule, employers should ensure that all records that contain medical information are kept confidential. These records should not be kept in the same file as personnel records that managers need to access. The Americans with Disabilities Act (ADA), the Rehabilitation and the

Family and Medical Leave Act (FMLA) require employers to keep information obtained from a medical examination or medical inquiry to be kept confidential except that:

- Employers may inform supervisors/managers of work restrictions that apply to an employee and of any accommodations that the employer will provide the employee.
- Employers may inform first aid and/or safety personnel of an employee's medical condition if it might require emergency treatment.
- Employers are also authorized to provide information about an employee's medical condition to government officials who are investigating compliance with the ADA, FMLA, etc.

Additionally, employers may disclose medical information as necessary in the context of workers' compensation claims and it may be used by insurance companies where the insurance carrier requires a medical examination to provide health or life insurance to employees.

OSHA provides that an employer can release medical records (defined as records concerning the health status of an employee that are made or maintained by a physician, nurse or other health care personnel or technician) only to a representative upon specific written consent. The consent form asks for the employee's name, the person authorized to receive the information, description of the information being asked for, the purpose of the request, the full name of the employee, the full name of the legal representative and the signature of the employee and legal representative.

The regulations also suggest that an employer may wish to add provisions dealing with:

- a specific expiration date for the authorization
- a description of medical information to be created in the future that the employee intends to be covered by the authorization letter
- a description of portions of the medical information in an employer's records that the employee does not intend to be released as a result of the letter.

Drug test results of interstate truck drivers conducted because of DOT regulations may not be released without the employee's written permission.

Handling outside requests for information

Employers should not disclose information regarding employees except to those who have a legitimate need for the information and the employer should consider securing a release from the employee before disclosing anything more than the most basic information about the employee. Information that should not be released to outsiders includes, but is not limited to, information provided by a consumer reporting agency, drug test results, medical information and payroll information. The employer should designate a person to handle all requests for information to ensure that the company takes a uniform approach to all such requests, which will help prevent liability.

Chapter 10

Employment contracts

In most states, employment is presumed to be "at will." This means employees can be discharged and can resign at any time, with or without cause or notice. Such discharge or resignation usually does not give the employee the right to sue unless the employee can establish that an exception to the general at-will rule applies. The most commonly recognized exceptions to at-will employment include:

- federal and state anti-discrimination laws
- the existence of a union contract requiring just cause for termination
- federal or state statutes prohibiting discharge in certain situations (such as whistleblower laws)
- violation of a state's public policy
- breach of an implied promise of good faith and fair dealing
- the existence of a contract, which puts the employer and employee in a relationship that is other than at will.

It is important to understand that state law primarily governs the employment relationship. While this chapter provides an overview of the ways in which the at-will relationship may be modified, state laws are very specific and can be complicated. Employers should consult with experienced employment counsel regarding the provisions of the laws of the states in which they have employees.

Elements of a contract

Most employees today do not have written employment contracts. Such contracts are usually limited to executive and other highly paid employees, employees with special knowledge and skill and sales personnel working on commission. Written employment contracts usually detail the terms and conditions of employment and identify any limitations on the employer's ability to discharge the employee (such as for just cause or notice requirements) as well as the employee's ability to resign (notice requirements).

These contracts may also include nondisclosure, noncompete and nonsolicitation provisions. However, employees who otherwise would be considered to be employed at-will often argue that they have an enforceable employment contract based on oral statements made by interviewers or supervisors, language contained in employee handbooks, disciplinary policies or other written documents prepared by employers, terms of benefits provisions, compensation agreements or the prior course of dealing between the employer and employee. When one of the parties claims there has been a breach of contract, the first issue to be resolved is whether a legally enforceable contract exists. To create an enforceable contract, two parties with legal capacity to contract must mutually assent (for instance, there must be an offer and acceptance of that offer) to the terms of the contract and there must be consideration.

Mutual assent

The parties to an employment contract must negotiate and agree to its essential terms for the contract to be enforced. The employee's testimony regarding his or her subjective belief that he or she entered into an employment contract with the employer is not evidence of such a contract. Where there is no evidence that the employer agreed to a specific term of employment or that it unequivocally indicated a definite intent to be bound not to terminate the plaintiff's employment except under clearly specific circumstances, there is no enforceable employment contract.

Oral statements

To establish mutual assent between the parties, there must be an offer and acceptance of that offer. Some states permit contracts to be created through oral statements. Whether these statements constitute a binding contract is often analyzed in the context of whether they are sufficiently definite to constitute an offer as to which there could be an acceptance that has legal ramifications.

Offers of permanent employment

Some state courts are generally hesitant to enforce claims of oral contracts for lifetime employment because such oral offers usually lack definiteness and mutuality of obligation, which are required to create an enforceable contract. Generally, courts construe such "contracts," which contain no express or implied restrictions as to duration, as being indefinite, general hirings terminable at the will of either party, where the employee furnishes no consideration in addition to the services incident to employment.

Statements of periodic compensation

An employer's statements concerning pay may result in a breach of contract claim. For instance, in Georgia, if an employment contract provides that wages are payable at a stipulated period, it is presumed that the hiring is for such period. Care must therefore be taken with respect to statements regarding pay.

Consideration

Consideration is another element required for an enforceable contract. Consideration consists of some detriment to the offeror and some benefit to the offeree or some bargained-for exchange between the two parties.

An implied contract

In the absence of specific language altering or limiting the at-will status of employees, general employment policies usually do not create a contract specifying that the employee can be terminated only for cause. In some states, however, employee personnel manuals or handbooks may create a contractual employment relationship if the handbook or manual contains clear promissory language that makes the handbook an offer that the employee accepts by continuing to work after receiving it. Additionally, if the language of the handbook is not clear, it may create a factual issue regarding whether there is an enforceable contract. A jury must decide that factual issue.

Definite language required

To establish enforceable rights, the handbook or manual must be sufficiently unambiguous to constitute an offer.

Consideration

In some states, continued employment is sufficient consideration to create a binding contract based on promises of job security contained in an employee handbook.

Disclaimers

A clearly worded disclaimer in the employee handbook has been viewed by the courts in some states as a complete defense to a suit for breach of contract based on an employee handbook. However, if the disclaimer does not clearly state that the employee is an at-will employee, the court may find that it is not a defense to a breach of contract claim or that the employee is entitled to a jury trial because the handbook is ambiguous.

Benefits upon discharge

Handbooks may also give discharged employees' rights to vacation pay or other job benefits, especially when the employer followed such a practice in the past.

Doctrine of good faith and fair dealing

Some state laws imply an obligation of good faith and fair dealing that may overcome the presumption of employment at-will. The law varies by state, but many states that recognize the covenant of good faith and fair dealing in contracts also recognize the covenant as a limitation on an employer's ability to discharge an at-will employee.

Public policy exception to employment at-will

Many states recognize a public policy exception to the employment at-will doctrine. To establish that the public policy exception applies, an employee must generally show the following:

- a clear public policy that existed and was manifested in the federal or state constitution, a statute, an administrative regulation or the common law
- a discharge involving facts that would jeopardize the public policy
- evidence to demonstrate an overriding legitimate business justification for the dismissal.

Most state courts have determined that, pursuant to this public policy exception, employers may not discharge at-will employees for refusal to participate or remain silent about illegal activity.

Contract provisions

Each written employment agreement should be prepared individually to specifically address the particular employment relationship. The following provisions should be considered:

- **Duration of employment**
  Duration of the contractual employment relationship should be expressly defined. If the employment is not for specific duration, but is "at-will," the contract should contain a statement to that effect. If the employment is for a specific duration, consider including a "for cause" termination provision.

- **Notice provision**
  If notice of termination is to be required by either party, it should be spelled out in a notice provision. If no notice is to be required, language to that effect should also be included to avoid a determination that reasonable notice is required.

- **Merger clause**
  An employer may rely on a merger clause providing that the written document constitutes the entire agreement between the parties, revokes and supersedes any prior agreements and that no representations or promises other than those set forth in it may be relied upon. The provisions of a written employment contract should state that it supersedes any alleged oral or implied agreements inconsistent with it. It should specifically provide that no oral assurances or implied contracts are valid.

- **Alternative dispute resolution**
  An internal complaint procedure and an arbitration or other alternative dispute resolution (ADR) clause may create a feeling of job security and may be combined with exclusive remedy language designed to prevent an employee from suing the employer until the internal complaint procedure has been exhausted. Such a provision may not totally bar administrative and judicial proceedings brought to enforce statutorily created rights.

- **Releases/consent**
  When not specifically prohibited by law, written contracts should include consents and releases of all claims for matters such as substance abuse testing. Employers should also consider including consent for a reference check and a clause holding the employer (and reference provider) harmless for any references.

- **Probationary period**
  Some employers choose to include acknowledgment of an "initial" probationary period. However, as discussed previously, this is not always a prudent decision.

- **Liquidated damages**
  The employer may also consider including a liquidated damages clause specifically limiting available remedies if the employment contract is breached. As a general rule, where such clauses are included merely as a penalty, they are unenforceable.

- **Noncompetition clauses**
  Consider including noncompetition or nonsolicitation provisions and/or nondisclosure provisions. However, employers should consult with counsel to account for requirements that vary by state, as some states may find these provisions void in certain circumstances.

- **Assignment of invention provision**
  Generally, an invention belongs to the inventor and the fact that the inventor is an employee does not mean the employer necessarily has any rights to the invention. It depends on the relationship of the parties and the circumstances under which the invention was developed. If the employer hired an employee for the specific purpose of inventing something, that invention most likely belongs to the employer. An employer likely has no legal interest, however, when an employee invents something that has nothing to do with his or her employment, on his or her own time and with his or her own resources. When the employee is not hired to invent, but on the employer's time and with some of the employer's resources develops an invention that somehow helps the employer, the general rule is that the employer has a "shop right," which is a non-exclusive license to the use of that invention. The "shop right" doctrine is fragile and of uncertain duration. An employer can ease uncertainty with a written agreement that specifically assigns inventions to the employer. As in the case of noncompete clauses, it is preferable to obtain the agreement at the beginning of employment.

- **Attorneys' fees**
  A provision for an award of attorneys' fees to the prevailing party should enforcement be necessary is often included in written employment contracts.

- **Forum selection clause**
  Employers may wish to specify the controlling state law in a written contract.

- **Jury trial**
  Some written employment contracts include a waiver of a right to a jury trial in the event that it is necessary to bring a court action to enforce the agreement. Some courts do not recognize such waivers.

- **Commissions**
  Generally, state law governs whether employees are entitled to earned commissions when discharged, but contractual terms may create valid standards to the employee's earning of the commission.

- **Severability clause**
  A severability clause is a provision that expresses the parties' intent that a court enforces the contract to the greatest extent possible, severing or limiting unenforceable provisions of the contract or portions thereof. Severability clauses are particularly important in contracts containing restrictive covenants such as noncompete and non-solicitation provisions.

Chapter 11

Noncompete agreements and trade secrets

Noncompete agreements

Businesses across many different industries use noncompete agreements. These agreements generally prohibit an employee from competing with the employer during and after the employment relationship. Employers also use confidentiality and non-solicitation agreements to protect against competition from former employees. Over the past several years, however, the law has witnessed a variety of changes to the landscape of restrictive covenants at both the state and federal levels. Increasingly, legislatures and courts have been taking an aggressive approach to limiting the type and scope of restrictive covenants that an employer can use in its relationships with employees.

For instance, noncompete agreements are invalid in California, North Dakota, the District of Columbia and Oklahoma, subject to few exceptions. Additionally, Colorado, Illinois, Maine, Maryland, New Hampshire, Oregon, Rhode Island, Virginia and Washington prohibit such agreements unless certain compensation levels are met. Many other states are considering new legislation on noncompetition agreements as well. Any business that has a legitimate interest to protect with a noncompete or nonsolicitation agreement should consult with counsel to account for requirements that vary by state.

Enforceability

Although noncompete agreements are generally not favored because they are a restraint on trade, courts determine whether such an agreement is enforceable by considering the following factors:

- **Reasonable in geographic scope and duration**
  Courts will review the terms of the noncompete to determine if the restriction on time period and geographic area qualify as reasonable. Most courts evaluate whether the restrictions imposed by the agreement on a case-by-case basis. In states that are willing to enforce noncompete agreements, it is not uncommon for courts to approve of one-year restrictions, but periods beyond one year are more likely to be declared unenforceable. Likewise, a court is less likely to enforce a noncompete that would apply to a large geographic area rather than one that is limited in its scope.

- **Legitimate business interest**
  Courts will not enforce a noncompete agreement unless the employer can show that it needs to utilize the noncompete to protect a legitimate business interest. A court is more likely to find that an employer has a legitimate interest to protect if the employer provided the employee specialized training and the employee needed access to confidential information such as trade secrets to perform his or her job. As a general rule, an employer must show a court that its legitimate business interest is more significant than its general desire to limit competition from former employees. What will qualify as a legitimate business interest will vary, but it can include the need to protect trade secrets, prevent the use of confidential customer information and the like.

- **Other factors affecting enforceability**
  Some courts have also considered whether the agreement would essentially prevent the employee from working in his or her chosen field, whether it would impose an undue hardship on the employee and whether the employer had taken steps to enforce the agreement against other employees in the past.

"Blue penciling"

If a noncompete agreement contains an unenforceable restriction, some jurisdictions hold that the entire agreement is invalid, but the law in some states, such as Tennessee, empowers judges to "blue pencil" or revise the unenforceable restriction so that the contract is enforced to the extent appropriate under the law. Non-compete agreements are more likely to be enforced in states where courts engage in blue-penciling than in states where one unreasonable restriction makes the entire contract unenforceable.

Consideration

Like any other contract, a noncompete agreement must be based on sufficient consideration. An employer can require an employee to enter a noncompete agreement in consideration for an initial offer of employment. Whether the agreement is supported by sufficient consideration generally becomes an issue when an employer requires its current employees to sign a noncompete agreement in exchange for continued employment. Some courts have found that the promise of continued employment qualifies as a sufficient condition to support the noncompete, but other courts have held that employers must offer an additional or "new" condition to bind current employees to a noncompete agreement.

Trade secrets

Trade secrets are very important to many employers. In very general terms, a trade secret is information that derives economic value from not being generally known to others who can obtain economic value from its disclosure or use and is the subject of reasonable efforts to maintain its secrecy. Because it may be difficult to prove that information an employer wants to protect rises to the level of a trade secret, employers should try to get employees who deal with confidential information to sign noncompete agreements. These agreements, if enforceable, may provide greater protection than relying on a claim of misappropriation of trade secrets.

"Reasonable" efforts to maintain secrecy

Generally, for information to qualify as a trade secret, the employer must make an effort to maintain the secrecy of the information. Some examples include:

- written employee confidentiality agreements
- conducting proper background checks on new employees and others who will have access to vital company secrets
- labeling or identifying trade secrets prominently with "confidential" or "proprietary"
- limiting distribution of documents to "need to know" or "need to use" personnel
- using numbering systems for documents that can be reasonably numbered along with a ledger system that accounts for each copy of the document
- limiting access to computer areas and computer systems
- using logs to monitor the dissemination of proprietary information
- having computer experts thoroughly search and examine laptops and desktop computers before they are recirculated to other employees
- requiring employees to encrypt sensitive computer files and data
- installing screensavers and server passwords to protect computer systems
- monitoring highly sensitive areas with closed-circuit television
- using a system of embedded codes to trace copies and faxes – controlling the circulation of copies of sensitive document
- conducting a comprehensive audit or inventory of trade secrets and other confidential information
- reviewing outgoing materials including documents being sent to vendors and customers, as well as articles for professional, scientific or business publications
- placing restrictions on photocopying through the use of logs or central photocopying
- periodic printed reminders to caution employees about protecting "confidential" and "proprietary" information
- use of document destruction systems including in-house shredding
- registration, identification and supervision of visitors
- fencing of premises and "lock and key" protection of sensitive work areas and document storage areas
- development of employee termination procedures including the return of all confidential documents, checklists and acknowledgment forms and reminders of

"continuing obligations" regarding non-use and nondisclosure of confidential information

- conducting exit interviews for every departing employee to make sure that all trade secrets or confidential information remain with the company and to re-emphasize the duty of confidentiality to the employee.

Affirmative action

Chapter

12

Executive Order 11246

Executive Order 11246 (EO11246) provides that contracts entered into by federal government agencies must include specific "equal opportunity clauses," one of which requires that those contracting with the government agree to "not discriminate against any employee or applicant for employment because of race, color, religion, sex or national origin" and to "take affirmative action" to ensure that applicants are employed and employees are treated during their employment without regard to their race, color, religion, sex, including sexual orientation or gender identity or national origin. The Department of Labor's (DOL) Office of Federal Contract Compliance Programs (OFCCP) enforces the EO11246.

Coverage threshold

A contractor is exempted from the EO11246 and the Rehabilitation Act (Rehabilitation Act) if it has less than $15,000 collectively in federal contracts or subcontracts in any 12-month period. This dollar threshold was raised to $150,000 in the case of the Vietnam Era Veterans Readjustment Assistance Act (VEVRAA) for contracts entered into on or after December 1, 2003. If these thresholds are exceeded, the employer is subject to the affirmative action obligations as well as OFCCP jurisdiction and the OFCCP is authorized to conduct complaint investigations and compliance reviews of the employer's employment practices. Bills of lading, federal fund depositories and issuing and paying agents of U.S. savings bonds are not exempted regardless of the amount.

Equal opportunity clauses

For a nonexempt contract, the EO11246 requires the contractor or subcontractor agree during the performance of the contract that:

- The contractor will not discriminate against any employee or applicant for employment because of race, color, religion, sex or national origin. The contractor will take affirmative action to ensure that applicants are employed and that employees are treated without regard to their race, color, religion, sex or national origin during employment. Such action shall include, but not be limited to the following:
    - employment
    - upgrading

- demotion or transfer
- recruitment or recruitment advertising
- layoff or termination
- rates of pay or other forms of compensation
- selection for training, including apprenticeships.

The contractor agrees to post in conspicuous places, available to employees and applicants for employment, notices to be provided by the contracting officer setting forth the provisions of this nondiscrimination clause.

- The contractor will, in all solicitations or advertisements for employees placed by or on behalf of the contractor, state that all qualified applicants will receive consideration for employment without regard to race, color, religion, sex or national origin.
- The contractor will send – to each labor union or representative of workers with which it has a collective bargaining agreement or other contract or understanding – a notice to be provided by the agency contracting officer, advising the labor union or workers' representative of the contractor's commitments under section 202 of EO11246 and shall post copies of the notice in conspicuous places available to employees and applicants for employment.
- The contractor will comply with all provisions of EO11246 and of the rules, regulations and relevant orders of the Secretary of Labor.
- The contractor will furnish all information and reports required by EO 11246 and by the rules, regulations and orders of the Secretary of Labor or pursuant thereto and will permit access to its books, records and accounts by the contracting agency and the Secretary of Labor for purposes of investigation to ascertain compliance with such rules, regulations and orders.
- In the event of the contractor's noncompliance with the nondiscrimination clauses of this contract or with any of such rules, regulations or orders, this contract may be canceled, terminated or suspended in whole or in part and the contractor may be declared ineligible for further government contracts in accordance with procedures authorized in EO11246 and such other sanctions may be imposed and remedies invoked as provided in EO11246 or by rule, regulation or order of the Secretary of Labor or as otherwise provided by law.
- The contractor will include the provisions of paragraphs one through seven in every subcontract or purchase order unless exempted by rules, regulations or orders of the Secretary of Labor issued pursuant to section 204 of EO11246 so that such provisions will be binding upon each subcontractor or vendor. The contractor will take such action with respect to any subcontract or purchase order as may be directed by the Secretary of Labor as a means of enforcing such provisions including sanctions for noncompliance provided, however, that in the event the contractor becomes involved in or is threatened with, litigation with a subcontractor or vendor as a result of such direction, the contractor may request the United States to enter into such litigation to protect the interests of the United States.

The Rehabilitation Act and VEVRAA require similar clauses.

Incorporation by reference

The equal opportunity clauses may be incorporated in the transaction merely by reference, perhaps by a citation to them or their implementing regulations in an agreement or purchase order or an addendum thereto.

Incorporation by law

The equal opportunity clauses are considered to be a part of every contract and subcontract required by the affirmative action laws and DOL regulations. This is so regardless of whether the clauses are physically incorporated in such contract and regardless of whether the contract between the agency and contractor is written.

Government contracts and contractors under EO11246

A "government contract" is an agreement with a contracting agency for the furnishing of supplies or services or the use of real or personal property, including lease arrangements. "Services" include, but are not limited to, utilities, construction, transportation, research, insurance and fund depositories. The term also includes any "federally assisted construction contract" or agreement for construction work paid in whole or in part with funds obtained from the federal government or borrowed on credit of the government pursuant to any federal program involving a grant, contract, loan, insurance or guaranty undertaken pursuant to any such program. Government contractors are any persons who hold a government contract.

Subcontracts and subcontractors

"Subcontract" means any agreement or arrangement between a contractor and any person for the furnishing of supplies, services or the use of real or personal property that, in whole or in part, are necessary to the performance of a federal contract or under which any portion of the contractor's obligation under a federal contract is performed, undertaken or assumed.

Corporate-wide coverage

A non-exempt contract will subject all of the operations of a contractor to the contractual obligations of the "equal opportunity clauses." The Secretary of Labor may exempt facilities that are separate and distinct from the activities related to performance of the government contract. Such facilities, however, are covered unless a successful application for exemption has been submitted. The OFCCP also takes the position that a separate corporate entity sharing common ownership and deemed to be under "common control" with a non-exempt contractor is subject to the same equal opportunity clauses as the contractor.

Rehabilitation Act

Section 503 of the Rehabilitation Act provides that contracts with the federal government for the procurement of personal property and non-personal services in excess of $15,000 (including construction) entered into by federal government departments and agencies must include specific "equal opportunity clauses." One of these clauses requires that contractors take affirmative action to employ and advance in employment qualified handicapped individuals. This law is also enforced by the OFCCP and handicapped individuals may file complaints with that agency.

Regulations effective March 24, 2014, revised the regulations implementing section 503 of the Rehabilitation Act. These regulations significantly changed the Rehabilitation Act obligations for federal contractors. Some of the more significant changes implemented include:

- Revising the definition of disability and its component parts to be consistent with the changes made by the Americans with Disabilities Act Amendments Act (ADAAA) and the Equal Employment Opportunity Commission (EEOC) regulations interpreting the ADAAA. Thus, under these regulations, disability is defined as:
    - a physical or mental impairment that substantially limits a major life activity
    - a record of such an impairment
    - being regarded as having such an impairment.
- Revising the mandatory equal opportunity clause that must appear in applicable subcontracts. The regulations provide the exact verbiage that must appear in the subcontracts.
- Requiring contractors to post the mandatory equal employment opportunity (EEO) poster in a conspicuous place for applicants and employees, including online.
- Requiring contractors to invite all applicants to self-identify as individuals with a disability before and after an offer of employment and extend similar invitations to employees. The OFCCP has issued a self-identification form that contractors must use.
- Requiring contractors to engage in outreach and recruitment efforts as to disabled persons.
- Establishing a 7% utilization goal for disabled persons for each affirmative action plan job group at each facility.
- Requiring contractors to collect data on the following:
    - the number of applicants who identify as an individual with a disability
    - the total number of job openings and total number of jobs filled
    - the total number of applicants for all jobs
    - the number of individuals with disabilities hired
    - the total number of applicants hired.
- Imposing a three-year recordkeeping requirement for the data collection and outreach and recruitment efforts.

Anti-discrimination provision

Section 504 of the law provides that no otherwise qualified disabled individual shall, solely by reason of his or her handicap, be excluded from participation in, be denied the benefits of or subjected to discrimination under any program or activity receiving federal financial assistance or under any program or activity conducted by executive agencies or by the U.S. Postal Service. Section 504 is enforced by private suit in court. It should be noted that it requires nondiscrimination in programs or activities receiving federal financial assistance, as distinguished from the affirmative action required of contractors subject to section 503. It is equivalent to Title VI, which prohibits race, sex and national origin discrimination in programs or activities receiving federal financial assistance.

Coordination with the American with Disabilities Act

The procedures by which a contractor employs handicapped individuals (and disabled veterans) have been made consistent with the Americans with Disabilities Act's (ADA) limitation on pre-employment medical inquiries.

Vietnam Era Veterans Readjustment Assistance Act

The Vietnam Era Veterans Readjustment Assistance Act (VEVRAA) generally requires employers with federal contracts or subcontracts that meet the threshold amount specified in the statute to take affirmative action to employ and advance in employment qualified covered veterans, to provide information regarding job openings to certain state or federal agencies and to fulfill certain reporting obligations.

Amendments

Until Congress passed the Veterans Employment Opportunities Act (VEOA), it applied to contractors and subcontractors with contracts of more than $10,000. In addition, only "special disabled veterans" and "veterans of the Vietnam era" were protected under the section.

In the VEOA, Congress raised the minimum contract amount to $25,000 and expanded the application to include other protected veterans. Effective January 3, 2006, the Office of Federal Contract Compliance Programs (OFCCP) revised its VEVRAA regulations to conform to the requirements of the VEOA.

In the Veterans Benefits and Health Care Improvement Act (VBHCIA), Congress separated veterans to those groups of veterans protected under VEVRAA. A "recently separated veteran" is any veteran separated from the military during the three-year period beginning on the date of the veteran's discharge or release from active duty.

In the Jobs for Veterans Act (JVA), Congress raised the minimum contract amount to $100,000 and changed the categories of veterans that are covered under VEVRAA. In addition, the JVA changed the manner in which federal contractors are to comply with the requirement when listing job openings with the state employment security agency.

The regulations require contractors to use the VETS-100A report form to provide the required information on their employment of protected veterans.

In September 2013, the OFCCP revised the regulations. Some of the significant regulatory changes are:

- The regulation provides four protected veteran categories:
    - disabled veteran
    - recently separated veteran
    - U.S. Armed Forces service medal veteran
    - active-duty wartime or campaign badge veteran.
- Protected veterans are protected under both the nondiscrimination and affirmative action provisions of VEVRAA. Veterans not included in these four categories are not considered "protected" veterans for affirmative action purposes. The regulations, however, still allow for such veterans to file discrimination complaints with the OFCCP against contractors. Contractors are required to:
- Establish hiring benchmarks for protected veterans using one of two methods.
    1. use a benchmark equal to the national percentage of veterans in the civilian labor force (8%)
    2. establish its own benchmark based on certain factors.
- List vacancies with the appropriate Employment Service Delivery System (ESDS) where the opening occur.
- Post the mandatory EEOC poster in a conspicuous place for applicants and employees.
- Invite persons to identify as a protected veteran at both the pre-offer and post-offer stages in the application process.
- Post an equal employment opportunity policy statement on company bulletin boards and provide this notice in a form that is accessible and understandable to a disabled veteran.
- Make the full affirmative action program, without the data metrics, available to employees for inspection.
- Undertake outreach and positive recruitment efforts to hire qualified protected veterans. Contractors are also required to send written notification of the company's affirmative action policy to subcontractors and request their cooperation.
- Document and update annually:
    - the total number of applicants for employment and the number of applicants who are protected veterans

    - the total number of job openings and the number of jobs filled
    - the total number of applicants hired and the number of applicants hired who are protected veterans.
- Retain data collection and outreach and recruitment efforts records for three years.

Coverage

The contractor is covered by affirmative action obligations if the contract is for $150,000 or more.

Type of contracts covered

VEVRAA covers contracts with the federal government for the procurement of personal property and non-personal services (including construction). The following contracts are not covered by VEVRAA:

- contracts that do not meet the statutory threshold amount
- contracts for indefinite quantities
- contracts for work that is performed outside the United States
- contracts with state or local governments, except for the specific government entity that participates in work on or under the contract.

Requirements

Covered contractors and subcontractors are required to take affirmative steps to employ qualified protected veterans.

- **Written affirmative action programs**
  The threshold for an affirmative action program (AAP) coverage is a contract of $150,000 or more. Therefore, each employer that has a federal contract (or subcontract) of $150,000 or more and 50 or more employees must prepare, implement and maintain a written AAP covering each of its establishments.
- **VETS-100A report**
  All contractors and subcontractors with contracts of $100,000 or more must file a VETS-100A report. This report must be filed annually on or before September 30.
- **Requirements applicable to all contractors**
  VEVRAA and its implementing regulations require all contractors to refrain from discrimination in employment against protected veterans and include a specific equal employment opportunity clause in their non-exempt contracts and subcontracts.

Subcontractors

Generally, the same principles are used in determining contractor or subcontractor status under the Rehabilitation Act and VEVRAA.

Dodd-Frank Act requirements

The Dodd-Frank Act requires certain federal financial agencies to establish an Office of Minority and Women Inclusion (OMWI) to "be responsible for all agency matters relating to diversity in management, employment and business activities."

The act requires each OMWI to monitor the diversity efforts of the agencies, the regulated entities and agency contractors. If an OMWI director determines that an agency contractor has failed to make a good faith effort to include minorities and women in their workforce, the agency head may refer the matter to the OFCCP or take other appropriate action, including termination of the applicable contract.

Government contractors

The obligation to annually develop and maintain a written affirmative action program (AAP) applies to each contractor or subcontractor that has 50 or more employees and:

- has a single contract or subcontract of $50,000 or more
- has government bills of lading that total or can reasonably be expected to total, $50,000 or more in any 12-month period
- serves as a depository of government funds in any amount
- is a financial institution that is an issuing and paying agent for U.S. savings bonds and saving notes of any amount.

Each contractor or subcontractor meeting the threshold must develop a written AAP program for each of its "establishments."

Contents of a written affirmative action plan

A written AAP under EO11246 must include at least the following:

- assignment of affirmative action responsibility
- organizational profile (organizational display or workforce analysis format)
- job group analysis
- availability analysis
- incumbency-to-availability analysis
- placement goals
- identification of problem areas
- action-oriented programs designed to eliminate problems and achieve goals
- an internal audit and reporting system.

Organizational profile

The OFCCP revised the regulations concerning certain written affirmative action plans in 2000. According to these revised regulations, the organizational profile can be in one of two forms. The employer may prepare an affirmative action plan that contains a traditional workforce analysis, a listing of jobs ranked within departments and lines of progression on the basis of pay, showing for each job the total number of workers, the total number of male and female workers and the total number of male and female workers in each of the following groups:

- African Americans
- Hispanics
- Asians/Pacific Islanders
- American Indians/Alaskan Natives.

Alternatively, the employer may provide an organizational display using graphs or text that shows:

- each of the company's organizational units and their relationships to one another
- the gender, racial and ethnic composition of each organizational unit.

Job group analysis

A worker-to-availability analysis must be conducted by "job groups," which are clusters of jobs having similar content, wage rates and opportunities. The regulations clarify the terms "similarity of content" and "similarity of opportunities," which are the two criteria most open to differing interpretations. The regulations state "similarity of content refers to the duties and responsibilities of the job titles that make up the job group."

The regulations also provide that "similarity of opportunities refers to training, transfers, promotions, pay, mobility and other career enhancement opportunities offered by the jobs within the job group." The regulations also require a list of job titles comprising each job group. Under the regulations, employers with fewer than 150 employees may use EEO-1 categories as job groups.

Availability analysis

Availability is an estimate of the number of qualified minorities or women available for employment in a given job group, expressed as a percentage of all qualified persons available for employment in the job group. The factors for determining availability are:

- the percentage of minorities or women with requisite skills in the reasonable recruitment area
- the percentage of minorities or women among those promotable, transferable and trainable within the contractor's organization.

The reasonable recruitment area is the geographical area from which the contractor usually seeks or could seek workers to fill the positions in question.

Trainable refers to those employees within the contractor's organization who could, with appropriate training, which the contractor could reasonably provide, become promotable or transferable during the AAP year. The regulations require contractors to use the most current and discrete statistical data to conduct availability analyses, such as census data, data from local job service offices and data from colleges and other training institutions.

Worker to availability analysis

For job groups, the contractor must compare the percentage of minorities and females actually employed in the job group with those determined to be available by using the factors discussed previously. Placement goals must be established if there are fewer minorities or females in a particular job group than would reasonably be expected given their availability.

Placement goals

When the area workforce does not reasonably approximate availability in job groups, the employer must establish placement goals. The OFCCP now interprets this as requiring only the declaration of annual percent of placement goals that equal the availability for the underutilized job group.

Construction industry

The construction industry is treated separately from other industries for the purpose of implementing affirmative action requirements. The goals for female and minority utilization in construction are issued by the OFCCP for specific geographic areas.

Determinations for contractor compliance

The Uniform Guidelines on Employee Selection Procedures were adopted in 1978 by the EEOC and the OFCCP. In the past decade, the OFCCP has departed to some degree from its emphasis on the "bottom line" numerical compliance with goals and shifted its focus to analysis of the impact of hiring and other personnel procedures. There has also generally been an increased emphasis on analyses of the impact of hiring and other personnel procedures in equal employment opportunity litigation. For contractors, this requires detailed recordkeeping and periodic statistical studies to compare the selection rates of non-minorities and minorities, as well as males and females. When substantial discrepancies in the selection rates exist, a contractor may incur significant liability.

Adverse impact

Contractors are required to compare applicants to hires to determine if any group has been adversely impacted. This analysis is calculated using several tests and analyzes gender and race information. When a contractor has not maintained data on adverse impact as required, the OFCCP may draw an inference of adverse impact in the selection process.

Other selection procedures

Impact determinations must also be accomplished for promotions, transfers and layoffs that are not based solely on seniority. The OFCCP also considers all terminations, including discharges, as "selection procedures," although this interpretation is questionable.

Compliance review procedures

Effective January 1, 2011, federal contractors became subject to active case enforcement (ACE) procedures. The ACE directive begins with a definitions section. In this section, the following processes are defined:

- compliance check
- compliance evaluation
- compliance review
- focused review
- full desk audit
- full compliance review
- offsite review of records
- pre-award compliance evaluation.

Should the OFCCP select a specific site for an audit, these various terms will define the scope of the audit. While the OFCCP may use different terms to describe each audit, the ACE directive makes it clear that all supply and service contractors selected for review will be required to submit their AAPs and supporting documentation to the OFCCP within the time specified in the scheduling letter. The next step after receiving a scheduling letter is a full desk audit.

Selection procedure

Under the ACE procedure, the OFCCP will continue to use the neutral Federal Contractor Selection System (FCSS) to select supply and service contractor establishments for compliance evaluations. Neutral selection criteria will then be employed to designate which type of investigative procedure will be conducted for each establishment.

For instance, the list will identify whether an establishment will undergo a compliance review, an offsite review of records, compliance check or a focused review. The directive further instructs each OFCCP regional/district/area office to schedule the establishments for review in the strict sequential order identified on the FCSS list.

Cooperation with other agencies

Simultaneous with mailing the scheduling letter to a selected contractor, the OFCCP will contact the EEOC and the state/local fair employment practice agency to determine the nature, status and outcome of any complaints filed against the establishment. The contractor will then submit its AAP and supporting data.

The OFCCP then conducts a full desk audit under EO11246, the Rehabilitation Act and VEVRAA. The OFCCP also will review its own records for the previous three years to assess the contractor's recent compliance history and determine if there are any "patterns of noncompliance." Patterns of noncompliance will be based on the OFCCP's data and information obtained from the EEOC, state/local agencies and/or any other agencies such as the DOL's Veterans Employment and Training Services (VETS) and the Wage and Hour Division.

Desk audit, to onsite, to audit closure

During the desk audit the OFCCP will determine whether there are "indicators of potential discrimination or violation," which will require an onsite investigation. In the past, the OFCCP considered statistical and anecdotal evidence to determine whether "indicators" exist. However, under the ACE procedure, indicators of potential discrimination and/or violations also will include:

- patterns of individual discrimination
- patterns of systemic discrimination
- patterns of major technical violations, such as recordkeeping deficiencies or the failure to maintain an AAP
- noncompliance with other labor and employment laws, such as wage and hour laws.

In addition, an onsite audit may occur if the OFCCP determines that the submitted AAP or supporting documentation is insufficient to determine compliance. If no indicators are found, the OFCCP may close the review. However, if the compliance review has been designated by the national office as a "quality control review" or "focused review," the compliance officer must conduct an onsite audit even in the absence of indicators. During an onsite review, the OFCCP will examine data and documentation relating to the indicator, but the ACE procedures make it clear that the scope of an onsite review is not limited to the indicators.

In addition, during an onsite review, the OFCCP will also determine the contractor's compliance with Executive Order 13496 (EO13496), which is the mandated posting that informs employees of their rights to organize and is discussed in the following paragraphs.

If, during the desk audit, the OFCCP identifies minor technical violations, but no indicators exist as to potential discrimination, the compliance officer will attempt to remedy the deficiencies. If the deficiencies have been remedied, a letter entitled "Closure for No Apparent Violations or Technical Violations" will be issued. If the conclusion of the review results in major technical violations and/or discrimination remedied through a conciliation agreement, the audit will close with the "Closure Letter for Substantive Violations."

Standards and guidelines regarding compensation

On February 28, 2013, the OFCCP issued a directive describing procedures for reviewing contractor compensation systems and practices. Directive 2013-03, formerly Directive 307, calls for a case specific review of compensation beyond base pay such as overtime, commissions, shift differentials, stock options, bonuses) for gender-race- or ethnicity-based differences. The directive also sets forth the procedure compliance officers will follow in performing an analysis. The directive may be found at:

- https://www.dol.gov/agencies/ofccp/directives/2018-05

Internet applicant rule

The OFCCP requires covered federal contractors to obtain gender, race and ethnicity data on employees and, where possible, on applicants. The OFCCP encourages contractors to seek such information through the use of "electronic tear off sheets" or similar automated means. Effective February 6, 2006, the OFCCP amended its regulations to include "Internet Applicants."

The OFCCP's "Internet applicant" rule establishes both record keeping and applicant tracking standards for certain applicants for employment. The OFCCP's existing record keeping standards continue to apply to jobs for which a government contractor does not obtain applicants through the use of the Internet or related technologies and for which it does not accept any electronic submissions of interest.

However, the Internet applicant rule applies to those jobs for which a government contractor obtains applicants through the acceptance of expressions of interest via the Internet or related technologies (for example, email, resume databanks, employer website). It also applies where the contractor considers both applications submitted electronically and those submitted on paper. The Internet applicant rule requires the contractor "where possible" to identify and record the gender, race and ethnicity of each applicant for the job, including each "Internet applicant."

Definition of Internet applicant

The rule defines "Internet applicant" as an individual who:

- submits an expression of interest in employment through the Internet or related technologies
- is considered by the government contractor for a particular position
- indicates in the expression of interest that he or she possesses the basic qualifications for the position
- the individual does not remove himself/herself from further consideration at any point in the selection process or otherwise indicate that he or she is no longer interested in employment in the position.

Basic qualifications

The "basic qualifications" that an applicant must possess are qualifications that the contractor advertised to potential applicants or criteria the contractor established in advance. These qualifications must be included in the contractor's advertisement for the job or, if the job is not advertised, must be established prior to the contractor's screening of an external or internal database. In addition, the qualifications must be:

- noncomparative features of a job seeker (such as three years' experience in a particular position, rather than a comparative requirement, such as being one of the top five among the candidates in years of experience)
- objective (such as a bachelor's degree in accounting, but not a technical degree from a good school)
- relevant to performance of the particular position and enable the contractor to "accomplish business related goals."

It is important to note that employment tests are not considered to be basic qualifications.

Record retention requirements

The Internet applicant rule requires employers to retain records pertaining to all expressions of interest through the Internet or related electronic data, for which the contractor considered the applicant for a particular position, such as online resumes or internal resume databases. Contractors must also retain records identifying job seekers contacted regarding their interest in a particular position regardless of whether the person qualifies as an Internet applicant. Also, for the purposes of recordkeeping with regard to an internal database, the contractor must maintain:

- a record of each resume added to the database
- a record of the date each resume was added to the database
- the position for which each search of the database was made
- corresponding to each search, the substantive search criteria used and the date of the search.

For purposes of recordkeeping with respect to external resume databases, the contractor must maintain a record of the position for which each search of the database was made and corresponding to each search:

- the substantive search criteria used
- the date of the search
- the resumes of job seekers who met the basic qualifications for the particular position who are considered by the contractor.

Contractors also must retain all tests, test results and interview notes.

Posting requirements

On May 20, 2010, the DOL issued a final regulation implementing Executive Order 13496 (EO13496), signed by President Obama on January 30, 2009. EO13496 requires non-exempt federal contractors and subcontractors to post a notice informing their employees of their rights under the National Labor Relations Act (NLRA).

The final regulation does not apply to public sector employers or employers covered by the Railway Labor Act. Effective June 21, 2010, all contractors with a contract in excess of $100,000 must post this new notice in a conspicuous area. Employers with subcontracts of $10,000 or less are exempt from this requirement.

Employers who generally post electronic notices are required to use specific language on their website that will contain a link to the full text of the notice. The DOL prints the required notice poster and provides it to federal contractors through the federal contracting agency. Alternatively, contactors can obtain it from the Office of Labor-Management Standards (OLMS). Contractors will need to follow the specific document requirements when printing their own copy of the notice.

The specific requirements are that no alterations can be made to the size, color or content of the poster provided by the DOL; thus, the poster must be printed on 11 x 17-inch paper (or in the 11 x 8.5 inch two-page format). This may make it more difficult (although not impossible) for federal contractors to simply buy an "all-in-one" poster that consolidates all the federally mandated labor and employment notices (since this is usually done by shrinking the posters to fit the layout).

In addition, if a "significant portion of the contractor's workforce" is not proficient in English, the employer must post the notice in the language of those employees. Finally, if an employer generally posts electronic notices and a significant portion of its workforce does not speak English, the employer must provide a website link to a copy of the notice in the language the employees speak.

The final regulation also sets out the four paragraphs that EO13496 requires to be included in all non-exempt government contracts and subcontracts (the "employee notice clause"). The employee notice clause be quoted verbatim; instead it can be included in the contract by citation to 29 C.F.R. Part 471, Appendix A to Subpart A.

Enforcement

The OFCCP issued a directive stating that it will share responsibility with the OLMS for ensuring that covered contractors and subcontractors comply with EO13496. The OFCCP's role will be to physically inspect contractors' and subcontractors' establishments at which employees covered by the NLRA engage in activities relating to the performance of the contract or subcontract, including plants, offices and worksites.

The OFCCP is responsible for examining government contracts and subcontracts to ensure compliance with EO13496's posting and contract clause requirements. The OFCCP is also charged with investigating a contractor's or subcontractor's compliance with EO13496 if a complaint is filed with the OFCCP that a covered contractor or subcontractor is not in compliance with the order.

The enforcement directive states that the verification process will be made a part of the onsite phase of compliance reviews that the OFCCP conducts under EO11246, the Rehabilitation Act or VEVRAA. Prior to an onsite review, the OFCCP will request that the contractor or subcontractor provide for inspection a minimum of the last three contracts, subcontracts or purchase orders resulting from solicitations that took place on or after June 21, 2010. Review of a greater number of contracts and purchase orders, however, may be necessary to ensure compliance.

During an onsite investigation, the OFCCP compliance officer will physically inspect a contractor's facility to determine whether the notices are posted in conspicuous places so that the notice is prominent and readily seen by employees.

Additionally, during the onsite investigation, the compliance officer will inspect the identified sample of contracts or purchase orders to determine whether they include the required contract clause. If a contractor customarily posts employee notices about terms and conditions of employment in an electronic format, the compliance officer will also view the electronic posting and ensure that the contractor's website states: "Important Notice About Employee Rights to Organize and Bargain Collectively with Their Employers."

Also, the employer must include a link to the OLMS's website on the contractor's website. If a significant portion of a contractor's workforce is not proficient in English, the OFCCP compliance officer will check to ensure that the poster is provided in the appropriate language. If a contractor is found to be noncompliant during the onsite investigation, the OFCCP will attempt to correct the violation.

In addition, the OFCCP will make reasonable efforts to obtain compliance through conciliation. The remainder of the enforcement order discusses the procedures for an EO13496 report of noncompliance and the administrative proceedings that relate to a compliance investigation. The enforcement directive remains in effect until superseded or rescinded.

Employee complaints

An employee of a covered contractor may file a complaint alleging that the contractor has failed to post the employee notice as required and/or has failed to include the employee notice clause in subcontracts or purchase orders. Complaints may be filed with the OLMS or the OFCCP. In investigating complaints, the director of the OFCCP will evaluate the allegations of the complaint and develop a case record. The record will include findings regarding the contractor's compliance with the requirements of EO13496 and, if applicable, a description of conciliation efforts made, corrective action taken and/or enforcement recommended. The bases for a finding of a violation may include, but are not limited to:

- the results of a compliance evaluation
- the results of a complaint investigation
- a contractor's refusal to allow a compliance evaluation or complaint investigation to be conducted
- a contractor's refusal to cooperate with the compliance evaluation or complaint investigation, including failure to provide information sought during those procedures.

If a violation is found, the contractor must correct the violation and must commit, in writing, not to repeat the violation, before the contractor may be found to be in compliance. If a violation cannot be resolved through conciliation efforts, the OFCCP director will refer the matter to the director of OLMS who may refer the matter to the Solicitor of Labor for implementing administrative enforcement proceedings.

Penalties

In enforcing EO13496, the director of the OLMS may direct a contracting agency to cancel, terminate or suspend any contract for failure of the contractor to comply with its contractual provisions. Contracts may be canceled, terminated or suspended absolutely or continuance of contracts may be conditioned upon compliance. Additionally, an order of debarment may be issued.

Chapter 13

Discipline

With the obvious exception of compensation and benefits, the administration of discipline is probably the single most important dimension of the employment relationship. Arbitrary and unfair imposition of discipline – even if legal – can have dramatic, adverse consequences for the employer.

Discipline is not and should never be the goal. Discipline is a tool to help the employer produce a happy, productive workforce.

The employer should think through what it wants to reward and what it wants to discourage and then communicate these thoughts. The imposition of discipline should never be a surprise to the employee. A well-developed policy that is implemented correctly should almost always result in an employee acknowledging that he or she knew better. Granted, that acknowledgement will not always happen, but if the documentation is in place, it will be evident to any third party looking at the documents that the employee should have expected some level of discipline.

Finally, the disciplinary policy and the administration of discipline should be perceived as fair from the perspective of the disciplined employee and his or her co-workers. This goal requires the employer to be mindful of:

- the specific offense before it
- prior "precedents" or past disciplines
- the future value of what it might do and what message the employer wants to send for future purposes.

Documenting discipline

Employers should ensure that managers are trained to document the facts that justify any disciplinary action so that there is consistency within the organization. It is important for any business to ensure that managers apply a uniform standard. An employee should not be written up for a minor violation when other employees are not written up for the same type of violation. Otherwise, the employer may appear to be building a case against a particular employee.

Common discipline/discharge pitfalls

- Constructive discharge, such as forcing an employee to quit by making conditions intolerable.
- Reducing an employee's hours as discipline without addressing the employee's poor performance.
- Transferring an underperforming employee to another supervisor.
- Failing to give underperforming employees appropriate performance evaluations.
- Acting out of anger or frustration.
- Coming up with false justification or explanations to soften the blow for the employee. For instance, it is a mistake for a manager to justify an adverse decision by stating that the decision was made by someone else.
- Expressing dissatisfaction to others.
- Mislabeling employees based on early performance, which could cause employees to live down to expectations.
- Failure to establish an internal system to ensure consistency of actions between supervisors of various departments and among employees supervised by the same supervisor. Consistency in management and discipline decreases the likelihood of a disparate treatment claim, helps avoid retaliation charges and supports an employer's defense against future charges.

Example
A senior employee, who has been a mediocre performer, has received inflated written performance reviews of average and above average. Among all of these ratings there may be one negative and it has been commented on annually. On a day-to-day basis the manager has frequently expressed dissatisfaction with the performance to the employee and to others. One day the manager has "had enough," and the manger terminates the employee "on the spot."

Although the employee has been consistently underperforming, all of the documentation in the employee's file indicates the employee has a long history of being an average employee. Although the records show that the employee has been underperforming in one specific area, the employee's manager has let the employee's behavior continue without discipline for years. Under the circumstances, one would have to question, "Why was the employee suddenly terminated for this same behavior now when it had been on-going for many years?" It will be difficult for the employer to provide a good answer to this question. Furthermore, the manager acted out of frustration or anger. The manger made the adverse employment decision before anyone had an opportunity to review whether similarly situated employees had been terminated for similar misconduct. Unfortunately, mistakes like these are common, but they can be prevented.

Practical tips for reducing the risk of an employee lawsuit

It is not possible to completely eliminate the risk of a lawsuit, but employers should take a proactive approach to ensure that they are in an advantageous position when an employee brings a claim. A successful defense begins with good company policies that are consistently followed and applied. Helpful steps include:

- Train management to be considerate of all employees and to treat all employees fairly and with respect.
- Educate supervisors to ensure that they understand protected categories of employees.
- Establish guidelines for dealing with employees, such as:
  - criteria for excessive absenteeism
  - how to deal with work performance problems
  - what actions justify immediate discharge.
- Follow established guidelines and be sure not to vary actions based on the identity of the employee.
- Set up a review procedure for personnel decisions. A review of disciplinary or termination decisions may safeguard against a problem before it occurs.
- Confirm all necessary facts, dates and documents used to support the decision making sure no sensitive areas are raised, such as age, sex and the like.
- Be consistent.
- Give careful consideration to decisions that negatively impact long term employees.
- Consider whether an affected employee has some type of protected status. For instance, did he or she just have an on-the-job injury?
- Be fair. All personnel actions should be reviewed for how a jury would feel about the action.
- Do not provide information about personnel decisions to persons other than those who have a need to know.
- Do not discuss disciplinary issues with employees in private. Such issues should be discussed in the presence of a management witness.
- Do not berate employees in front of co-workers – an embarrassed, humiliated or angry employee is more likely to fight and bring a lawsuit.
- Document all disciplinary actions, even verbal reprimands.
- Investigate all sides to a story and, if multiple employees are involved, give them equal opportunities to present their side of the case.

- Consider severance pay in exchange for a release of liability.
- Be considerate of the employee during the termination interview and in all circumstances surrounding the employee's departure.
- Limit reference information to neutral reference only (dates of employment and position held) unless a signed release is obtained.
- Include "at-will" disclaimers everywhere (in handbooks, on acknowledgment pages signed by employee, on employment applications and anywhere else feasible).

Polygraph testing

The Employee Polygraph Protection Act (EPPA) prevents most private employers from using polygraph tests for pre-employment screening and it places substantial restrictions on the use of polygraphs for current employees. Employers generally may not require or request any employee or job applicant to take a lie detector test; or discharge, discipline or discriminate against an employee or job applicant for refusing to take a test or for exercising other rights under the act. In addition, employers are required to display the EPPA poster in the workplace.

The law does provide a few exceptions of instances when it may be appropriate for an employer to use a polygraph test, but the employer must first take a number of specific steps, which if not properly completed can lead to liability. If an employer believes that circumstances justify the use of a polygraph examination, the employer should consult with counsel to avoid violating the law.

Exemptions

Ongoing investigation

The EPPA prohibits employers from discharging, disciplining, discriminating against or denying employment or promotion to an employee solely on the basis of the results of a polygraph test or for refusing to take the test, except pursuant to the ongoing investigations exemption and then only when there is other supporting evidence. Ongoing investigation means that the investigation is of a current, specific and identifiable incident in which company money or property is missing and in which there are identifiable suspects.

Employers may test employees whom they reasonably suspect of workplace theft if these employees had access to the property involved. Before the test can be administered, the worker must be given a signed, written statement that specifically describes the incident under investigation, the basis for testing particular employees and the basis of the employer's reasonable suspicion, in addition to other requirements.

While the EPPA does not prohibit medical tests to determine the presence of controlled substances in the body, the regulations state that the ongoing investigation exemption does not allow an employer to give an employee a polygraph test to learn whether he or she has used drugs or alcohol. This is true even when possible substance abuse leads to economic loss such as an accident caused by a drunken employee driving a company vehicle.

Manufacturers and distributors

The act permits limited use of polygraph examinations by employers authorized to manufacture, distribute or dispense certain controlled substances. Regulations provide that this exemption does not apply to common or contract carriers and warehouses, whose possession of the controlled substance is in the usual course of their business and who are not required to register with the U.S. Drug Enforcement Agency.

Employers providing security services

The act permits testing of prospective employees of companies whose primary business purpose consists of providing armored car, security alarm and security guard services for the protection of "facilities, materials or operations having a significant impact on" the health or safety of a state, a political subdivision or the national security of the United States or "currency, negotiable securities, precious commodities or instruments or proprietary information."

This exemption only permits testing of prospective employees employed to protect facilities, materials, operations or assets as described in the regulations. Some types of employees, such as custodial and maintenance employees, would not be covered by the exemption.

Public employers

The act exempts federal, state and local governments and does not apply to certain testing administered by government agencies for national defense or security reasons. The 11th Circuit Court has held that the national defense exemption does not apply to private contractors.

Penalties

Federal courts have the power to award legal and equitable relief for violations of the act, including reinstatement, promotion, lost wages and benefits and attorney fees. Additionally, the U.S. Department of Labor (DOL) may seek civil fines of up to $10,000 against employers who violate the act.

Posting requirements

The law requires all employers engaged in (or affecting) commerce to post and maintain a notice where notices to employees and applicants are customarily posted that sets forth the pertinent provisions of the act. Copies of the notices are available online at:

- https://www.dol.gov/agencies/whd/posters/employee-polygraph-protection-act

State laws

Some states also have their own laws regulating the use of polygraph tests in employment.

Employer monitoring

In certain situations, an employer may desire to place an employee under surveillance who is suspected of criminal activity against the employer. Although it is generally appropriate to place employees suspected of wrongdoing under video surveillance or to hire a "spotter" to masquerade as an employee to observe employees, employers should generally avoid conducting audio surveillance with any type of electronic device. Both federal and state law generally prohibits audio surveillance.

Federal wiretap law

The federal wiretap law, adopted as part of the Omnibus Crime Control and Safe Streets Act, imposes criminal liability on the illegal use of technology to intercept and record telephone calls and other communications. The act has also been the basis for civil claims by employees who discovered their telephone conversations or other communications were recorded, monitored or both, by employers.

In 1986, Congress amended the statute to extend the prohibition to the interception of electronic communications. The Electronic Communications Privacy Act provides for a private cause of action permitting the recovery of actual damages or statutory damages at $100 per day or $10,000, whichever is greater. Aggrieved individuals may also recover punitive damages, attorney fees and court costs. As applied to employers, the statute prohibits:

- intentionally intercepting, trying to intercept or procuring another person to intercept employees' wire oral or electronic communications
- intentionally using, trying to use or procuring another to use an electronic, mechanical or other device to intercept an employee's oral communications
- intentionally disclosing or trying to disclose to another person the contents of a wire oral or electronic communication, knowing or having reason to know that the information was obtained in violation of the act
- intentionally using or trying to use the contents of a wire oral or electronic communication, knowing or having reason to know that the information was obtained in violation of the act.

Although the interception and use of an employee's conversation or other communications are generally prohibited, it is not a violation of the act if:

- a party to the conversation is the one who intercepts the communication
- one of the parties to the communication consents before interception occurs
- the circumstances do not justify an expectation of privacy and the employee does not exhibit such an expectation.

Consent may be implied from the circumstances, such as when the employee's language and acts tend to show that the employee knows of or agrees to exceptions to the expectation that conversations are private. Nevertheless, because lack of consent may result in significant liability to the employer, if the employer desires to intercept the communications of its employees, the employer should explain to employees in advance why communications will be monitored and obtain express written consent to the interception from each employee. Although this procedure will most likely do little to help uncover the source of employee theft, under such circumstances, the employer will avoid exposing itself to liability.

If an employer believes it is necessary to use wiretapping or other audio interception methods to keep track of employee theft and/or other criminal activity, the employer should include a wiretapping policy in its employee handbook, which each employee should be required to sign at the time he or she accepts employment with the company. Although all employees will be properly put on notice of the potential for audio surveillance, this approach will not likely create the same suspicion as announcing the policy shortly after a criminal incident occurred.

Although direct interception of an employee's conversations is clearly prohibited by the act (subject to the exceptions listed previously), there has been some concern over whether messages stored on computers such as computer files or email messages are similarly protected by the act.

Many states also have laws regarding wiretapping as well as privacy.

The value of performance appraisals

Performance appraisals often figure prominently in litigation, so employers should conduct employee reviews with an understanding of how the document would be used in the context of litigation. If an employer decides to discharge an employee, performance appraisals should support the adverse employment decision. Supervisors should give honest performance appraisals and these reviews should be recorded accurately and in a timely fashion. Providing an employee with the opportunity to comment on a performance appraisal, in writing, may help avoid a later claim that the appraisal was unfair or inaccurate or that the employee never received it. Employers may also require employees to sign performance appraisals.

Guarding against defamation and discrimination

Sensitive information, such as unflattering performance evaluations, should be kept secure and shared only with those who "need to know" the information because of their job duties.

The performance evaluation may become evidence to support a claim of discrimination under either a disparate impact or disparate treatment theory of discrimination. To avoid disparate impact claims, employers must ensure that their performance appraisal system is administered even-handedly. Employers should continually evaluate the process to ensure no protected groups are disadvantaged.

To guard against disparate treatment claims, employers must give accurate appraisals, even if the truth hurts. An employer's failure to criticize poor work by a member of a protected group can backfire. For instance, in one case, the employer did not criticize an African-American employee's poor work for fear she would sue. When the employee was discharged, she claimed she had not been given the same opportunity to improve as had white employees and successfully sued for discrimination.

Termination

Chapter

14

More and more often, employers who discipline or discharge an employee find themselves in the midst of litigation over the action. Decisions made by employers during the discipline process can either protect the employer in the event of litigation or build a case for the terminated employee. It is essential that employers handle discipline and discharge in a way that reduces exposure to claims.

Essentials of the termination procedure

Initial considerations

Evaluating termination procedures should begin well before an employee is terminated. That is, the employer can begin to protect itself when employees are hired by having them sign a written disclaimer of permanent employment or employment for a specific period of time. The waiver should state that representations to the contrary must be in writing and signed by the employer or a specific officer of the employer, such as the company president or CEO. The disclaimer should also state that employment is at-will.

Arbitration or jury waiver clause

Employers may consider having employees sign an arbitration or jury waiver clause as a condition of employment during the hiring process. A jury waiver clause helps employers avoid the uncertainty of litigating employment related claims before a jury.

Under a jury waiver agreement, employees retain all rights to sue their employers, except the right to request a jury and all potential statutory remedies. Bench trials (trials by a judge) are usually shorter and much less expensive than jury trials. Additionally, a study released by the U.S. Department of Justice shows that employers fair better in verdicts returned by judges than juries. Finally, the decision of a trial judge is subject to full review on appeal, unlike an arbitrator's decision, which is subject to extremely limited review. Employers should confer with local counsel before relying on these clauses as some courts will not enforce.

Avoid implied contracts

Train interviewers to avoid making promises or implied promises of tenure, longevity or continued employment. Avoid making promises or implied promises of job tenure in handbooks, personnel policies or written work rules.

Avoid "for cause" statements

Termination polices should not refer to discharge "for cause" and should not limit management's right to discharge employees. Review any statements of the potential grounds for discharge to ensure that they give the employer flexibility and provide notice to the employee.

Document performance

Identify potential problems early. Establish and police employee evaluation systems. Give honest evaluations, including weak points and circulate those evaluations only to those with a "need to know." Evaluations should offer specific examples and explain the conclusions. Evaluations may be the basis for a wrongful discharge suit if they do not support the reason for the discharge by establishing a pattern of employee conduct.

Establish, distribute and enforce standards of conduct

Establish, distribute and enforce a general nondiscrimination policy that addresses all forms of prohibited discrimination, including harassment.

Establish a complaint procedure

Establish a specific complaint procedure (consider requiring all complaints be reduced to writing but maintain some flexibility with this) that:

- provides alternative avenues for complaints
- does not require an employee to complain only to his or her immediate supervisor (in case the supervisor is the problem)
- assures the employee that he or she may use the complaint procedure without fear of retaliation.

A complaint procedure is a particularly effective method for dealing with potential whistleblowers because it gives them a place to air their grievances.

Train supervisors and managers

Ensure that supervisors and managers are sensitive to potential wrongful discharge claims and are trained regarding the use of personnel documents to avoid litigation.

Review terminations

Appoint an individual to review all factors relating to terminations to ensure consistency. Evaluate the strength of the evidence and whether policies are being applied consistently. Consider whether the employee has had a chance to tell his or her side of the story.

Be honest regarding the reason for termination

Candidly state the reason for discharge, but avoid defamation. Keep the explanation factual and brief. If the reason for discharge is documented, ensure the documented reason is the real reason because any subsequent change in the stated reason may allow a plaintiff to argue that the employer's proffered reason is pre-textual.

Designate reference providers

Designate a particular individual to respond to inquiries by subsequent potential employers. Many employers have the designated individual limit the information provided to a confirmation of the previous employee's employment dates and their position. However, in light of an increasing effort to hold employers liable who fail to disclose information about potentially dangerous employees to subsequent employers, some employers provide additional information where appropriate. Additionally, if the former employee has signed a release that includes an agreement regarding references, employers may consider providing additional information.

Insurance coverage

Check liability insurance coverage and make sure that the carrier is given timely notification of any potential claims.

Pre-termination considerations

In most states, the employment relationship is "at-will" except as modified by statute and court decisions. This generally means that an employer can fire an employee, in the absence of an employment contract, for any reason as long as it is not an illegal reason, such as termination based upon race or any other protected category.

Similarly, the employee is free to resign at any time. Accordingly, in most states an "at-will" employee who has been discharged cannot sue unless an exception to the at-will rule applies.

Exceptions to the basic at-will rules

The exceptions to the rule of employment at-will include contractual limitations. The employer and employee may have entered into a contract that states that employment is for a specific duration or that the employer can only terminate the employee for "just cause." Employers should guard against inadvertently creating employment contracts in employee handbooks or by making promises to employees regarding the duration of their job.

Public policy exception

Additionally, some courts have created public policy exceptions to the employment at-will doctrine. The public policy exception to the at-will employment doctrine "provides that an at-will employee who has been discharged by an employer in violation of a clear mandate of public policy has a cause of action against the employer for wrongful discharge."

An employee has a cause of action for wrongful discharge if he or she was discharged for:

- refusing to perform an illegal act or an act contrary to a strong mandate of public policy
- reporting wrongdoing or violations of law or public policy by the employer or fellow employees to superiors or third parties
- acting in a manner public policy would encourage
- filing a workers' compensation claim.

Implied covenant of good faith and fair dealing

Additionally, some state courts have held that in all employment contracts (written but not oral) there is an "implied" agreement that each side will deal with the other "fairly" and in "good faith."

Public employers

A public employer's ability to discharge an employee may be limited by civil service or similar laws or by constitutional restrictions, such as due process requirements.

Equal employment opportunity

Discrimination statutes make it illegal for an employer to discharge or otherwise discriminate against an employee because the employee belongs to a statutorily protected class, such as age, race or sex. When making a termination decision, employers should consider the following areas of potential discrimination:

- sex discrimination/harassment
- pregnancy/abortion and child related considerations
- race, color, national origin and/or religious discrimination
- disability discrimination
- marital status discrimination
- discrimination based upon veteran status or military participation
- alienage or citizenship discrimination
- discrimination based on status as a debtor or filing bankruptcy under the Bankruptcy Code
- discrimination because of the employee's wages have been garnished.

Although discrimination on the basis of sexual orientation is not prohibited by federal law (at least with regard to private employers), the EEOC has ruled otherwise and many states and municipalities have enacted laws prohibiting sexual orientation discrimination.

Protected concerted activity

The labor laws, specifically the National Labor Relations Act (NLRA) and most public-sector labor laws, apply to both union free and unionized employers. The NLRA prohibits acts by the employer against employees who engage in "protected concerted activities" – these need not be union-related. The NLRA gives employees the right to "engage in other concerted activities for the purpose of collective bargaining or other mutual aid or protection ..."

Protected concerted activities involve employees acting together to affect wages, hours or other terms and conditions of employment.

Whistleblowers and retaliation

A variety of laws protect employees who choose to blow the whistle on employer wrongdoing. In addition to the federal laws discussed herein. Some states have laws prohibiting employers from terminating employees who refuse to participate or remain silent about illegal activity.

The Civil Service Reform Act and the Whistleblower Protection Act

The First and Fourteenth Amendments to the U.S. Constitution prohibit federal, state and local governments from retaliating against employees who blow the whistle on matters of public importance. Federal employees are protected by the Civil Service Reform Act (CSRA), which prohibits various employment actions, such as the discharge of whistleblowers. The Whistleblower Protection Act (WPA) and its 1994 amendments expanded the CSRA. The CSRA, as amended by the WPA, provides the "exclusive remedial scheme" for civil service employees to seek relief for whistleblower claims. This means that an employee who pursues a claim under the WPA may not be able to sue under other statutes.

Occupational Safety and Health Act

Individuals who have made safety related complaints are protected under the Occupational Safety and Health Act (OSH Act). Individuals who exercise their rights under the OSH Act regarding toxic substances are protected from discharge. An employer that violates this section may be liable for attorney fees and costs. The OSH Act does not pre-empt state criminal prosecutions. Additionally, the Occupational Safety and Health Administration (OSHA) is charged with investigating complaints of numerous federal whistleblower laws.

Title VII of the Civil Rights Act

Title VII of the Civil Rights Act (Title VII) protects individuals who have opposed unlawful employment discrimination.

Fair Labor Standards Act

Individuals who have filed claims or have participated in investigations of violations of the Fair Labor Standards Act (FLSA) are protected under that act.

National Labor Relations Act

Individuals who have filed charges or given testimony under the National Labor Relations Act (NLRA) are protected.

Protecting the public interest

State laws vary in the extent to which they protect whistleblowers for acting in the public interest.

In addition, there are a host of federal statutes that specifically provide such protection including:

- Clean Air Act
- Energy Reorganization Act
- Safe Drinking Water Act
- Solid Waste Disposal Act
- Comprehensive Environmental Responsibility, Compensation and Liability Act (CERCLA)
- Toxic Substances Control Act
- Water Pollution Control Act.

Sarbanes-Oxley Act

The Sarbanes-Oxley Act (SOX), as amended by the Dodd-Frank Wall Street Reform and Consumer Protection Act, provides a civil cause of action to protect employees of publicly traded companies who provide information or assist in a federal fraud investigation. A "publicly traded company" includes any "subsidiary or affiliate whose financial information is included in the consolidated financial statements of such company." This whistleblower provision prohibits any officer, employee, contractor, subcontractor or agent of a publicly traded company from taking certain retaliatory actions. Thus, under SOX, there can be individual liability. The prohibited retaliatory actions include discharging, demoting, suspending, threatening, harassing or discriminating against an employee who engages in protected whistleblowing activity.

The act protects two types of whistleblowing activities:

1. **Assisting investigation of violation of federal law**
   SOX protects a person who provides information or assists in the investigation of conduct that the employee reasonably believes to be a violation of federal mail, wire, bank or securities fraud statutes, rules or regulations of the SEC or any other federal law relating to fraud against shareholders. To be protected, this information must be disclosed to a federal regulatory or law enforcement agency, a member or committee of

Congress or a person with supervisory authority over the employee or who has the authority to investigate or terminate the misconduct.

2. **Filing proceeding regarding alleged violation of federal law**
The act also protects an employee who files, causes to be filed, testifies, participates in or otherwise assists in a proceeding filed or that is about to be filed, regarding an alleged violation of federal mail, wire, bank or securities fraud statutes, rules or regulations of the SEC or any other federal law relating to fraud against shareholders.

Elements of a SOX claim

To establish a SOX claim, the complainant must show that:

- he or she engaged in protected activity as defined by the act
- the employer was aware of the protected activity
- the employee suffered an adverse employment action
- the circumstances are sufficient to raise an inference that the protected activity was likely a contributing factor in the unfavorable action.

If a claimant establishes these elements by a preponderance of the evidence, a respondent may avoid liability by presenting clear and convincing evidence that it would have taken the same unfavorable personnel action had there not been any protected activity.

Remedies

SOX authorizes an award to a prevailing employee of make-whole relief, including reinstatement with the same seniority status that the employee would have had but for the discrimination, back pay with interest and compensation for any special damages sustained, including litigation costs, expert witness fees and reasonable attorney fees.

Administrative procedures

Responsibility for handling complaints under SOX has been delegated to OSHA, which has published a final rule establishing procedures for handling whistleblower complaints under the act. The act provides that proceedings under SOX will be governed by the rules, procedures and burdens of proof of the Wendell H. Ford Aviation Investment and Reform Act for the 21st Century (AIR21).

Timeliness of a SOX complaint

An individual who believes he or she has been subjected to retaliation in violation of SOX must file a charge of discrimination against the employer with the Assistant Secretary for OSHA within 180 days of the violation.

Investigations

OSHA will investigate the complaint if it finds that the complaint states a prima facie case that protected behavior or conduct was a determining factor in an unfavorable personnel action. However, if this prima facie showing is not made or if the named person (the entity accused of violating SOX) demonstrates by clear and convincing evidence that it would have taken the same unfavorable personnel action regardless of the complainant's protected behavior or conduct, notwithstanding the prima facie showing of the complainant, OSHA will not investigate the complaint.

Preliminary order

Within 60 days of the filing of the complaint, OSHA will issue written findings as to whether there is reasonable cause to believe that the named person has discriminated against the complainant in violation of the act. If a reasonable cause determination is made, it will be accompanied by a preliminary order for relief. If OSHA determines that a violation has not occurred, it will notify the parties of that finding.

Objections to a preliminary order

The parties can file objections to the findings and preliminary order and request a hearing with a U.S. Department of Labor (DOL) administrative law judge (ALJ). The findings and preliminary order will be effective 30 days after receipt by the named person unless an objection and request for hearing is filed. However, any order of reinstatement will be effective immediately upon receipt of the findings and order.

Hearings and decisions of the ALJ

If a timely objection is filed, the ALJ will conduct a hearing. The ALJ will not review OSHA's determination to dismiss a complaint without an investigation and will not remand the complaint until after completion of the investigation or receipt of additional findings. Instead, the ALJ will hear the case on the merits. If the ALJ concludes that the party charged has violated the law, the order will provide all relief necessary to make the employee whole. If, upon the request of the party charged with the violation, the ALJ determines that a complaint was frivolous or was brought in bad faith, the judge may award that party a reasonable attorney fee, not to exceed $1,000.

Administrative Review Board decisions and orders

The Administrative Review Board may review the ALJ's decision if a written petition for review is filed within 10 business days of the date of the ALJ's decision. The ALJ's decision will become final if the Administrative Review Board does not notify the parties within 30 days of the filing of the petition for review that the case has been accepted for review. If the Administrative Review Board concludes that the party charged violated the law, it will order that party to provide all relief necessary to make the complainant whole. The parties may seek review of the Administrative Review Board's order by filing a petition for review in the U.S. Court of Appeals for the circuit in which the violation allegedly occurred or the circuit in which the complainant resided on the date of the violation.

Judicial enforcement

If either party fails to comply with a preliminary order of reinstatement or a final order or the terms of a settlement agreement, the Secretary or a person on whose behalf the order was issued may file a civil action seeking enforcement of the order in the U.S. district court for the district in which the violation was found to have occurred.

District court jurisdiction of discrimination complaints

If the DOL fails to issue a final decision within the specified 180-day period and there is no showing that the delay is due to any bad faith on the part of the claimant, the claimant may file suit in federal district court.

Criminal provisions of SOX

In addition to civil penalties, SOX makes it a crime punishable by a fine and up to 10 years in prison to knowingly retaliate against any person, including interfering with the person's lawful employment or livelihood, for providing truthful information relating to the commission or possible commission of a federal crime to a law enforcement officer. This provision protects every employee, including those employed by non-publicly traded companies, from adverse action based on reporting a criminal matter to local, state or federal law enforcement.

Additionally, SOX makes it a crime punishable by a fine and up to 20 years in prison to knowingly alter, destroy, conceal or falsify any record, document or tangible object with intent to impede, obstruct or influence the investigation or administration of any matter within the jurisdiction of any department or agency of the United States or any bankruptcy case under Title 11 of the U.S. Bankruptcy Code.

Confidentiality

SOX requires publicly traded companies to establish audit committees, which must establish procedures for filing internal, confidential and anonymous complaints concerning financial irregularities. The SEC has adopted rules directing national securities exchanges and national securities associations to prohibit the listing of any security of a public company that fails to comply with this requirement. While each company has discretion in deciding what type of complaint procedure it will adopt, at a minimum, the company should have a well-publicized hot line or other system for employees to make anonymous complaints. The company must keep a record of the complaints, including the initial report and resolution.

Miscellaneous employment protections

Various federal and state laws may limit an employer's ability to discharge an employee.

Jury duty

Under federal law, it is illegal for an employer to discharge, threaten to discharge, intimidate or coerce any employee because of the employee's jury service or the attendance or scheduled attendance in connection with such service in any federal court. An employer who discharges an employee because of the employee's jury service may be liable to the employee for the amount of wages lost due to the discharge and may be ordered to reinstate the employee. The employer may also be subject to other injunctive relief and a civil penalty of not more than $1,000 per employee per violation. Additionally, the court may award the prevailing employee attorney fees and costs.

The employer, however, can recover attorney fees only if the action was frivolous or in bad faith. A claim by an employee alleging wrongful discharge can be brought in state or federal court. The statute does not require employers to pay employees for the time spent on jury duty, unless the non-payment is a method of coercion or intimidation. The employee must also be allowed to participate in insurance and other benefits as if he or she had been away on a leave of absence during the term of service. Many states also have laws that prohibit employers from terminating or discriminating against employees because of jury duty. In fact, many states have laws, similar to voting leave laws, requiring employers provide paid leave to employees serving jury duty.

Garnishment

Individuals with one or more garnishments of one debt are protected from discharge under the Consumer Credit Protection Act. An employer that violates this law may be fined not more than $1,000 or imprisoned not more than one year. The Secretary of Labor enforces this statute and courts are split on whether the individual employee can sue under the statute. The federal wage garnishment law only prohibits the discharge of employees for the garnishment of one debt. Employers should be aware, however, that Title VII may prohibit a policy of discharging employees for garnishment of more than one debt if the policy has a discriminatory impact on a protected category of employees.

Family and medical leave

The Family and Medical Leave Act (FMLA) permits covered employees to receive up to 12 weeks of unpaid leave per year for the birth or adoption of a child, serious health condition of an employee or family member or a qualifying exigency based on a covered servicemember's active duty or call to active duty status. The FMLA also provides for 26 weeks of military or caregiver leave.

If employees are discharged for taking this leave, they may sue for back pay and benefits, reinstatement, attorney fees and actual losses sustained. In addition, employees may recover double damages for willful violations.

Layoffs and plant closings

Individuals are protected under the Worker Adjustment and Retraining Notification Act (WARN), which requires 60-days' notice be given to employees and state and local governments before layoffs of 50 or more employees. Penalties include payment of 60-days' wages and benefits to employees and a $500 per day civil penalty paid to the local government for up to 60 days. Additionally, some states have their own WARN-type statutes that may impose different obligations on employers.

Consumer reports

Under the Fair Credit Reporting Act (FCRA), before taking any adverse employment action against someone based in whole or in part on a consumer report, the employer must provide the affected person with a copy of the report and a written description of the person's rights under the FCRA.

Bankruptcy

Employers may not discharge an employee solely because the employee is or has been a debtor in bankruptcy. An employee who is discharged prior to filing is not protected, however. Discharge of an employee who has filed bankruptcy may be permissible if the employer can prove there is a non-bankruptcy reason for the discharge.

Other laws

In addition to the federal law protections described herein, some states provide additional protection. For instance, some states, including Illinois and North Carolina, have enacted laws prohibiting discrimination against victims of domestic or sexual violence. In most states, protections available at the pre-employment/interview stage remain available throughout the entirety of employment, including termination. Employers should check the law of the state in which they are located.

Steps of termination

Suspension

Employers may consider suspension pending investigation. Suspension allows the employer to avoid mistakes and irrational decisions. It also gives the employer time to collect the information necessary to determine the appropriate action and to support the ultimate decision. Screening, reviewing and discussing preliminary decisions provides the opportunity for input from higher management and review of documentation to ensure the termination decision is supported. Screening also permits the employer to ensure the discharge is consistent with company policies and comparable cases.

In some cases, it may be appropriate to question the supervisor regarding the reasons for the proposed discharge and question witnesses and the employee at the screening stage, to ensure the termination is appropriate and that all facts have been considered. This is also the time to review the pre-termination checklist and obtain input from labor counsel, if appropriate.

Handling the termination

- Conduct the termination meeting privately.
- Have at least one trustworthy management witness with a "duty to know" at the termination conference.
- Consider whether any reason should be given. When stating the reason for the termination, avoid false reasons, such as "economic layoff." Consider possible defamation and defamation by self-publication claims and whether the statement of the reason will make it more or less likely the employee will file a complaint.
- Consider whether the reason for termination should be given to the employee in writing.

  Note:
  In the public sector, a written reason may be required. Additionally, some state laws may require written reasons for the termination.

- Consider giving the employee the opportunity to speak. Properly handled, this may reduce animosity between the employer and the employee and head off a potential lawsuit.
- Consider the "Weingarten Right" to an employee representative. The National Labor Relations Board (NLRB) has overturned its decision that the right to an employee representative, when requested by a non-supervisory employee in an investigatory interview, applies to non-union employees as well as union employees; this right only applies to unionized employees.
- Make sure the employee obtains information and documents needed to receive benefits, if any, including COBRA continuation coverage. Additionally, consider offering separation and outplacement counseling/benefits.
- Consider describing the nature of the reference to be given and obtaining the employee's agreement regarding the intended reference.
- Consider obtaining a release as a condition of providing a reference.
- Consider whether the post-meeting memo should be confidential, at the direction of counsel and in anticipation of litigation.
- Determine whether the final paycheck must be presented when the employee is discharged. Some states require this.

Final paycheck regulations

State	Final paycheck rules
Alabama	None
Alaska	If an employee is discharged, pay is due within three working days. If an employee quits, the final paycheck is due on the next regular payday that is at least three days after the employee gives notice of quitting.

State	Final paycheck rules
Arizona	If an employee is discharged, pay is due within seven working days or by the end of the next regular pay period, whichever is sooner. If an employee quits, the final check must be given on the next scheduled payday.
Arkansas	The final paycheck is due on the next regularly scheduled pay date, unless the employee demands or requests payment, in which case, the payment must be made within seven days after the termination date.
California	If an employee is discharged, pay is due immediately. If an employee without a written contract quits, the paycheck is due within 72 hours (unless the employee gave 72-hours' notice of quitting, in which case the paycheck is due immediately).
Colorado	If an employee is discharged, pay is generally due immediately, although more time may be allowed in certain circumstances. If an employee quits, the paycheck is due on the next regular payday.
Connecticut	If an employee is discharged, pay is due on the next business day. If an employee quits, pay is due on the next regular payday.
Delaware	Due on the next regular payday.
District of Columbia	If an employee is discharged, pay is generally due the next business day, subject to a few exceptions. If an employee quits, pay is due on the next regular payday or within seven days, whichever is earlier, subject to certain exceptions.
Florida	None
Georgia	None
Hawaii	If an employee is discharged, pay is due on the same day or the next day if conditions prevent immediate payment. If an employee quits, pay is due on the next regular payday, unless the employee gives at least one pay period's notice of quitting, in which case payment is due the same day.
Idaho	Due on the earlier of either the next regular payday or 10 days after layoff or termination. If an employee makes a written request for an earlier payment, then pay is due within 48 hours of the employer receiving the request.
Illinois	Due at time of separation, if possible. If not, no later than next regular payday.
Indiana	Generally, where an employee is discharged or quits, pay is due at the next regular pay day in the pay period in which the separation occurs.
Iowa	On the next regular payday if the employee is suspended or discharged.

State	Final paycheck rules
Kansas	Due on the next regular payday on which the employee would have been paid if employment had not ended.
Kentucky	If employee is discharged or quits, pay is due no later than the next regular payday or 14 days following the termination date.
Louisiana	Due on the next regular payday or within 15 days after employment ends, whichever is earlier.
Maine	Final check must be given on the next scheduled payday or within two weeks after a demand from the employee, whichever is earlier.
Maryland	Due on the next regular payday.
Massachusetts	If an employee is involuntarily terminated, he or she must be paid on the date of termination. If an employee leaves voluntarily, the final pay is due on the next regular payday or on the Saturday that follows an employee's resignation if there is no scheduled payday.
Michigan	Due as soon as can be paid with due diligence, but no later than the next regular payday.
Minnesota	If an employee quits, pay is due on the next regular payday, unless it is less than five calendar days from the employee's final day. If so, he or she can be paid the earlier of the following regular payday or within 20 days of the employee's final day. If discharged, all unpaid wages must be paid within 24 hours.
Mississippi	None
Missouri	Due on day of termination if fired. No law if employee voluntarily resigns, but according to the state labor department final pay should be made no later than the next regularly scheduled payday.
Montana	If an employee quits, pay is due on the next scheduled payday or within 15 days, whichever is earlier. If an employee is discharged or laid off, pay is due immediately, but the employer has the option of maintaining a written policy that extends this time to the next scheduled payday or within 15 days, whichever is earlier.
Nebraska	Due the next regular payday or within two weeks of when employee discharged, whichever is earlier.
Nevada	If an employee is discharged, pay is due within three days. If an employee quits, the final pay is due on the next regular payday on which employee normally would have received it or within seven days of employee's resignation, whichever is earlier.
New Hampshire	If an employee is discharged, the final pay is due within 72 hours. If an employee quits, pay is due on the next regular payday, unless the employee gives at least one pay period's notice of intention to quit, then pay is due within 72 hours.
New Jersey	If an employee is discharged, suspended or quits, the final pay is due on the next regular payday from the pay period.

State	Final paycheck rules
New Mexico	If an employee is discharged, he or she must be paid within five days of the discharge if the employee is paid in a fixed and definite amount (not based on a task, piece, commission or other method of calculation) or within 10 days of the discharge, for all other employees. Employees who quit or resign their employment must be paid by the first payday following the resignation.
New York	Due on the next regular payday.
North Carolina	Due on the next regular payday.
North Dakota	Due on the next regular payday.
Ohio	A terminated employee should receive their final paycheck on their next scheduled pay date or within 15 days, whichever is earlier. Employees who voluntarily quit are required to be paid on their next regularly scheduled payday.
Oklahoma	Due by the next regular payday for the pay period in which the work was performed.
Oregon	If an employee is discharged or employment ends by mutual agreement, the paycheck is due on the first business day thereafter. If an employee quits without giving 48-hours' notice, pay is due on the next payday or within five days, whichever is earlier, subject to certain exceptions. If an employee resigns with at least 48-hours' notice, the paycheck is due on the final day worked, unless that day is on a weekend or holiday, then it is due on the next business day.
Pennsylvania	Due on the next regular payday.
Rhode Island	If an employee voluntarily or involuntarily separates from employment, the final pay is due on the next regular payday.
South Carolina	Due either within 48 hours or next regular payday, but cannot be more than 30 days after employment ends.
South Dakota	Due by the next regular payday or as soon thereafter as the employee returns all company property.
Tennessee	Due no later than the next regular payday or within 21 days.
Texas	If an employee is discharged, pay is due within six days. For employment ending for other reasons, pay is due by the next regular payday.
Utah	If an employee is discharged, pay is due within 24 hours. If the employee quits, pay is due by the next regular payday.
Vermont	If an employee quits, pay is due on the next regular payday or the following Friday if there is none. If an employee is discharged, pay is due within 72 hours.
Virginia	Due on or before the date the employee would have been paid if not terminated.

State	Final paycheck rules
Washington	Due at the end of the established pay period, unless a labor agreement provides otherwise.
West Virginia	Final wages, including any fringe benefits that are payable directly to the employee, must be paid on or before the next regular payday on which the wages would otherwise be due and payable.
Wisconsin	Due on the next regular payday.
Wyoming	Payment must be made no later than the employer's usual practice on regularly scheduled payroll dates.

Note:
These rules may be altered where there is an employment contract or a collective bargaining agreement in place. Additionally, some states regulate when commissions must be paid. Some states also require that accrued vacation time be included in a final paycheck. In certain instances, an employer may be permitted to withhold a final paycheck until the employee has returned all of the company's property. The relevant state law must be consulted to ensure compliance with these statutory requirements.

Employer mistakes

In discriminatory discharge cases, it usually is not very difficult for a plaintiff to establish a case of discrimination or for the employer to furnish a legitimate nondiscriminatory reason for the discharge. Accordingly, the issue most often litigated is whether a plaintiff can demonstrate that the employer's stated reason for discharge is a pretext for discrimination.

A plaintiff usually tries to prove a pretext by showing that the employer's asserted justification for discharge is untrue. Management mistakes can make a plaintiff's job of proving pretext much easier, even if discrimination was not the reason for discharge. The following is a list of common management mistakes and fixes that may help an employer furnish a legitimate nondiscriminatory reason for its actions:

- It is important to treat similarly situated individuals in a consistent manner. Address the following questions prior to discharging an employee:
  - What is the company policy?
  - How has it been applied in the past?
  - How can I credibly explain different treatment?
- Examine what the manager was doing before the spotlight was on him or her. Does the personnel file tell the same story about the employee as the manager? Is there "an empty file" issue?
- Words are a window to the mind. Examine whether the manager's past comments reflect what he or she is now saying about the employee (for example, about the employee's performance, conduct and the like). Examine whether the manager's comments demonstrate bias or prejudice.

- Timing is everything. Examine whether the manager's actions coincide with recent protected activity by the employee. Also determine whether the manager has information about the employee, such as knowledge of a disability or serious health condition, which can be identified by the employee as a protected reason for the manager's adverse actions.
- Employers frequently try to avoid difficult discharge decisions by classifying the discharge as a "layoff." Calling a discharge a layoff can be dangerous if a true layoff did not occur. A plaintiff will be entitled to conduct discovery on the layoff and the reason for his or her inclusion in the layoff. If an investigation shows a layoff did not occur, that may be enough for a reasonable juror to determine the employer's reason is a pretext for discrimination.
- Neither state nor federal discrimination laws require an employer to have more than one reason for discharging an employee. If the reason for discharge is an employee's conduct, it is unnecessary for the employer to identify anything else as a reason. Many employers gild the lily by identifying a number of reasons, which make them susceptible to proof that one or more of the reasons is false.

Constructive discharge

The constructive discharge doctrine originally developed under the NLRA, allows employees to sue if they feel their employer forced them to resign. To show constructive discharge under Title VII, the employee must prove that his or her working conditions were so difficult or unpleasant that a reasonable person in the employee's shoes would have felt compelled to resign. The U.S. Supreme Court has held that a constructive discharge may be a tangible employment action if a supervisor's official act precipitates the constructive discharge.

However, where an official act does not underlie the constructive discharge, it will not be treated as a tangible employment action.

The impact of termination

Employers may find themselves subject to various administrative complaints for discharging an employee. The following discussion details how the various proceedings may interact in a discharge situation.

Unemployment compensation

Employers should respond cautiously to inquiries on routine unemployment compensation forms because the initial response may be used against the employer later. Evidentiary hearings may be conducted and recorded. Such a proceeding provides early discovery opportunities for the employee and employer. Because testimony in such a hearing is made under oath, it may be admissible in later litigation.

Civil service proceedings

For public sector employers with civil service, evidentiary hearings may be conducted when a discharged employee appeals his or her termination. This provides both the employer and employee an early opportunity to gather evidence that may be used against the other party in a subsequent lawsuit. If a civil service decision in favor of the employer is reviewed in the state courts, it may preclude certain subsequent claims.

Workers' compensation

An employee may begin workers' compensation proceedings or maintain an ongoing workers' compensation proceeding while litigating a termination claim. In the workers' compensation proceeding, both the employer and the employee have the opportunity to gather evidence that could be used against the other. Evidence as to the injuries claimed by the employee can have an impact on the exposure and relief sought in a discrimination case.

Similarly, any disability determinations in the workers' compensation case can have an impact on the relief available and the exposure in the termination case. Also, it may be possible to settle both matters simultaneously.

Migrant farm workers are prohibited under the federal Migrant and Seasonal Agricultural Worker Protection Act (AWPA), from suing their employers under AWPA if a state's workers' compensation law applies and coverage is provided for migrant or seasonal agricultural workers. It provides that a state's workers' compensation law is the exclusive remedy for loss as a result of bodily injury or death. However, statutory damages of up to $500 per plaintiff per violation or up to $500,000 in class action suits are still available along with other equitable relief when the court finds that a violation of AWPA was intentional.

Arbitration

If an employer has a collective bargaining agreement (CBA) providing for arbitration of terminations, the arbitration proceeding may also provide a means for each side to gather information that can later be used to impeach the other party's position in termination litigation. An arbitration agreement contained in a CBA that clearly and unmistakably requires union members to arbitrate statutory discrimination claims is enforceable as a matter of federal law.

Equal Employment Opportunity Commission proceedings

Once an Equal Employment Opportunity Commission (EEOC) charge is filed, the EEOC will attempt to elicit information from the employer including a position statement outlining the reasons for the action and supporting documents. Much of the EEOC file material may become available to counsel for both the employee and the employer in later litigation. Accordingly, the employer should be careful about what documentation is submitted to the EEOC. In some cases, witnesses' statements may be deemed confidential by the EEOC for the protection of the witnesses. Such a designation may prevent the employee from "discovering" the statements. Neither a determination of "cause" nor "no cause" by the EEOC will preclude further litigation in court. Under federal law, an employee is not bound by an EEOC determination unless a court has reviewed it. Courts may, however, exclude agency determinations in jury trials because these determinations may confuse and prejudice the jury.

The value of releases to employers

Consider obtaining a release from a terminated employee in exchange for consideration such as additional pay. An effective release should include the following:

- a clear release of each protected right (with an explanation of the terms and consequences written in plain language)
- an acknowledgment that the employee consulted with or had the opportunity to consult with an attorney.

There is no bright-line test for determining a sufficient amount of time for an employee to consider a release and consult with an attorney before the employee is considered to have signed the release knowingly and voluntarily.

Employees 40 years of age or older

For a release to be knowing and voluntary under the Age Discrimination in Employment Act (ADEA), which protects those 40 and older, it must meet the requirements set forth previously and must state that:

- the individual is not waiving rights or claims that arise after the date the agreement is executed
- the consideration is in addition to that to which the individual is already entitled
- the individual is advised in writing to consult with an attorney prior to executing the agreement
- the individual is given a period of at least 21 days within which to consider the agreement
- the agreement gives the individual seven days following execution to revoke his or her agreement.

The employer has the burden of proving that the release was knowing and voluntary according to the Older Workers Benefit Protection Act (OWBPA), which amended the ADEA in 1990. Discharged employees may bring age discrimination suits even though they received and kept the extra money specified as consideration for their signing of invalid releases of possible ADEA claims.

Example
The U.S. Supreme Court reversed an award to an employer who claimed that the employee had ratified a defective release by failing to return or offer to return the release money that she received. The Court held:

- that the release was not enforceable as to the employee's ADEA claims because the release did not comply with the requirements of the OWBPA
- the employee's retention of the severance pay did not ratify the release as to the ADEA claims
- the employee was not required to return the money as a precondition to filing suit on her ADEA claims.

The Equal Employment Opportunity Commission (EEOC) subsequently issued regulations that state that a penalty or liquidated damages provision in a release of ADEA or OWBPA claims is invalid. The EEOC regulations state the court's "no tender back" position. The regulations also state that an employer cannot include any provision in a settlement agreement that limits an individual's right to challenge the agreement. Prohibited provisions include tender back provisions and requirements that the individual pay damages or the employers' attorney fees incurred in defending the suit if the individual files suit challenging the agreement.

If an employer includes a liquidated damages provision (a provision that if either party breaches the agreement, the breaching party will pay a certain amount, which is a good faith estimate of the actual damages resulting from the breach) in a settlement agreement, the agreement should clearly state that the liquidated damages provision does not apply to ADEA or OWBPA claims. The Eighth U.S. Circuit Court of Appeals has held that a release of claims signed by an employee as part of an involuntary termination program was not valid under the OWBPA because it was not written in a manner calculated to be understood by the person signing the release.

Covenants not to sue

Employers may consider including a covenant not to sue in the release. If such a provision is included, an employer may file a counterclaim for its attorney fees and costs incurred in defending against a suit in breach of the covenant not to sue. The Sixth Circuit Court of Appeals upheld this approach. In drafting releases and covenants not to sue, the agreement should expressly provide that the employer is entitled to attorney fees in the event of a breach of the release.

When an agreement provides for a release of claims but no covenant not to sue, courts have been less willing to enforce counterclaims. As discussed previously, however, employers will want to refrain from using covenants not to sue in a release of ADEA or OWBPA claims or, if such provisions are included, ensure that the agreement is clear and easy to understand.

Restrictive covenants

Consider including restrictive covenants, such as covenants not to compete, solicit customers or solicit employees.

Post-termination

Be wary of defamation claims

Avoid giving defamatory or derogatory reasons for termination to anyone not in a need to know or privileged position. An ex-employee may bring a defamation claim if an employer gives information to prospective employers without a release. Employers should also be aware, however, that a subsequent employer may sue the former employer for negligent referral if the employee commits the same type of wrongful conduct he or she committed at the previous job.

Replacement employees

An employee who is replaced by someone outside the protected category may use this fact to bolster a discrimination claim. Distributing the employee's duties to other employees or replacing him or her by someone in the same protected category may make it more difficult to prove discrimination but may not completely preclude a claim.

Appeals

Consider allowing the employee the opportunity to appeal the termination to a higher official within the company. Doing so may provide the employer with helpful evidence.

Recording witness statements

Any written records of witness interviews should be prepared immediately and should accurately reflect what the witness said. Do not include legal conclusions or personal opinions in these records. (Legal conclusions may include terms such as "unauthorized action," "violation," "negligent" or "wrongful.")

All written records should be dated when they are made and not at some later point in time. The records should reflect when they were written. For instance, whether it is notes taken during the meeting or notes written immediately after the meeting, the document should identify the writer and all persons in attendance at the meeting. The documents should contain verbatim statements to the extent possible, not summaries of what the attendees said.

Consider obtaining signed statements from witnesses, especially crucial witnesses and those who may change employment in the near future. Avoid any appearance that the statements were obtained by coercion or undue influence. Be aware that the employer will probably be required to produce any written records and witness statements if the employee sues over the discharge. Maintain consistency regarding the reason for the termination decision. The U.S. Supreme Court ruled that a discrimination plaintiff may be able get to a jury by showing that the employer's reason for the adverse employment action was false. Previously, some courts held that a plaintiff had to show both:

- the reason for the action was false
- some additional evidence of discrimination.

The Supreme Court overruled these cases. The Supreme Court also held, however, that proof the employer gave a false reason for the employment action will not always be enough for the employee to get to a jury. The Court pointed out that it is possible for a plaintiff to present a "weak issue of fact as to whether the employer's reason was untrue" while the employer presents "abundant and uncontroverted evidence that no discrimination had occurred." Such cases will not get to a jury. This decision further emphasizes the importance of giving a truthful, consistent reason for discharge.

Handling lawsuits

Lawsuits can be costly. A successful plaintiff may recover back and front pay; compensatory, punitive and mental distress damages; and attorney fees. Even if the employer wins, the cost of defending a wrongful discharge suit can be considerable. The employer will probably find it difficult to recover its attorney fees from the plaintiff. Additionally, litigation involves numerous "soft costs," such as the drain on management time and the effect on employee morale.

Furthermore, if the employer is unsuccessful and a court orders it to take certain actions as part of the order in favor of the employee, the cost of monitoring these actions and re-training supervisors can be extensive. There may be individual liability for some claims, so the cost to the individual supervisor may be significant.

Settlement may or may not be beneficial to an employer. Considerations include the cost of proceeding with the action compared with the cost of settlement. The employer should also consider the effect of a settlement on employee morale and whether the employer wants to support the decisions of the managers involved. Other factors include whether:

- reinstatement is an option
- the case can be settled for non-monetary consideration
- the settlement amount realistically can be expected to remain confidential
- a settlement will be perceived negatively by other employees
- whether a settlement is likely to encourage future claims
- some states are now voiding settlement agreements with provisions preventing disclosure of certain factual information.

Layoffs

Chapter

15

The focus of this chapter is primarily on the effects a layoff has on the company and those employees who are "let go." However, employers should also consider the impact that a reduction in force (RIF) has on employees who remain with the company. Those "let go" had job duties that the remaining employees must assume. This may require the remaining employees to work longer hours and to perform job functions that they may lack the skills to complete. In such situations, employees can become frustrated and customers can become irritated. When circumstances require a layoff, planning must also take place to determine how best to move forward with the employees being retained.

Considerations prior to executing a reduction in force

Before embarking on a workforce reduction, employers should plan their actions carefully, consider alternatives to a reduction in force (RIF), analyze any potential discriminatory impact and articulate a nondiscriminatory and legitimate business rationale for the decision. Employers should lay a fact-based foundation for any RIF to protect against the costs associated with discrimination charges and wrongful discharge litigation. In many situations, a permanent layoff will not be in an employer's best option and employers should consider all such options before deciding on a course of action. If a RIF is challenged in court, it is imperative for the employer to be able to show the judge and jury that it seriously considered other options before implementing the RIF. If a proper foundation is laid, including effective and fully informative communications regarding the employer's plan, an employer's main problem should be dealing with the remaining employees' emotional reactions to the workforce reduction.

Before embarking on a RIF, employers should candidly assess the needs and goals of the business. Employers should first set forth the overall cost cutting goals and senior management should develop and document a business justification to support the decision for the RIF. An organizational plan should then be designed to meet the identified cost cutting goals. Employers should avoid inconsistent statements or actions, such as when cutbacks are preceded by significant capital expenditures or compensation increases, which can be difficult to explain.

Alternatives

Employers would be wise to consider modified staffing plans to enhance cost-cutting measures, as well as alternatives to permanent RIFs, such as:

- rightsizing by attrition
- reductions in or a freeze on pay or benefits
- use of unpaid vacation time
- use of shorter work hours or workweeks and restrictions on the amount of overtime
- conversion of some staff to part time employees or consultants
- use of job sharing, which may be considered desirable among current or prospective single parent and two-worker households
- computerization to speed up processing and productivity
- constructive leaves of absence
- use of an employer-wide job posting system notifying those employees in affected areas of other available opportunities
- use of temporary/part time people to supplement staffing needs, avoiding the high cost of benefit payments
- "renting" professionals and other employees instead of hiring them full time
- buying services from outside vendors when the cost of providing that service for inside or outside use is too costly
- seeking input from employees on where waste is and what the company can do to cut costs
- participation in state work sharing programs
- temporary shutdowns.

Rightsizing

If, after due consideration, management assesses that rightsizing is deemed necessary, there are two basic ways it can proceed:

1. **Voluntary**
   Management can institute a voluntary RIF, often known as a voluntary severance plan. Employers who implement voluntary severance plans generally do so in an effort to streamline their businesses and improve performance. Employers often offer attractive economic incentives, such as increased pension benefits, to induce employees to voluntarily leave their positions.

2. **Involuntary**
   Management can institute an involuntary RIF, sometimes offering no incentives to entice employees to retire. Under this plan, management decides who goes and who stays. Usually, involuntary RIFs are caused by economic factors that threaten the employer's existence.

Preparation

Once rightsizing is deemed necessary, a small RIF management team should be established, consisting of respected managers who have the support of top management. This team's job is to either recommend or set policy and then oversee the implementation and the administration of the RIF itself. Preparations include:

- identification of the departments in which reductions are required
- definition of the present and projected responsibilities and work product of the affected departments
- establishment of a RIF timetable
- construction of a current, statistically based organizational chart for the employer
- review of any collective bargaining agreements
- construction and comparison of the equal employment opportunity (EEO) statistically based organization charts before and after the planned reduction (such analysis should be prepared by counsel, or at the direction of counsel, in anticipation of litigation and not by members of the RIF management team to avoid discrimination claims)
- preparation of an EEO workforce disparate impact analysis
- implementation of alternative programs based on the results of the disparate impact analysis
- review of any affirmative action plan (if the employer is a federal contractor) to avoid deviation from the plan's goals
- decisions concerning how best to inform employees about the RIF
- determination of whether to retain a public relations firm to handle adverse publicity.

In addition to the provisions of any collective bargaining agreement or affirmative action plan, the employer's past practices or policies may also affect a RIF. Employers should expressly reserve the right to revise such policies to maintain maximum flexibility. The RIF management team should be responsible for recommending the positions and departments that should be eliminated. The team should include representatives of affected categories of employees by race, age and sex. Members of the team must be able to dedicate the appropriate amount of time to their tasks. Managers involved in the RIF should be told how to handle human resource issues properly and consistently and should have a clear understanding of the overall program. The employer should have an upper level management control mechanism to monitor company-wide hiring during the RIF process.

Carrying out the reduction in force

Issues to be considered when carrying out the RIF include:

- salary continuation versus lump sum severance
- maintenance of fringe benefits in addition to mandated benefits, such as the Consolidated Omnibus Budget Reconciliation Act (COBRA) and determination of how long the benefits will be maintained and who will pay for them
- pension consequences, such as unfunded withdrawal liability from multi-employer plans
- waivers or general releases signed by employees to minimize legal exposure and compliance with Age Discrimination in Employment Act (ADEA) and Older Workers Benefit Protection Act (OWBPA) provisions concerning waivers and releases
- "stay pay" or bonus incentives to keep employees on the job as a particular operation is wound down
- the applicability of plant closings/mass layoff laws and WARN
- timely distribution of final paychecks.

Voluntary severance plan

The employer should identify the number of positions that must be eliminated and determine which employees will be eligible for the voluntary severance/retirement program (for instance, employees having a certain minimum level of service with the employer). Eligible employees, other than key employees, generally are offered an early retirement package. If the number of surplus positions is greater than the number of eligible employees, the employer may offer voluntary retirement to all of its eligible employees. If the number of eligible employees exceeds the number of surplus positions, however, the employer may offer voluntary retirement to the eligible employees based on criteria such as longevity or on a first come, first serve basis until the surplus goal is met or the eligible list is exhausted.

Typically, a voluntary severance plan offers financial and other incentives to a segment of the workforce to entice employees to voluntarily resign or retire early. Often voluntary severance plans offer enhanced severance benefits, the addition of years to an employee's period of service for the purpose of calculating pension benefits and vesting rights or a one-time lump sum bonus paid to an employee if he or she agrees to retire early. As a downsizing device, voluntary severance plans are generally considered legal vehicles for reducing an employer's workforce, if they are properly administered and are nondiscriminatory.

Age discrimination considerations

Under the ADEA, as amended, an employer may not discharge any individual who is more than 40 years old because of age. In 1978, Congress amended the ADEA to explicitly outlaw mandatory early retirement. Because of the concern that early retirement incentive plans were not truly voluntary, Congress passed the Older Workers Benefit Protection Act (OWBPA) in 1990. This legislation was designed to overturn the U.S. Supreme Court's decision in *Public Employees Retirement System v. Betts*. In *Betts*, the U.S. Supreme Court held that the ADEA does not prohibit age discrimination in providing employee benefits except in rare situations. The OWBPA specifically authorizes voluntary early incentive programs, but only so long as those programs are truly voluntary and consistent with the ADEA's purpose and as long as they are not used as a subterfuge for discrimination against older workers. The OWBPA changes or clarifies the law in several respects.

> **Example**
> Employers cannot structure early retirement incentive programs to allow only those employees below a certain age to participate in or receive all of the benefits offered, without a showing that such distinctions are cost justified. It is unclear whether an early retirement plan that, on its face, does not violate the statute by excluding older workers could nevertheless be found discriminatory because it is applied to a particular department or facility in which the average age is younger than the average age of the employer's total workforce.

Such a claim might now be easier for plaintiffs to prove since the OWBPA requires disclosure of the categories of employees included in the program if a waiver or release is requested in connection with receipt of the benefits under an early retirement incentive program.

Rules governing early retirement

The OWBPA has specific rules governing voluntary early retirement incentive plans, including:

- An employer has the burden of proving that its conduct with respect to a benefit plan is lawful if the plan is challenged in court.
- An employer may set a minimum age as a condition of eligibility for normal or early retirement benefits.
- An employer may provide pension subsidies that supplement pension benefits and it may make social security "bridge" payments until the affected employees reach the age at which they are eligible for social security benefits.
- An employer cannot discriminate with respect to severance pay on the basis of age or deny severance pay to employees who choose to retire during a RIF. An employer may, however, offset severance payments by the value of any retirement health benefits received by an individual who is eligible for an immediate pension, as well as the value of any additional pension benefits provided to employees who are eligible for not less than an immediate and unreduced pension. OWBPA provides rules for determining the value of retirement health benefits to be reduced.
- An employer may offset severance benefits with "shutdown sweeteners," which provide additional retiree health and pension benefits to laid off employees, when, on the date of plant layoff or shutdown, the employee is entitled to immediate, unreduced pension benefits. The offset only applies to the additional retiree

health and pension benefits over that to which the employee is already entitled.

- An employer may reduce long term disability benefits by either the amount of pension benefits that an employee elects to receive or for which he or she is eligible after attaining the later of age 62 or normal retirement age.

Employee Retirement Income Security Act considerations

Employers who set up a voluntary severance plan should remember that such plans are normally subject to the requirements of the Employee Retirement Income Security Act (ERISA). In a one case, the U.S. Supreme Court held that an ERISA severance plan exists when:

- an employer establishes an administrative system that requires protracted, individual payments to employees based on a determination of their eligibility to participate in the plan
- the severance agreement provides that the employee is entitled to benefits only upon the occurrence of a triggering event requiring administrative interpretation, such as termination of the employee "for cause."

In contrast, the court held that ERISA does not apply to a one-time, lump sum severance payment triggered by a single, external event, such as a plant closing, which requires the employer to do little more than write a check.

Involuntary reduction in force

In the event that all surplus positions are not eliminated by a voluntary RIF and the employer determines that an involuntary RIF is necessary, it is important that it protect itself from possible claims of discrimination by building a record that supports its decision to reduce its workforce. Specifically, an employer should document why the RIF was taken and why other non-personnel related, cost cutting measures would not have been able to achieve management's desired objectives. The employer should demonstrate that it took various steps to lessen the impact created by the layoff. Often this can be accomplished by allowing the affected employee to remain on temporarily to provide the employee with an income while the employee attempts to relocate. The employer may wish to offer outplacement services to the employee. Employers should guard against making discriminatory decisions to lay off employees. To protect itself from the possibility of legal liability in the event a discrimination claim or suit is filed, an employer may follow certain guidelines, such as those discussed in the following paragraphs.

- Consider establishing a team, in which minorities, women and older employees participate, with specific responsibility for developing and implementing the RIF plan. This team should consider the impact of various options on protected categories of employees.
- Articulate sound business reasons for the decision to implement the RIF. Develop a media communications package.

- Document the need for the RIF in a legally defensible manner. Use labor counsel in the preparation and review phases. Well-documented reasons for a RIF will greatly assist the employer if defending itself against a discrimination claim.
- Predicate reductions on job functions (not individual employees) and on the relationship to articulated business needs.
- Clearly define the criteria for selection of employees for layoff and evaluate individual employees against those criteria by looking at job functions and job performance.
- Rank all employees according to the criteria selected, placing the more productive at the top and listing the reasons why those employees are considered to be more productive. Compare the profile of the pre-RIF workforce against the post-RIF workforce and the relationship of the latter to the work functions that will remain and to the goals of the RIF.
- Have labor counsel review all rankings of employees done in the performance evaluation level. This will further enhance the legal soundness of the RIF. Be honest in evaluating the employees' performances.
- Analyze for adverse impact on a protected group by race, sex, age and the like. Account for the adverse impact and make a workforce adjustment if legally appropriate.
- Prior to instituting the RIF, consider conducting a training program for supervisors and managers to inform them of the mechanics of the employer's reorganization plan. Supervisors and managers should be alerted to the fact that they will be faced with questions from employees prior to or during the voluntary phase of its program and should be told what information should be disseminated to employees concerning the RIF.
- Prepare and implement an exit interview program so that there is early identification of possible problems and the capability for timely intervention.
- Implement the reductions according to the RIF plan. Do not deviate without good reason. Document the reason for any deviation.
- If bumping, transfers or demotions are allowed immediately prior to or during the RIF, ensure that there is objectivity and consistency in those actions.
- Consider the implications of WARN and whether there is any duty to give notice to employees of the RIF.
- For employers with collective bargaining agreements, consider whether there is a bargaining obligation with respect to a RIF or the effects of a RIF or whether there is a provision in the union contract covering layoffs, manning levels and the like.
- Consider providing each involuntarily terminated employee with a form on which the employee can indicate whether he or she is interested in re-employment with the employer.
- Consider the implications of COBRA. A plant closing or RIF will result in termination of employment for some employees and reduction in hours for

others (both qualifying events) that generally result in a loss of health coverage to the employees. If the employer maintains other health benefit plans for other plants or divisions, it must offer continuation coverage to the terminated employees. Employers should check with their carriers to ensure that coverage is available for inactive employees to assess the burdens of continuing coverage for terminated employees.

- Consider the impact of ERISA, which prohibits discrimination against an individual in connection with his or her entitlement to pension benefits. Allegations of ERISA violations arise when an individual claims he or she was included in a reduction or was terminated for reasons related either to vesting in a pension program or approaching eligibility for a higher level of benefits.

Discrimination concerns

Federal and state laws protect employees from discrimination in employment on the basis of:

- race (including protected hairstyles)
- color
- sex
- sexual orientation
- gender expression and identity
- age
- national origin
- citizenship
- handicap
- religion
- genetic information.

In planning a job elimination program, management should consider the potential impact on all statutorily protected groups. Allegations of discrimination resulting from RIFs most frequently involve age, sex and race. In planning a RIF, management should maintain a profile of the age, sex and race of the workforce. Employers who do not have such data available when planning a RIF cannot know whether a reduction will have an adverse impact on a protected group. If an employer must adopt an involuntary plan to cut its workforce, the plan should be in writing. Under the adverse or disparate impact theory, an employment practice may be unlawful if it has a disproportionate impact on any protected category. If the practice has a disproportionate impact on any protected group, the employer must prove that the practice is justified by business justification or job-relatedness and is consistent with business necessity.

Age discrimination

Age discrimination complaints are the most common claims brought in the wake of RIFs. Although the ADEA does not bar the termination of older workers, it forbids discriminating against them because of their age. In the context of a RIF, employees need to show that the employer's reduction decisions were based on consideration of the ages of the terminated workers. It is not unlawful for an employer to make decisions based on reasonable factors other than age. Frequently, when a court upholds an age discrimination claim arising out of a RIF, the RIF is accompanied by statements and comments made to the older plaintiff that suggest that the employer harbors a company-wide animosity toward older employees. However, stray remarks containing isolated or ambiguous comments are generally insufficient to create a jury issue in an ADEA case. In addition to derogatory age-related comments, employers may subject themselves to liability for age discrimination in other ways. For instance, the Sixth Circuit has indicated that a company's failure to find another position within the company for an older executive whose position was eliminated during a corporate restructuring may constitute a violation of the ADEA.

Courts have set forth a test for allowing a prima facie case of age discrimination in RIFs to be proven by circumstantial evidence indicating:

- that the plaintiff was in a protected age group and was adversely affected by the layoff decision
- that the plaintiff was qualified for the current position at the time of the layoff
- that a fact finder might reasonably conclude that the employer intended to discriminate on the basis of age in reaching a layoff decision.

Where a particular job position is eliminated, the plaintiff must show qualification for another available job at the time of the layoff in order to prevail. In a recent case, the U.S. Supreme Court held that a plaintiff does not have to show he or she was replaced by someone outside the protected class (less than 40 years of age) to make out a prima facie case under the ADEA; he or she need only show that he or she was replaced by someone "substantially younger." The court, however, expressly limited its review of the case as a non-RIF case.

Severance pay and ongoing benefits

Even when severance pay is not mandated by an existing collective bargaining agreement, a union may bargain with an employer that has announced plans to close or lay off employees in an attempt to obtain the employer's agreement to pay severance pay. The employer will likely be obligated to the union to bargain on that subject if the union requests the employer to do so under the general "effects" bargaining duty. An employer may also have unanticipated severance pay obligations to non-union employees. Courts have found that severance pay plans are subject to the reporting and disclosure requirements of ERISA and the fiduciary responsibility standards. In one case, the U.S. Supreme Court resolved a conflict among the circuit courts regarding the appropriate standard of review to be applied in actions challenging benefit eligibility determinations. Unless the plan gives the fiduciary "discretionary authority to determine eligibility for benefits or construe the terms of the plan" a court will review a decision to deny a claim for benefits on a de novo basis. If, however, the plan documents confer full discretionary authority on the fiduciary, the court will generally defer to the fiduciary's decision provided there has not been an abuse of discretion.

Severance obligation of successors

The strict language of a severance pay plan can shield successor companies from liability for severance pay. The Sixth Circuit Court of Appeals has held that employees who accepted offers for substantially similar positions with a company that purchased their employer were not released from employment and, thus, not entitled to severance benefits. The employee argued that the severance plan was ambiguous because it used "etc." following a list of conditions under which an employee would be considered released. The court rejected this argument, noting that this word refers to "others of a like kind." The court held that the phrases preceding the term "etc." (lack of work and economic reduction in force) were so unlike the plaintiffs' situations that the term did not bring them within the scope of the severance agreement. The standard announced in this case can also result in unanticipated liability for severance pay for successor companies.

Liability under the Family and Medical Leave Act

The FMLA provides, among other rights, a total of 12 workweeks of leave during any one year to an eligible employee "unable to perform the functions of [his or her] position" due to a serious health condition." An eligible employee is one employed for at least 12 months or 1,250 hours in the previous 12 months with the employer from whom he or she seeks leave. Employer, in the context of the FMLA, "means any person engaged in commerce or in any industry or activity affecting commerce who employs 50 or more employees for each working day during each of 20 or more calendar workweeks in the current or preceding calendar year." The regulations explain that "[e]mployers covered by FMLA also include any successor in interest of a covered employer. The regulations lay out eight factors to consider in the determination of whether an employer is a "successor in interest." These factors "include" (and, by the use of that word, the regulations suggest that these are not the only factors to be considered):

1. continuity of operations
2. use of same facility
3. continuity of the workforce
4. similarity in working environment
5. similarity of supervisory personnel
6. similarity of equipment and methods
7. similarity of services
8. ability of the predecessor to provide relief.

The regulations further explain: When an employer is a "successor in interest," employees' entitlements are the same as if the employment by the predecessor and the successor was continuous employment by a single entity. For instance, the successor, whether or not it meets FMLA coverage criteria, must grant leave for eligible employees who had provided appropriate notice to the predecessor or continue leave begun while employed by the predecessor, including maintenance of group health benefits during the leave and job restoration at the conclusion of the leave.

A successor that meets the FMLA's coverage criteria must count periods of employment and hours worked for the predecessor for purposes of determining employee eligibility for FMLA leave. Therefore, under the FMLA, once an employer is found to be a successor in interest, it inherits the FMLA duties of its predecessor. The examples provided by the regulation only suggest the types of duties and liability that the successor acquires. The Sixth Circuit has held that a merger or transfer of assets is not always a precondition to successor liability under the FMLA.

"Successorship" under Title VII of the Civil Rights Act

"Substantial continuity" is the link between predecessor and successor that leads to liability on the part of the successor for alleged Title VII of the Civil Rights Act violations by the previous employer. If substantial continuity exists, the successor is deemed to have notice of the actions of the predecessor that have given rise to potential liability. Without substantial continuity, the imposition of liability would interfere with the goal of maintaining the fluidity of corporate assets, which is impeded if assets sold piecemeal are each encumbered by the liabilities of their previous owner. Courts examine the particular facts of a case to determine whether the successor had notice of the predecessor's act that gave rise to liability, including the following factors:

- whether the successor company had notice of the charge
- the ability of the predecessor to provide relief
- whether there has been a substantial continuity of business operations
- whether the new employer uses the same plant
- whether the new employer uses the same or substantially the same workforce
- whether the new employer uses the same or substantially the same supervisory personnel
- whether the same jobs exist under substantially the same working conditions
- whether the new employer uses the same machinery, equipment and methods of production
- whether the new employer produces the same product.

Impact of the Bankruptcy Act

Key employee retention plans (KERPs) have become quite common in cases filed under Chapter 11 of the U.S. Bankruptcy Code. These are generally an effort to encourage key managers to remain employed by the debtor during bankruptcy and help establish the successful reorganization or sale of the debtor. The Bankruptcy Abuse Prevention and Consumer Protection Act made significant changes to the U.S. Bankruptcy Code and, for the first time, placed stringent limits on the ability of a court to approve KERPs and severance payments in a bankruptcy case. Specifically, the act provides that payments to induce insiders of a debtor to continue work for the debtor are not allowed unless:

- the payment is essential to retain that person because the person has a bona fide job offer from another business at the same or a greater rate of compensation
- the services provided by the person are essential to the survival of the business
- the amount of the transfer or obligation is not greater than 10 times the amount "of the mean transfer or obligation of a similar kind given to non-management employees for any purpose during the calendar year in which the transfer is made or the obligation is incurred"
- if no such similar transfers were made to - or obligations were incurred for - the benefit of non-management employees during such calendar year, the amount must not be greater than 25% of the amount of any similar transfer or obligation made to - or incurred for the benefit of - such insider for any purpose during the calendar year before the year in which such transfer is made or obligation incurred.

Additionally, a severance payment to an insider of the debtor will not be approved unless the payment is part of a program that is generally applicable to all full-time employees and its amount is not greater than 10 times the mean severance pay given to non-management employees during the calendar year in which the payment is made. Further, the court will not approve other payments that are outside the ordinary course of business and not justified by the facts and circumstances of the case, including payments made to officers, managers or consultants hired after the filing of the bankruptcy petition. If a debtor is a corporation, the law defines an "insider" to include, among other parties:

- a director of the corporation
- an officer of the corporation
- the person in control of the corporation
- a relative of any of the foregoing
- an insider of any "affiliate" of the corporation.

Unionized employers

Transactions altering ownership

The form and nature of the transaction that alters or restructures corporate ownership determines, to some extent, the rights and obligations of the purchaser or succeeding owner of the corporation. Courts generally focus less on the form of the corporate transaction and more on the competing equities between employers and employees. Accordingly, courts balance the employer's right to freely transfer assets and reorganize its business with employees earned or vested benefits acquired through the duration of their employment with a prior employer. The U.S. Supreme Court has endorsed the view that the form of the corporate transaction offers less guidance in determining successorship than the impact of the reorganization on the employee and the actual business operations: "So long as there are other indicia of 'substantial continuity,' the way in which a successor obtains the predecessor's assets is generally not determinative of the 'substantial continuity' question." Despite this de-emphasis on the form of the corporate transaction, certain corporate forms remain relevant to the determination of the purchaser's rights and obligations with respect to an organized workforce.

Sale or transfer of stock

When there is a sale or transfer of stock and no change in corporate form, successorship principles give way to the doctrine of a "continuing employer." The continuing employer is obliged to adopt the substantive provisions of the collective bargaining agreement, as well as to recognize and bargain with the incumbent union. Thus, the general rule for a sale or transfer of stock is that the status of the labor contract and an incumbent union are unchanged. In short, one set of stockowners is simply substituted for another and the enterprise continues.

Asset purchase

Different rules apply in an asset purchase, depending on the composition of the buyer's workforce and whether the seller's business continues without "substantial change." Union representation, but not necessarily the union contract, may pass from seller to buyer. Thus, with an asset purchase, union representation may pass from seller to buyer, but only if a majority of the buyer's workforce is comprised of the unionized seller's former employees and provided that the business of the seller or substantial portions of it continue substantially unchanged after the asset sale. Thus, since the buyer has control over the workforce it hires, the buyer has significant control over whether union representation passes from seller to buyer. If a majority of the buyer's workforce is not comprised of the seller's unionized former employees, union representation does not pass automatically.

There is, however, an exception to this hiring rule. Even before a buyer hires anyone, union representation passes to the buyer if the buyer expresses an intention to take all or a majority of, the seller's unionized workers. A buyer cannot base its hiring decisions on a desire to avoid union representation, which is unlawful discriminatory motivation. Rejection by a buyer of a seller's trained workers who are willing to work under the buyer's employment terms can be difficult to explain and can lead to National Labor Relations Board (NLRB) unfair labor practice findings.

Considerations regarding successorship in asset purchase context

As the U.S. Supreme Court ruled, the buyer is largely the master of its own destiny on the question of being a "successor" to the seller's bargaining obligation. In summary, the considerations are:

- If a buyer establishes its own terms and conditions of employment and hires its own workforce, a majority of whom are not the seller's unionized employees, there is no duty to recognize or bargain with the union regardless of other indicia of continuity of the workforce.

- If a majority of the employees hired by the buyer come from the seller's unionized workforce, they are presumed to continue to support the union and the buyer becomes a "successor" to the seller's duty to recognize and bargain with the union. Neither a hiatus in, nor a radical restructuring of, operations will relieve the buyer of the duty to bargain if the buyer's workforce is comprised of a majority of its predecessor's unionized employees.
- Even if a buyer hires a majority of the seller's unionized workforce, the buyer is under no duty to assume the terms of that collective bargaining agreement unless the buyer makes the mistake of not setting its own initial terms and conditions of employment and, by implication, promises to maintain the terms and conditions of employment existing in the collective bargaining agreement.

Previously, an asset purchaser had to recognize and bargain with the seller's union for a "reasonable period" of time, even though it might have suspected or even known that most of its employees wanted the union gone. Under the NLRB's "successor bar" rule, employers acted at their peril by challenging whether such a union continued to enjoy majority support because the "reasonable period" standard was so imprecise. The NLRB's decision in *MV Transportation* overturned *St. Elizabeth's Manor* and removed the uncertainty of the successor bar rule for a purchasing employer. In light of this reversal, employees of an acquired business are free to seek to decertify their union at any time after an acquisition, as long as the union has been their certified bargaining representative for more than one year and there is no collective bargaining agreement in effect.

"Alter ego"

If the purchaser is deemed to be the "alter ego" of the predecessor, the purchaser is bound by the substantive terms of the collective bargaining agreement between the predecessor employer and the union. Alter ego status is often found when, subsequent to a change in corporate form, substantially identical management, business purpose, operations, equipment, customers, supervision and ownership remain. In order to make a finding of alter ego status, the Sixth Circuit has held that intent may be considered but is not essential. A hiatus between the predecessor and the newly formed company also has been found to negate alter ego status.

Bankruptcy petitions

The U.S. Supreme Court has held that an employer (or other debtor-in-possession under the Bankruptcy Code) could reject a collective bargaining agreement without the prior approval of a bankruptcy court. Although the ruling permitted employers to escape onerous collective bargaining agreements, it was never a means to escape the obligation to bargain with a certified or a recognized union. In response to the decision, Congress amended the Bankruptcy Code. The Bankruptcy Amendments of 1984 require prior court approval before an employer may repudiate its collective bargaining agreement and provide that an employer must bargain with the union over modifications in the agreement before applying to the bankruptcy court for approval of contract rejection. The court may permit rejection of the contract only if it finds that the union refused to accept the proposed changes "without good cause" and that the balance of equities "clearly favors" rejection of the contract. Also, the debtor-in-possession may then unilaterally reject the contract pending further court action if the court fails to act within 30 days of the hearing on the application.

In enacting the 1984 amendments, Congress recognized that a debtor may require emergency relief from a collective bargaining agreement prior to rejection and included a provision whereby a bankruptcy court may authorize a trustee to make interim changes to the contract if essential to the continuation of the debtor's business or in order to avoid irreparable damage to the estate.

Employees may, in any event, picket to protest nullification of a collective bargaining agreement pursuant to an order of a bankruptcy court. The trustee in bankruptcy may be ordered to remedy the employer's violations of the act. An "alter ego" firm that succeeds to the business of a bankrupt predecessor may also have to remedy the predecessor's unfair labor practices. The automatic stay provisions of the Bankruptcy Code, which suspend most court proceedings against entities that have filed for bankruptcy, do not prevent contempt proceedings brought by the NLRB to enforce its regulatory powers.

When a bankrupt employer promises to pay severance to its employees, then attempts to escape this liability in bankruptcy, the employer's motion to amend its bankruptcy schedules may be denied under certain circumstances. The Bankruptcy Abuse Prevention and Consumer Protection Act amended numerous provisions of the Bankruptcy Code, many of which affect corporate reorganizations. The amendments relating to key employee retention plans were discussed previously.

Additionally, the revisions amended the Bankruptcy Code to include payment of wages and benefits awarded according to a judicial proceeding or a proceeding of the NLRB as back pay attributable to any period of time occurring after commencement of the case under this title as a result of a violation of federal or state law by the debtor, without regard to the time of the occurrence of the unlawful conduct on which such award is based or to whether any services were rendered, if the court determines that payment of wages and benefits by reason of the operation of this clause will not substantially increase the probability of layoff or termination of current employees or of non-payment of domestic support obligations. The amount of pre-petition wage claims that can be treated as priority claims is $10,000.

Also, the calculation date was expanded from 90 to 180 days prior to the start of the case. Priority claims receive payment ahead of general unsecured claims and typically are paid at the beginning of the case. This amendment deals with the complaints of employees in highly publicized bankruptcy cases who received only small payments on their claims.

Subcontracting, partial closings and relocation of work

Mandatory subjects of bargaining

In *Fibreboard Paper Products Corp. v. NLRB*, the U.S. Supreme Court addressed the issue of subcontracting under the National Labor Relations Act (NLRA). The company's employees performed maintenance work and were represented by a union. Without negotiating with the union, the employer subcontracted the bargaining unit work. The court held "that the type of 'contracting out' involved in this case – the replacement of employees in the existing bargaining unit with those of an independent contractor under similar conditions of employment – is a [mandatory] subject of ... bargaining[.]" Significantly, the court determined that the company subcontracted because it "was concerned with the [labor] cost of its maintenance operation."

The U.S. Supreme Court revisited the issue of whether an employer must negotiate with a union over the elimination of bargaining unit work, this time in the context of a partial closing of a company's business. The Court held that a decision to shut down part of a business purely for economic reasons was not subject to mandatory bargaining, because the decision in that case was based on entrepreneurial concerns unrelated to labor costs. The Court's decision established a balancing test regarding the duty to bargain over certain fundamental business decisions. The concept of mandatory bargaining is premised on the belief that collective discussions backed by the parties' economic weapons will result in decisions that are better for both management and labor and for society as a whole.

This will be true, however, only if the subject proposed for discussion is open to resolution through the bargaining process. Management must be free from the constraints of the bargaining process to the extent necessary for running a profitable business. In view of an employer's need for unencumbered decision making, bargaining over management decisions that have a substantial impact on the continued availability of employment should be required only if the benefit, for labor-management relations and the collective bargaining process, outweighs the burden placed on the conduct of the business. An employer's decision to subcontract or engage in a partial closing is a mandatory subject of bargaining when it is based on labor costs.

If, however, it represents a fundamental change in the scope and direction of the business and is unrelated to labor costs, the employer is not obligated to bargain over the decision. The NLRB has adhered to this distinction. In one case, the NLRB established a different test for determining whether an employer's decision to relocate the business is a mandatory subject of bargaining:

- General counsel must establish a prima facie case by showing that the employer's decision involved a relocation of unit work unaccompanied by a basic change in the nature of the employer's operations.
- The employer can rebut a prima facie case by showing:

- work performed at the new location varies significantly from work performed at the former plant
- work performed at the former plant is discontinued and will not be performed at a new plant location
- the decision involved a change in scope and direction of the business.

Under this test, the employer is allowed to rebut a prima facie case that the relocation decision is subject to mandatory bargaining by showing that labor costs were irrelevant to the decision or, if such costs were considered, that relocation would not have been affected by the union's offer of cost concessions.

This decision was upheld by the Circuit Court of Appeals for the District of Columbia. In its decision, the court held that the test protects management's prerogatives with respect to those relocations that are entrepreneurial in nature and exempts decisions that were motivated by something other than labor costs. The court also held that the NLRB properly excused employers from attempting to negotiate when doing so would be futile or impossible. The employer filed a petition for review with the Court, contending that the test and the appeals court holding ignored the requirements and arguing that it is improper to apply the standard to an employer decision implemented more than 10 years before the current standard was adopted. The Court initially agreed to review the decision, but when the NLRB and the company achieved a settlement, the case was dismissed.

Mid-term relocation and subcontracting decisions

The terms of a current collective bargaining agreement may have a significant impact on an employer's ability to relocate or subcontract work. Considerations include whether the employer has, in a current contract, explicitly or implicitly agreed not to close the facility, relocate or dissolve the bargaining unit, in whole or in part, during the contract term. Another consideration is whether the union has expressly waived its right to further bargaining regarding the decision or its effects, by agreeing in the current contract, that management has the unilateral right to close, relocate or consolidate without bargaining over the decision or over the effects of that action.

The NLRB held that the employer had no duty to bargain over the decision to subcontract work, where the management rights clause in the contract specifically stated that the employer had "the exclusive right to ... subcontract." The NLRB determined that this clause was a clear and unmistakable waiver by the union of its right to bargain over the issue of subcontracting. The NLRB also determined, however, that the employer was in violation for failing to bargain over the effects of subcontracting.

The impact of a current collective bargaining agreement on such decisions and the duty to bargain was addressed in a previous case. In this case, the NLRB announced the principles that apply when a collective bargaining agreement is in place establish an employer's obligation to bargain in good faith with respect to "wages, hours and other terms and conditions of employment." Generally, an employer may not unilaterally institute changes regarding these mandatory subjects before reaching a good faith impasse in bargaining.

The law imposes an additional requirement when a collective bargaining agreement is in effect and an employer seeks to "modify the terms and conditions contained in" the contract:

> The employer must obtain the union's consent before implementing the change. If the employment conditions the employer seeks to change are not "contained in" the contract, however, the employer's obligation remains the general one of bargaining in good faith to impasse over the subject before instituting a proposed change.

Under these guidelines, the first issue is whether an employer would be modifying a provision of the collective bargaining agreement. If so, it is legally inhibited from implementing the proposed change without first obtaining the union's consent.

If, on the other hand, no contractual clause would be affected by the decision, then the employer would be required to bargain to impasse before taking unilateral action. It was noted that the contract at issue in that case contained a zipper clause, which is essentially a contractual provision that precludes mid-term bargaining. It asserted that a zipper clause normally relieves both parties from any obligation to bargain on any subject, whether or not included in the contract, during the term of the contract.

The court further asserted that zipper clauses generally prohibit the employer from making a unilateral change regarding a subject not specifically referred to in the contract. From this, the court concluded that a zipper clause generally has the effect of incorporating all mandatory subject of bargaining (without union assent) a violation of the NLRA. As defined by the court, a zipper clause is a clause that: "purports to close out bargaining during the contract term and to make the written contract the exclusive statement of the parties' rights and obligations." The court, after reaching this conclusion, phrased the issue as: "Does the current contract permit a mid-term relocation without bargaining?"

The court agreed with the NLRB's decision because it found that the union had conceded that the parties' management rights clause gave the company the right to relocate unilaterally and without bargaining. The NLRB itself had not explicitly addressed this possibility. The management rights clause reserved the right not only to "manage the plant and business" and to "plan, direct and control operations," but also to "change existing methods, materials or facilities" to the company. The court called this a very "broad" clause, permitting relocation during the contract term.

Unfunded pension liabilities

If the employer contributes to a multi-employer pension plan that is less than fully funded, a closing or even partial closing or layoff could trigger a withdrawal from the plan and may result in liability for the company for such under funding under the Multi-

Employer Pension Plan Amendments Act (MPPAA). The U.S. Supreme Court has upheld the constitutionality of the MPPAA, saying that is does not violate employers' procedural due process rights. Courts have extended withdrawal liability from a multi-employer pension plan to enterprises under the common control of an employer.

Runaway shops

The U.S. Supreme Court held that an employer may close its entire business for any reason it chooses, including anti-union motivation. The court also stated, however, that a partial closing or closing of a particular facility, intended "to chill unionism" at other surviving plants, can result in a violation of the NLRA, which gene

rally prohibits anti-union discrimination. In a number of cases, the NLRB and the courts have found that an employer's:

- partial closing of an operation
- closing of a part of its business
- relocation of an operation
- consolidation of one operation into another

was motivated by a desire to avoid a union relationship or in retaliation for employees for choosing a union.

These types of scenarios are commonly known as "runaway" shops. The critical issue in such cases is whether the business reasons the employer has for the closing, relocation or consolidation are sufficiently compelling and not merely a desire to escape the union. If the reasons are directly related to labor costs and a desire to escape the labor costs under a collective bargaining agreement, an issue may arise as to whether a relocation is "inherently" destructive of employee rights and therefore unlawful notwithstanding the question of motivation.

Collective bargaining agreements

Many collective bargaining agreements contain "successorship" clauses, purporting to require a successor or purchaser to abide by the terms of the agreement. Purchasers and successors are not necessarily bound by such agreements since they were never parties to them. The predecessor employer (seller), however, may be liable for breach of its agreement if it fails to obtain an agreement from the successor employer to be bound by the collective bargaining agreement. A union may also seek injunctive relief under the Labor-Management Relations Act (LMRA) against the predecessor employer for breach of the successorship clause where the successor employer indicates that it will not accept the existing agreement. The seller of the assets of a business may also be liable for damages caused by the failure of a purchaser to assume the terms of a union contract for the duration of the agreement under a "successors and assigns" provision in a collective bargaining agreement.

Discrimination in rehiring

Although a successor employer need not hire all or even most, of the employees of a unionized predecessor, the successor employer cannot refuse to hire an individual because of union involvement. If any laid off employees apply for work at surviving operations, they need to be considered. If the work to be performed will be the same as the work previously performed by these employees, their experience (compared to a new hire without any related experience) may make it difficult to avoid hiring them without risk of being found in violation of the NLRA.

Effects of bargaining and duty to supply information

If requested by a union, a seller is obligated to bargain concerning the effects on employees of its decision to terminate part or all of its operations. The union must be notified of the commercial transaction and afforded a meaningful opportunity to bargain over the effects of the sale. Of course, a seller may not transfer all or part of its operations if it is motivated by anti-union animosity. Employers often are concerned about when a union must receive notice of a transaction that may trigger effects bargaining. The NLRB has not formulated a hard and fast rule on the number of days' advance notice an employer is required to give a union prior to the sale or transfer of the employer's business.

The NLRB has, however, determined that, in order to afford a "meaningful opportunity" to bargain, notice must be given at a time when the employer is still in need of the bargaining unit's labor and the union thus retains its bargaining power. In a purchase and sale context, the NLRB held that the union must be notified sometime between the period when the sale is "under active consideration" and the period of time when it has become a fait accompli. In most cases, this appears to mean that notice should be provided at least between the signing of a purchase agreement and closing. In order to meaningfully bargain regarding the effects of the corporate transfer transaction, the union is entitled, upon its request, to information relevant to the effects of a transfer of operations. Information that is often requested and typically must be provided includes:

- job openings at other plants, including wages and benefits
- plans for benefits to be provided to non-union employees, including severance, relocation and retirement options
- a profile of the bargaining unit
- location of the new worksite and anticipated timetable for relocation
- copies of internal studies or reports on the plans for relocation
- copies of the sales/purchase agreement
- identity of the officials involved in the purchase/sale
- seller's plans for the existing building and equipment
- notice, if any, provided by the seller concerning the existence of a collective bargaining agreement
- timetable for the closing or relocation.

Notice requirements for a mass layoff

In general, employers are covered by the Worker Adjustment and Retraining Notification Act (WARN) if they have 100 or more employees, not counting employees who have worked less than six months in the last 12 months and not counting employees who work an average of less than 20 hours per week. Regular federal, state and local government entities that provide public services are exempt. Employees entitled to notice under WARN include hourly and salaried workers, as well as managerial and supervisory employees.

WARN requires employers to provide notice 60 days in advance of covered plant closings and covered mass layoffs. This notice must be provided to affected workers or their representatives (such as a labor union), to the state dislocated worker unit and to the appropriate local government. A covered plant closing occurs when a facility or "operating unit" is shut down for more than six months and 50 or more workers lose their jobs as a result during a 30-day period. A covered mass layoff occurs when a layoff of six months or longer affects 500 or more workers or 33% or more of the employer's workforce when the layoffs affect between 50 and 499 workers. The number of affected workers is the total number laid off during a 30-day or in some cases, 90-day period.

WARN does not apply to the closing of temporary facilities or the completion of an activity when the workers were hired only for the duration of that activity. WARN also provides for less than 60-days' notice when the layoffs were the result of the closing a faltering company, unforeseeable business circumstances or a natural disaster. These exceptions to WARN are very narrowly defined by the statute, so caution is recommended in asserting these as a justification for what otherwise may be considered noncompliance with the statute. WARN applies to any business enterprise that employs:

- 100 or more employees, excluding part time employees
- 100 or more employees, including part time employees, who in the aggregate work at least 4,000 hours per week, exclusive of hours of overtime.

Employees on temporary layoff who have a "reasonable expectation of recall" are counted in determining whether an employer has at least 100 employees. Not only are temporarily laid off employees counted for threshold numerical purposes of WARN, they may also be entitled to the 60-day notice requirements of WARN as an affected employee. In determining whether an employee on layoff has a reasonable expectation of recall, courts rely upon the factors utilized by the NLRB to determine whether an employee is eligible to vote in an NLRB election. These factors include:

- past experience of the employer
- the employer's future plans
- the circumstances of the layoff
- the expected length of layoff
- industry practice.

Coverage

If the number of employees to be laid off is anywhere close to the critical threshold numbers, the employer should pay close attention to the finer points under WARN:

- the calculation must include all employment losses during a rolling 30-day period (therefore including the 30 days before and after the actual shutdown date)
- employment losses during a rolling 90-day period must be included under some circumstances
- part time employees are excluded (those who average fewer than 20 hours per week and those with less than six months' service are not counted in determining whether the threshold numbers have been reached)
- employees terminated as a result of a discharge for cause, voluntary departure or retirement are excluded from the threshold computations.

Employment loss

An employee suffers an employment loss if:

- the individual's employment ends for any reason other than a discharge for cause, voluntary departure or retirement
- the person is laid off for more than six months
- the person's work hours are reduced by more than 50% during each month of any six-month period.

Employees who transfer to other employer facilities with no break in employment do not suffer an "employment loss" and therefore should not be counted towards the 50 employees required by WARN.

Consolidating groups

Job losses affecting two or more groups at a single employment site, which occur within any 90-day period, may be consolidated for purposes of determining whether the requisite number of employees have been affected, "unless the employer demonstrates that the employment losses are the result of separate and distinct actions and causes and are not an attempt by the employer to evade the requirements of the act." The employer has an affirmative burden to prove that employment losses at a single site during a 90-day period should not be combined.

Transfers to other locations

The job loss is not counted if it is the result of a relocation or consolidation and the employer offers to transfer the employee to a different job site, subject to certain limitations. In a layoff situation, the court does not look at the number of eliminated positions to determine whether or not there has been a "mass layoff" or a "plant closing" under WARN, but rather at the number of employees actually terminated.

Sale of business

Employers who are considering the sale of all or part of their business must be cognizant of potential layoffs by the purchaser. The act provides that the seller is responsible for providing notice for any plant closing or mass layoff up to and including the effective date of the sale. An employment loss occurring after the sale of a business is the buyer's responsibility. When a transfer of assets, liabilities and employees to a successor employer occurs and the successor continues operations of the predecessor with no loss of employment and no change in the terms and conditions of employment, no plant closing or mass layoff occurs and no action for damages may be maintained under WARN.

Notice requirements

WARN imposes a 60-day advance notification requirement with respect to either a "plant closing" or a "mass layoff." A "plant closing" requiring notice means a permanent or temporary shutdown of a single site of employment or one or more facilities or operating units within a single site of employment, if the shutdown results in an employment loss at the site of 50 or more employees during any 30- day period (excluding part timers). If a covered "plant closing" causes some employees to be laid off earlier than that actual plant closing date, the 60-day notice must be given 60 days in advance of the layoff of the first employee whose layoff is caused by the plant closing.

A "mass layoff" requires notice if 50 or more full time employees at a single site of employment are going to lose their jobs within any 30-day period and the affected workers constitute 33% or more of a workforce. If the affected workers do not constitute a third of the workforce, notice of layoffs must still be provided whenever 500 or more employees are affected. The WARN act does not define a "single site of employment." Whether multiple work locations constitute a single site of employment is a mixed question of law and fact. Generally, proximity and contiguity are the most important criteria for making single site determinations. However, once a court makes the contiguous/non-contiguous determination, operational, managerial and labor variables become decisive factors and can defeat or reinforce the presumptions established by proximity and contiguity.

If WARN is applicable, the employer must give 60-days' advance notice to each representative of the affected employees as of the time of the notice or, if there is no such representative at that time, to each affected employee, to the chief elected official of the unit of local government within which the closing or layoff is to occur and to the state's Dislocated Worker Unit designated under the Job Training Partnership Act. In most states, the appropriate official to receive the notice can be located by contacting the state's department of labor. Part time employees are "affected employees" and they are entitled to notice under WARN, even though they were not counted in deciding whether the company had 100 or more employees and qualified as an "employer" within the meaning of the act. U.S. Department of Labor (DOL) regulations set forth the information that must be included in such notices.

Often, the most troublesome aspect of the notice is the requirement to identify, with some specificity, when the job losses will occur. With respect to the notice to employees not represented by a union, notice must be written in language understandable to the employees and must contain:

- a statement as to whether the planned action is expected to be permanent or temporary and, if the entire plant is to be closed, a statement to that effect
- the expected date the plant closing or mass layoff will begin and the expected date the individual employee will be separated
- an indication of whether bumping rights exist

- the name and telephone number of the company official to contact for further information.

For employees represented by a union, the notice must contain:

- the name and address of the employment site where the plant closing or mass layoff will occur and the name and telephone number of a company official to contact for further information
- a statement as to whether the planned action is expected to be permanent and, if the entire plant is to be closed, a statement to that effect
- the expected date of the first separation and the anticipated schedule for making separations
- the job titles of positions to be affected and the names of the workers currently holding affected jobs.

In either case, the notice may include additional information useful to the employees such as information on available dislocated worker assistance and, if the planned action is expected to be temporary, the estimated duration, if known. Laid off workers are "affected" employees who must be notified about impending plant closings under the same terms as active employees. In addition to requiring that WARN notices be given to the laid off employees, the court noted that its reasoning "applies equally to employees laid off for more than six months, provided they can establish that they held a legitimate and reasonable expectation of recall up to the time of the plant closing."

"Stay pay"

If advance notice of a closing is to be given for any reason, consideration should be given to offering some kind of "stay pay" incentive to induce employees to remain at work during the time period immediately preceding the shutdown.

Exceptions to 60-day notice requirement

Faltering business exception

An employer may order a "shutdown" with less than 60-days' notice if, as of the time that notice would have been required, the employer was actively seeking capital or business that, if obtained, would have enabled the employer to avoid or postpone the shutdown and the employer reasonably and in good faith believed that giving the notice required would have precluded the employer from obtaining the needed capital or business. An employer asserting this exception, however, will be required to prove every required element.

Additionally, this exception applies only in the plant-closing context, not the mass layoff context. Also, the employer must still give as much notice as is practicable and must give a brief statement of the basis for the reduced notification period. The faltering business exception is applied on a company-wide basis. If a company has access to capital markets or cash reserves, it may not use this exception by looking solely at the financial condition of a particular facility, operating unit or site to be closed.

Unforeseeable circumstances

An employer may also order a plant-closing or mass layoff before the conclusion of the 60-day period in the event of business circumstances that were unforeseeable at the time notice would have been required. Again, the employer must give as much notice as is practicable and a brief statement of the basis for reducing the notification period. The DOL has provided some guidance regarding when the "unforeseen business circumstances" exception applies. There is no steadfast rule regarding what constitutes "unforeseen business circumstances," but rather, the DOL prefers a case-by-case examination of the facts.

A business circumstance may be reasonably unforeseeable if it was caused by some sudden, dramatic and unexpected action or by conditions outside the employer's control. When determining whether a mass layoff was caused by unforeseeable business circumstances, courts evaluate whether a similarly situated employer exercising reasonable judgment could have foreseen the circumstances that caused the layoff. Thus, a company will not be liable if, when confronted with potentially devastating occurrences, it reacts the same way that other reasonable employers within its own market would react.

Natural disaster exception

WARN notice is waived if a plant closing or mass layoff is caused by a natural disaster, but the employer must give as much notice as possible (including notice after the fact) and the notice must explain why less than full notice is being given. The law provides that floods, earthquakes, droughts, storms, tidal waves, tsunamis and similar effects of nature qualify as natural disasters. The regulation further provides that:

> "While a disaster may preclude full or any advance notice, such notice as is practicable, containing as much of the information required in § 639.7 as is available in the circumstances of the disaster still must be given, whether in advance or after the fact of an employment loss caused by a natural disaster."

Impact of the COVID-19 pandemic

The speed with which businesses reacted to the COVID-19 pandemic, mostly in compliance with emergency declarations requiring non-life sustaining businesses to cease physical operations no doubt serve as a defense to claims based on the failure to provide the 60-days' advance notice ordinarily required by WARN. But even when the original decision to close or engage in a mass layoff is unforeseen at the outset, businesses must still provide WARN notices as soon as practicable. As COVID-19 cases continued to affect workplaces, many businesses may be hit with new reasons to curtail their operations. Thus, employers need to be vigilant about providing WARN notifications "as soon as practicable" if new shutdowns occur.

Waiver of rights

Release forms signed by employees in return for enhanced layoff benefits may serve as a waiver of the right to sue under WARN, even where the release does not specifically mention the statute.

Paid leave of absence

An employer may give employees a paid leave of absence in lieu of advance notice of layoff, although before doing so it should consult with experienced labor counsel since this plan of action is not without some risks. For instance, an employer may not want to give employees advance notice of a mass layoff because it is concerned that laid off employees may engage in acts of sabotage. The employer, therefore, may notify them of their layoff, to be effective 60 days hence and immediately place the employees on a leave of absence for 60 days with full pay and benefits. Employers should consult with experienced labor and employment counsel before utilizing a paid leave of absence in lieu of WARN notice.

Violations

An employer that violates the WARN provisions is liable to each employee for an amount equal to back pay and benefits for the period of the violation, up to 60 days. This may be reduced by the period of any notice that was given and any voluntary payments made by the employer to the employee. An employer who fails to provide the required notice to the unit of local government is subject to a civil penalty not to exceed $500 for each day of violation. This may be avoided if the employer satisfies the liability to each employee within three weeks after the closing or layoff. Employees or their representatives and units of local government may bring individual or class action suits in federal district court for violations of the act. The court may include reasonable attorney fees as part of any final judgment.

Penalties include liability to each employee consisting of back pay and benefits "including the cost of medical expenses incurred during the employment loss, which would have been covered under an employee benefit plan if the employment loss had not occurred," attorney fees and a civil penalty up to $500 for each day of violation with respect to a failure to notify the appropriate unit of local government.

- Failure to provide WARN notice will result in the employer having to pay the mandated monetary penalties.
- Earnings from subsequent employment are not included in the statutory list of amounts that may be used to offset the employer's back pay liability.
- Vacation, severance pay and other such payments are not to be applied against back pay liability due under WARN.
- The $500 per day penalty will be waived if the employer "pays to each aggrieved employee the amount for which the employer is liable to that employee within three weeks from the date the employer orders the shutdown or layoff."

Reduction of amount owed

Certain payments may reduce the damages owed for WARN violations. The amount for which an employer is liable shall be reduced by:

- any wages paid by the employer to the employee for the period of the violation
- any voluntary and unconditional payment by the employer to the employee that is not required by any legal obligation
- any payment by the employer to a third party or trustee (such as premiums for health benefits or payments to a defined contribution pension plan) on behalf of and attributable to the employee for the period of the violation.

In addition, any liability incurred with respect to a defined benefit plan may be reduced by crediting the employee with service for all purposes under such a plan for the period of the violation. The act specifically excludes ERISA payments from payments that may be deducted from damage awards for violations of WARN. Additionally, payments legally owed under other laws, such as state laws, do not reduce amounts owed for WARN violations.

Parent corporation's liability for noncompliance

A parent company may be held liable for its subsidiary's failure to follow the requirements of WARN. The DOL has issued a regulation setting forth relevant factors for courts to use when considering whether to impose WARN liability on a parent corporation. WARN is applicable only to business enterprises and not to individual persons. In a recent case, the District Court for the Eastern District of Michigan denied the plaintiffs' attempt to hold the owner personally liable for the alleged WARN violations. The court held that WARN's legislative history "clearly provides" that the act intended "employer" to mean "business enterprise," which is synonymous with "company, firm or business."

State-specific laws that regulate closings and layoffs

Several states also have laws regulating plant closings and mass layoffs.

State	State notice laws
Alabama	Employers with 25 or more employees being laid off for at least seven days within the same time period are required to call the nearest unemployment office to report the layoffs.
Alaska	No law
Arizona	No law
Arkansas	No law

State	State notice laws
California	State law generally parallels federal law but applies to employers with 75 or more employees and relocation is included as a triggering event for notice requirements. The law also applies to a plant closing, layoff or relocation of 50 or more employees within a 30-day period, regardless of the percentage of workforce.
Colorado	No law
Connecticut	Connecticut doesn't have a WARN-type law, but it requires certain employers to continue paying for employee health insurance following certain layoffs.
Delaware	Delaware law applies to all employers with at least 100 employees (excluding those working part time) who work an aggregate of at least 2,000 hours per week. Employers are required to provide a 60-day notice in the event of a mass layoff that will exceed six months in duration or where there will be a reduction in work hours of more than 50% during each month of any consecutive six-month period. Plant closings and relocations are also covered events.
District of Columbia	State law only applies to nursing homes, community residence facilities and contractors.
Florida	No law
Georgia	Georgia law requires that employers with layoffs of 25 or more employees on the same day for the same reason expected to last more than seven days are to fax the Georgia DOL Forms 402 and 402A within 48 hours of the event.
Hawaii	Employers with 50 or more employees must provide written notice required for a closing or divestiture. Some workers must be paid a dislocated worker allowance for four weeks.
Idaho	No law
Illinois	Employers with 75 or more employees must give a 60-day notice of a relocation, mass layoff or temporary or permanent employment loss.
Indiana	No law
Iowa	Employers are covered by Iowa's layoff law if they have at least 25 full-time employees. Employers must give 30-days' notice if they are closing a business (shutting it down permanently or temporarily) or conducting a mass layoff that will affect 25 or more full-time employees.

State	State notice laws
Kansas	No requirement for private employers
Kentucky	No requirement for private employers
Louisiana	No law
Maine	Employers with 100 or more employees must give 90-days' notice prior to closing or relocating out of state, unless due to unforeseen circumstances or a physical calamity and must provide severance to employees who have been with the company for at least three years. A seven-day notice must be provided in the event of a mass layoff.
Maryland	Employers with at least 50 employees must provide a 90-day notice of relocations or shutdowns that reduce the number of employees by at least 25% or 15 employees, whichever is greater, over any three-month period.
Massachusetts	Employers with 50 or more employees at a facility must provide notice; the state bills employers for employment assistance it provides up toa 13-week maximum, which is reduced for every week of advance notice provided by the employer.
Michigan	No law
Minnesota	If notice is required under federal WARN, employer must report the names, addresses and occupations of persons being discharged to the state commissioner of employment and economic development.
Mississippi	No law
Missouri	No law
Montana	No requirements for private employers
Nebraska	No law
Nevada	No requirements for private employers
New Hampshire	If the company employs 100 or more employees who work at least 3,000 hours per week in aggregate, it must give 60-days' notice prior to a temporary or permanent plant closing or layoff.

State	State notice laws
New Jersey	Employers with 100 or more employees must provide 90-days' notice before a termination of operations, mass layoff or transfer of operation. Employers are required to pay a mandatory severance equal to one week of pay for each year of service.
New Mexico	No law
New York	Employers with 50 or more employees must give 90-days' notice before a mass layoff, employment loss or relocation.
North Carolina	No law
North Dakota	No law
Ohio	If laying off or discharging 50 or more employees within a seven-day period due to lack of work, notice must be given to the Director of Jobs and Family Services.
Oklahoma	No law
Oregon	State law mirrors federal law, but employers also must provide notice to the Office of Community Colleges and Workforce Development.
Pennsylvania	No state law; however, employers with 50 or more employees in Philadelphia are required to submit a letter to the Philadelphia Director of Commerce specifying the anticipated economic impact associated with the impending and involuntary closure or relocation of their facilities.
Rhode Island	No law
South Carolina	No law
South Dakota	No law
Tennessee	If employer employs between 50 and 99 employees, it must give notice of a reduction in operations.
Texas	No law
Utah	No law

State	State notice laws
Vermont	If an employer employs 50 or more employees, it must give at least 30-days' advance notice to affected employees and at least 45-days' advance notice to Agency of Commerce and Community Development and the Vermont Department of Labor.
Virginia	No law
Washington	No law
West Virginia	No law
Wisconsin	Subject to certain exceptions, employers with 50 or more employees in the state must give 60-days' notice before a mass layoff affecting: • at least 25% of the workforce or 25 employees, whichever is greater • 500 employees.
Wyoming	No law

Foreign workers

Mergers, acquisitions or changes in corporate ownership can affect the status of an existing foreign employee/prospective employee. A merger or acquisition could cause a change in the foreign employee's job location, position, job duties and compensation. Employers need to recognize their obligations in such situations.

Successor employer obligations

Successor employers may have an obligation to amend the visa petition of a foreign worker involved in the corporate transaction. The surviving entity must often submit documentation to the bureau of U.S. Citizenship and Immigration Services (USCIS) establishing that it has assumed the rights, duties, obligations and assets of the predecessor employer and that it will continue to operate the same type of business. The rationale behind this requirement stems from the fact that most foreign nationals who wish to work in the United States must be sponsored by a U.S. employer and are allowed to work only for that employer under the terms specified in the visa petition.

Depending on the circumstances, a merger, acquisition or significant change in ownership can alter the terms specified in the original petition, requiring an amendment to maintain the immigration status an individual. Two examples of temporary work visas that are employer specific, authorizing employment only by the sponsoring employer, are the H-1B Specialty Workers visa and the L-1 Intra-Company Transferees visa. These visas may be used by foreign businesses to send employees to affiliated companies within the United States or by domestic employers wishing to hire foreign employees.

H-1B visas for specialty workers

The H-1B category of visas may be used for new employees of existing U.S. businesses. The prospective employee must have a bachelor's degree or equivalent work experience. Examples would include professionals in the engineering, computer software and healthcare industries. The successor employer should be aware that it must amend or file a petition with USCIS for the H-1B worker when there is a change in the terms and conditions of employment.

L-1 visas for intra-company transferees

To qualify for an L-1 status, the prospective worker must have been continuously employed abroad for at least one of the past three years by a parent, affiliate or subsidiary of the U.S. company. Additionally, the worker must have been employed as an executive, manager or in a position involving "specialized knowledge" abroad and be coming to the United States to assume such a position. The person must meet specific criteria to qualify as an executive, manager or an individual with specialized knowledge. The successor employer of an L-1 intra-company transferee should be aware that it must amend or file a petition notifying USCIS that there has been a change in the original petitioning corporate entity. As with other non-immigrant visas, the successor employer assumes the rights, duties and obligations of the predecessor employer.

I-9 requirements

Successor employers who retain all or part of the predecessor's employees are not required to re-document or execute new I-9's on all retained employees. The successor employer should, however, obtain the predecessor's I-9 documentation. The successor employer can be held responsible for the predecessor's failure to complete or its defective completion of, the required documentation. In comparison to retaining existing employees in an acquisition, if the successor employer rehires the predecessor's employees, the courts may deem those employees to be new hires and thus require the successor to execute new I-9's. I-9 requirements do not apply to employees who were hired prior to November 7, 1986, unless "continuity of employment" is broken. If so, a new I-9 must be completed.

Employers, however, must be aware that these employees may still be subject to deportation if they are in the country illegally. Continuity of employment is deemed broken if the employee:

- quits
- is discharged (including seasonal hires)
- is employed by a different employer in a multi-employer bargaining unit
- is excluded from the United States, deported or departs under an order of voluntary departure.

Because the successor corporation may be liable for its predecessor's I-9 paperwork violations, the successor and its labor counsel should add an I-9 audit to the due diligence list. Counsel may also want to include indemnification provisions within the purchase agreement protecting against any sanctions, penalties or charges that result from any of the predecessor's defective I-9 documentation.

Preventive measures

Failure to consider these immigration issues can have severe consequences for an employer, such as the loss of the employee, revocation of the employee's visa or monetary penalties. Therefore, employers should take the following precautions:

- Conduct an I-9 audit during the "due diligence"/pre-transaction phase.
- Identify workers with immigration issues.
- Designate, in the agreement, who will be responsible for employment issues involving alien workers.
- Consider the possibility that the alien(s) will be transferred to another geographic location.
- Keep your immigration attorney informed of all changes in the conditions and terms of the H-1B employees (such as duties, salary, location and the like) and any changes in the employer's corporation (such as name, tax I.D. and geographic changes).

Avoiding a lawsuit

There are many steps an employer can take to avoid a lawsuit in the event layoffs within its workforce, such as those described in the paragraphs that follow:

- Ensure that specific employer representatives are designated as the primary sources of information regarding the voluntary severance plan and make these individuals easily accessible to the employees. Employers may also wish to provide the services of an independent financial or tax advisor depending upon the complexities of the plan. Ensure that inquiries from employees eligible to participate in the plan are answered. Document any conversations by confirming memorandum or letter. Ensure that those charged with administration and implementation of the plan have files that are complete and catalogued as to content.
- Instruct subordinate managers and supervisors as to what information should be relayed to employees, if asked.
- Make full disclosure regarding the voluntary severance plan and all proposed amendments.
- Implementation of the plan on a nondiscriminatory basis is critical to its legal viability.
- Whether a plan is deemed sufficiently voluntary depends on a number of factors including:
  - whether employees are pressured to take the early retirement option
  - whether employees are given adequate time to make a considered choice on whether to accept or reject the information from the employer concerning the option.

- Statements made to induce employees to accept the severance plan must not be false or misleading. Management's intent at the time the statements are made is significant.
- The employer must ensure that employees are afforded an ample amount of time to choose whether they wish to participate in the plan. Courts are more likely to uphold an early retirement plan when the employees had adequate time to consult with attorneys, financial advisors and their families concerning the details of the offer.
- Ensure that the voluntary severance plan clearly disqualifies individuals who have engaged in certain kinds of misconduct from receiving any benefits under the plan. If terminations during the pre-window period (the time between the proposal of the voluntary severance plan and its acceptance) must be made due to misconduct, ensure that such acts are carefully documented.
- If possible, announce the implementation of the voluntary severance plan separately from the enactment of any involuntary RIFs. However, frank discussions to the general target group about the employment risks (the likelihood of an involuntary RIF) are not in themselves unlawful and may encourage employees to accept the separation package who might not otherwise do so.
- Consider obtaining a written release or waiver of claims from employees accepting a voluntary severance plan, but exercise caution in this area. Courts have ruled that if waivers do not meet certain statutory requirements, older workers could not only keep their severance pay but also pursue their claims in court. The EEOC has also issued regulations that set out additional steps an employer must follow when drafting a waiver to comply with the OWBPA. Many employment law claims can be relatively easy to waive, but an age claim waiver is not valid unless it meets the tough standards of the OWBPA.

Chapter

16

Employment litigation

It is uncommon for an employee to file a lawsuit against their employer if they:

- have been properly selected
- have been effectively trained
- trust management
- are well informed
- feel that they will be listened to.

Therefore, the best way to avoid a lawsuit is to create a productive employee relations climate in which sound management practices occur every day. This chapter briefly explains many of the theories under which employers and employees sue each other.

Wrongful discharge

In a wrongful discharge suit, an employee claims that he or she was terminated for some wrongful purpose. Most employees are employed "at-will," which means that, generally, they can be discharged for a good reason, bad reason or no reason as long as it is not for an illegal reason. Illegal reasons include sex, race, religion or other protected category, as defined by federal, state or local law and may include retaliation and violations of public policy.

The public policy exception to the at-will employment doctrine "provides that an at-will employee who has been discharged by an employer in violation of a clear mandate of public policy has a cause of action against the employer for wrongful discharge." An employee has a cause of action for wrongful discharge if he or she was discharged for:

- refusing to perform an illegal act or an act contrary to a strong mandate of public policy
- reporting wrongdoing or violations of law or public policy by the employer or fellow employees to superiors or third parties
- acting in a manner public policy would encourage
- filing a workers' compensation claim.

Fraudulent misrepresentation

Promises to hire or retain an employee may become the subject of a fraud suit if the promises were made with no intention of performance and the employee relied upon the promises. To prevail in a suit for fraud, an employee must prove five essential elements:

1. the employer misrepresented or concealed a material fact
2. the employer knew the fact was false when the statement was made
3. the employer intended to induce the employee's reliance
4. the employee took action based upon reliance on the accuracy of the representation
5. the employee sustained damages.

Fraudulent inducement

In some states, an employer may be liable for inducing an employee to leave one job for another, if the employer misrepresents the essential aspects about the new job and the misrepresentation induces the employee to leave his or her current job.

Promissory estoppel

The doctrine of promissory estoppel is used to enforce promises that have been made and subsequently relied upon. Most of the time, contract law dictates the terms of how promises should be enforced. Promissory estoppel usually comes into play when there is no formal contract, but the parties involved have nevertheless acted as if there was one. Courts use the doctrine in these circumstances to impose a contract on the agreement, usually in the interest of fairness.

In common language, "promissory" means "related to a promise," and "estoppel" is a legal term that essentially means an enforced bar or ban. Judges use the doctrine to ban one person from going back on a promise. Seen from a different angle, the doctrine is a tool to enforce promises, effectively requiring both parties to do the things they said they would. It is often seen as an exception to black-letter contract law. The elements of promissory estoppel include:

- a clear promise
- reliance
- substantial detriment
- damages measured by the extent of the obligation assumed and not performed.

Defamation

In its most basic sense, defamation occurs whenever a speaker or writer communicates a false statement to a third person and that statement injures the reputation of the person identified in the statement. The defamation is called libel if it is written or otherwise tangible and slander if it is spoken. Although the two may differ slightly in some technical respects, for the purposes of these materials, both are treated as one issue.

Elements of defamation

The essential elements of defamation are as follows:

- a false and defamatory statement, (a statement that injures the reputation or community standing of another person or discourages others from associating with that person)
- concerning the plaintiff
- that is "published" or communicated to a third party
- with fault amounting to at least negligence (some states have not required a showing of fault or negligence if the plaintiff is a private person and the defendant is not a member of the media)
- with proof of damages or a presumption of damages to the plaintiff as a matter of law.

Claims arising from termination

Publication

Because publication is an element of defamation, employers should not publish the reasons for discharge of an employee.

Conduct as publication

While a claim for defamation may be supported by actions, merely escorting an employee off the premises after termination generally does not constitute defamatory publication.

Internal communications

Some state laws view the corporation as merely communicating with itself for defamation law purposes, if communicated without malice and to those with a need to know. Thus, the fact that an employer placed adverse information in a former employee's personnel file, without more, may be insufficient to support a defamation claim.

Claims arising from investigations of theft

Employers should be concerned about defamation in employer investigations and actions related to employee theft for an obvious reason: Any statement that is communicated about an employee accused or suspected of theft raises the possibility of injury to an employee's reputation and the risk of a lawsuit. A claim may arise from statements made:

- in the course of the investigation
- in interviews
- in discussions among security officers, employees and supervisors

- in the process of responding to requests for references
- during judicial or administrative hearings
- in response to questions from the news media or co-workers
- in any other context in which negative information about the employee is communicated.

In light of the potential for defamation claims, including defamation by self-publication where recognized and the U.S. Supreme Court's ruling that a plaintiff is not required to always produce evidence of discrimination in addition to evidence that the employer's reason for the adverse employment decision was false to get to a jury, employers should explain the reasons for an employee's discharge carefully. For instance, if an employee is discharged for a potentially defamatory reason, such as theft, it may be wise to phrase the reason for the discharge in terms of a violation of policy (such as, violation of the employer's cash control policies).

Privilege defense

While the truth of a statement is always a defense to claims of defamation, some types of statements and information are privileged as a matter of law. In certain situations, employers who communicate privileged information cannot be held liable for defamation even though the employer communicated information that is false and defamatory, if the requirements of the privilege are satisfied. Privileges may be absolute or qualified. A statement that is absolutely privileged cannot be the basis for defamation regardless of the truth or falsity of the statement, the injury caused or the motives of the person who made the statement. Absolute privileges are relatively rare. A qualified privilege covers statements made in good faith, without bad motives, made only to those with a legitimate business interest in the information. A plaintiff may overcome a qualified privilege by showing an abuse of the privilege.

Absolute privilege

Statements made in the course of giving testimony in criminal cases, in judicial proceedings and in pleadings filed in a judicial proceeding are absolutely privileged in some states. If the statements were not relevant to the judicial proceeding at hand or were made in the context of pre-litigation settlement discussions, the privilege is qualified, not absolute, under some states' laws. The laws of the states in which employers have employees should be reviewed to determine whether information in a particular proceeding is privileged.

Qualified privilege

In some states, employers have a qualified privilege from liability for false statements made to persons with a legitimate common interest in the information. The following are the essential elements in finding a qualified privilege:

- good faith
- an interest to be upheld
- a statement limited in its scope to the interest to be upheld

- a proper occasion
- publication in a proper manner.

For example, effective January 1, 2019, California allows employers to inform a prospective employer whether or not the employer would rehire the employee. Such a communication is deemed privileged and protected from a lawsuit for defamation under Civil Code Section 47 if done without malice.

Further, some states apply a qualified privilege to communications made as part of internal investigations, provided publication is not made to persons who do not have a legitimate interest in the information.

Precautionary measures

Employers should follow several rules designed to preserve the privilege:

- Statements about employees should be limited to the purpose of the common business interest at stake. Avoid excessive publication or needless repetition of the statements, because this may dilute and ultimately destroy the privilege. Limit or avoid publication to co-workers who do not have an interest in the matter.
- Employers should take appropriate steps to ascertain the facts before making statements. This will promote accuracy and lessen the risk of making damaging inconsistent statements. Fellow employees or supervisors who may have had a personal problem with the employees being investigated should be cautioned and perhaps should be excluded from responding to any inquiries from third parties regarding the employee.
- Employers and their representatives should avoid any tendency to be colorful in the descriptions of the employee and should remain factual at all times. Limit statements, particularly employment references, to information that can be verified and documented. Limit statements to those that are relevant to the job involved and responsive to the questions asked by the prospective employer and to another person's need to know.
- Whenever possible, former employers and prospective employers should obtain a signed, full consent or release from the employee for the purposes of references and investigations.

Invasion of privacy

Most states recognize some form of the common law invasion of privacy tort. Courts in other states have declined to recognize a common law right to privacy.

Unreasonable intrusion

Unreasonable intrusion may include:

- surveillance

- unauthorized physical presence
- breaking and entering
- unauthorized photography
- intrusion into private activities
- similar matters, which are detailed below.

Unreasonable intrusion can extend to some form of investigations or examinations of a person's private life and can lead to liability if the intrusion would be highly offensive to a reasonable person. Generally, publication or communication of the information obtained, if any, is not a necessary element of the claim. The claim is based upon the psychological distress caused by the intrusion, regardless of publication or whether any information was obtained.

- **Surveillance**
  Workplace surveillance may subject an employer to liability for invasion of privacy, depending on the facts of the situation and whether the employee was notified of and consented to the surveillance.

- **Medication information**
  A company's request, as part of its drug-testing policy, that an employee provide medication information does not violate the employee's right to privacy without an allegation that information gleaned from a medication information form is being disseminated or published.

Public disclosure of private facts

This type of invasion of privacy generally involves employees suing employers for publicly disclosing true but embarrassing private facts about the employee. If that publicity would be highly offensive to a reasonable person and if it is not a matter of legitimate public concern, the employer may be liable. Unlike a defamation claim, an employer may be liable under this theory even if the statement is true. In fact, unwarranted publication of the truth is the essence of this statute. Mere publication to any third party is not sufficient under this theory even though it generally is sufficient for defamation claims. Disclosure to a small group of persons who have an obvious interest in the subject matter of the disclosure is not sufficiently public to state a cause of action for invasion of privacy. The focus of this claim is disclosure of private facts, whether true or not, to a large number of people.

Consent is a defense. Because a person may waive his or her right to privacy, the use of releases and consent forms should be considered before the information is gathered and when a prospective employer or other party subsequently requests it.

False light

This type of privacy tort involves liability for giving publicity to a matter concerning another that places the other before the public in a false light. To be actionable, the false light in which the plaintiff is placed must be highly offensive to a reasonable person and the defendant must have acted with knowledge or reckless disregard as to the falsity of the publicized statement. Some examples would be:

- falsely attributing a statement or opinion to the plaintiff
- filing suit in the plaintiff's name without authorization
- falsely accusing the plaintiff of a crime.

As with Public Disclosure of Private Facts, the heart of this tort lies in the publicity rather than the invasion into the plaintiff's physical seclusion or private affairs and many jurisdictions limit the tort to information that would normally be considered "private." A statement may be actionable under a false light theory without rising to the level of defamation, however, because there is less emphasis on public reputation under a false light theory than under defamation. In addition, at least one court has held a corporate employer liable for compensatory damages for false light based upon the actions of its employee, even though the corporation bore no fault of its own.

As with the other privacy lawsuits, consent can be an affirmative defense to a claim of false light. Consent should be to the use actually made of the subject matter by the defendant, because some courts do not extend a general consent agreement to include use of such information for any purpose not specifically contemplated by the consent.

Appropriation of name or likeness

Another privacy tort involves the appropriation of the name or likeness of another for one's own use or benefit. The interest protected by the tort is the exclusive interest in one's own identity as it is represented by his or her name or likeness. The most common cause of action for this tort involves use of the plaintiff's name or likeness in advertising. Incidental mention of the plaintiff's name or publication of his or her name or likeness for purposes other than taking advantage of his or her prestige or other value associated with his or her name or image, does not give rise to liability.

Employer searches

The Fourth Amendment to the U.S. Constitution protects "the right of the people to be secure in their persons, houses, papers and effects against unreasonable searches and seizures." Because the Fourth Amendment protects private citizens against governmental intrusions, most searches by private employers do not implicate constitutional concerns. When an employer is acting in concert with the government, however, an unreasonable search may give rise to a claim under the Fourth Amendment. Additionally, the constitutions and statutes of a few states protect employees from unreasonable searches by their employers. Therefore, before conducting a search of an employee's workspace, private employers should be aware of state privacy laws.

Search of desks and file cabinets

The U.S. Supreme Court has held that the search of a public employee's desk and file cabinet is legal if it is reasonable under all of the circumstances. What is considered "reasonable" is measured on a case-by-case basis and depends upon balancing the public, governmental and private interests at stake in a given situation. An employer's search may be considered unreasonable if the employer does not have a policy with regard to searching employees' desks, lockers, etc., especially if the employer does not have a practice of conducting such searches.

Reducing exposure to invasion of privacy claims

An employer can reduce exposure by limiting disclosure of:

- investigative information
- applicant history
- medical testing or screening results
- background check results
- other private or possibly private information to as few people as possible.

Additionally:

- In accumulating information, be aware of state and federal statutes restricting the use of pre-employment inquiries, lie detector tests or credit reports.
- Limit the information accumulated to that which can be justified as truly job-related.
- Impose a "need to know" standard.
- Obtain information in as narrow an inquiry as possible. Do not ask for any information beyond that which can be justified and documented for legitimate business reasons.
- If the information is obtained as part of the hiring and screening process, access should, if possible, be limited to those involved in that process (this is also true of the investigative process).
- If the information is requested by a prospective employer, the former employer may wish to request a release signed by the former employee.
- Consider using releases and consent forms before gathering information and when it is subsequently requested by and released to a prospective employer or other party.
- Inform employees in advance that they may be searched or questioned at management's discretion and that they will be expected to cooperate.

Intentional infliction of emotional distress

In extreme cases, an employer may be found to have committed the tort of outrageous conduct inflicting emotional distress.

Elements of

- **Extreme and outrageous conduct by an employer**
  To commit the tort of intentional infliction of emotional distress, the conduct must be so outrageous in character and extreme in degree as to go beyond all

possible bounds of decency and be regarded as atrocious and utterly intolerable in a civilized society. It does not extend to mere insults, indignities, threats, annoyances, petty oppression or other trivialities. Sexual harassment may constitute "outrageous conduct" and a supervisor who assists the harasser in covering up harassment may be liable for intentionally inflicting emotional distress, but a supervisor who does nothing probably will not.

- **Intentionally or recklessly causes**
  The intent element means that the actor desires the consequences of the act or believes the consequences are substantially certain to result from the act.
- **Severe emotional distress**
  Because of this strict standard, cases alleging this tort are usually dismissed. Where the facts are sufficiently egregious, however, a jury verdict on an intentional infliction of emotional distress claim can be significant.

Workers' compensation retaliation

A workers' compensation retaliation claim typically is filed by an employee who claims that the employer discharged, threatened to discharge, intimidated or coerced the employee by reason of the employee's valid claim for compensation or attempt to claim compensation.

State jurisdiction in termination claims

The National Labor Relations Act (NLRA) blocks any state claim that requires interpretation of a labor agreement. In 1988, the U.S. Supreme Court ruled that a tort action for retaliatory discharge for filing a workers' compensation claim was not prevented by "just cause" language or the grievance and arbitration provisions of a union contract, even if the reviewing court must interpret the collective bargaining agreement.

The Railway Labor Act

In 1994, the U.S. Supreme Court held that the state law claims of wrongful discharge of an airline mechanic covered by a collective bargaining agreement, who refused to sign off on a maintenance record of a plane he considered to be unsafe, were not blocked by the Railway Labor Act (RLA). The employee, who was fired for insubordination, was allowed to bring his claim because it was not dependent on interpretation of the collective bargaining agreement.

"Whistleblower" protection

Many states have laws that protect "whistleblowers," covering either public or private sector employees or both. Check the case law of the state in question. Additionally, many federal laws, such as the Occupational Safety and Health Act (OSH Act), Title VII of the Civil Rights Act (Title VII), the Fair Labor Standards Act (FLSA), the National Labor Relations Act (NLRA) and the Energy Policy Act have retaliation provisions that protect employees from adverse actions for "whistleblowing" under those laws.

Criminal Antitrust Anti-Retaliation Act

The Criminal Antitrust Anti-Retaliation Act became law on December 23, 2020, and makes it unlawful for employers to take adverse action against employees covered by the act who provide information relative to criminal antitrust violations to their employer or to the federal government. The act prohibits retaliation against individuals in participate in a federal investigation or a proceeding filed or about to be filed for criminal antitrust violations.

Covered individuals include:

- an employee
- a contractor
- a subcontractor
- an agent of the employer.

The burden of proof for covered individual seeking relief is that their protected activity was a contributing factor in the adverse action the employer took against them. If the employer demonstrates by clear and convincing evidence that it would have taken the same personnel action int he absence of the protected activity, the DOL cannot provide relief for the covered individual.

The act specifically includes that any relief shall include:

- reinstatement with the same seniority status that the individual would have had, but for the adverse action
- an award of back pay with interest
- compensation for any special damages sustained as a result of the discrimination, including:
    - litigation costs
    - expert witness fees
    - reasonable attorney's fees.

Fair dealing requirements

In some states, discharges have been deemed improper when they were accomplished to avoid an obligation owed to the employee by the employer or when other extreme and outrageous conduct of the employer has been deemed intolerable.

Civil conspiracy

To establish a civil conspiracy claim the plaintiff must generally prove:

- two or more people were involved
- with an objective to be accomplished
- a meeting of the minds on the objective or course of action to be taken

- the commission of one or more unlawful acts
- damages as a result of the conspiracy.

A civil conspiracy is, fundamentally, an agreement to commit a crime. This is a state cause of action and the specific elements to be established may vary per each state's law.

Illegal immigration practices

Some courts have recognized civil Racketeer Influenced and Corrupt Organizations Act (RICO) claims by plaintiffs alleging an illegal criminal enterprise comprised of employers, recruiters and staffing companies engaged in a scheme to bring illegal workers to the United States in order to suppress the wages of legal workers. Whether a court will recognize such claims is dependent on a highly fact specific inquiry.

Negligent employment and retention

Negligent employment

In a negligent employment case, a third party sues an employer for injuries caused by its employee. Unlike claims based on vicarious liability, which seek to make the employer indirectly liable for an employee's negligence, negligent employment theories are based on the negligence of the employer. Liability turns on an act by the employer that made injury to the third party reasonably foreseeable. An employer may be liable, even for acts of an employee (and sometimes an ex-employee) outside the scope of employment, if the employer knew or should have known that the employee posed an unreasonable risk of harm.

Elements of a negligent employment claim

Just as in all negligence suits, the injured party must prove certain elements in order to establish a valid claim. The basic elements are:

- duty
- breach
- cause in fact
- proximate cause
- damages.

Duty

A duty was owed by the employer if:

- an employment relationship existed between the defendant employer and the person who caused the injuries
- a sufficient connection existed between the plaintiff and the employer's business activities to impose a duty of care.

Breach

The duty owed by the employer is breached when:

- the employee was incompetent and the employer had actual knowledge that the employee was incompetent
- the employer failed to adequately investigate the employee's background, provide adequate training or adequately evaluate the employee's job performance, when an incompetent employee created a well-known risk of harm.

Cause in fact

The employer's negligence is a cause in fact of the plaintiff's injury when the injury was caused by the same characteristic that rendered the employee incompetent.

Proximate cause

The employer's negligence is the proximate (that is, legal) cause of the plaintiff's injuries if:

- the injury was reasonably foreseeable considering the information that an adequate personnel policy would have uncovered
- the failure to investigate itself created a specific type of risk and the plaintiff's injury falls within this risk
- the plaintiff's injury was the direct outcome of the employer's negligence.

Damage

Plaintiff was damaged by the employer's negligence.

Application

The direct negligence of the employer may be based on its decision to hire, retain, assign or promote an employee to a position for which he or she was unfit or on the employer's inadequate training or supervision.

When negligent employment theory applies

Negligent employment claims are brought when the injury occurs outside the usual workplace and when:

- the nature of the job makes an injury arising from contact between an incompetent or dangerous employee and a third party foreseeable
- the nature of the job either makes active supervision impracticable or necessarily places control in the hands of the employee, which typically allows the employee to engage in contact with the public without active supervision

- the nature of the job necessarily places the safety of third parties in the hands of the employee.

Some lawsuits seek damages for injuries that occurred after normal working hours, away from the job site or under circumstances clearly removed from work related tasks, duties and responsibilities. The success of most negligent employment claims depends on whether the employer knew or should have known of the employee's propensity to commit whatever action or inaction gave rise to the suit.

How to minimize exposure to claims

The following paragraphs contain information on how to minimize exposure to negligent hiring, retention or supervision claims.

- Develop an effective employment application form based on negligent employment concerns. Require the applicant to list every employer for the past seven to 10 years and explain any periods of unemployment. Require the applicant to list each supervisor at each prior employer. Review the applicant's employment application, specifically looking for gaps in the applicant's employment record and other unusual entries or omissions. However, as mentioned, employers should check the laws of the state in which they have operations to determine whether questions regarding unemployment status are permissible.

- Obtain the applicant's authorization to gather information from all former employers, educational institutions and personal references. This authorization should be included on the job application form and perhaps on separate, individual forms for each prior employer. Indemnification of prior employers and the prospective employer for liability arising out of such inquiries should also be included in the authorization.

- Contact each prior employer and each supervisor listed on the application. If the information provided by the applicant is insufficient, obtain further information, such as forwarding addresses. If a former employer is reluctant to give a reference, be sure to at least document that the reference has been contacted and an attempt was made to get the necessary background information regarding the applicant.

- Contact each personal reference listed on the application. Document all information received from personal references.

- Ask all former employers and personal references whether there is any reason for them to doubt the applicant's competency, honesty, trustworthiness or reliability. Also, ask whether they are aware of anything in the applicant's background that would affect their suitability for your employment, including whether the applicant has engaged in any violent, criminal or improper conduct in the past.

- Require that all employees who have served in the U.S. Armed Forces provide a copy of their DD-214 form to show that they were "honorably discharged." However, employers should be cautious and check their local and state laws, as questions that inquire into the existence, nature and extent of the applicant's service in the U.S. Armed Forces could pose problems.

- Check the driver's license and the driving record of any applicant who, if hired, will be required to drive in the course of their employment. Some states restrict inquiries into driving history. Check the applicable state laws.

  Note:
  Such a search may be covered by the Fair Credit Reporting Act (FCRA) if conducted by an outside agency.

- Determine whether it is necessary to conduct a criminal record search, based on the job that is to be filled, the information provided by the applicant on the application form, information learned from previous employers or personal references and information learned through the initial interview. Employers should keep in mind that the EEOC takes the position that arrest records "alone" cannot be used as "an absolute bar to employment" because a greater percentage of African-Americans and certain minorities tend to have arrest records than do whites.

- Conduct reference checks on employees referred by employment agencies. Do not rely solely on employment agencies to check references.

- Conduct reference checks even on temporary employees who will have employer sponsored access to the public.

- Do not offer any applicant employment until the pre-employment screening process has been completed.

- Consider informing applicants that employment is contingent upon a satisfactory reference check.

The employer's duty

An employer has a duty to make an adequate investigation of an applicant's fitness before hiring. The extent of the duty may vary with the circumstances as discussed herein. When an employer breaches this duty, the employer may be held liable for negligent hiring. The duty is breached when the employer hires an employee it knew or in the exercise of reasonable care should have known, was incompetent or unfit for the work assigned. "Incompetence" means that the employee possessed certain personal or physical characteristics that created an unreasonable risk to third parties.

The notion of risk creation implies that the injury producing conduct of the employee was predictable. In order to recover, the injured party may have to show a pattern of such conduct to establish that the past behavior had practical predictive value and justifies the conclusion that the particular employee was "incompetent." In some cases, plaintiffs have been awarded punitive damages if they are able to prove that the employer had knowledge of the prior behavior in question.

What constitutes adequate investigation of a prospective employee

A judge or jury must decide, after the fact, what would have constituted an "adequate investigation" given the particular situation. The scope of the duty to investigate is relative to the magnitude and likelihood of risk associated with a particular job. Jobs that pose the greatest risk to the public, like law enforcement, require the most extensive background checks. In some situations, an employer may face a no-win situation. If an initial investigation raises serious questions about a particular applicant's fitness, the employer may be found liable if it fails to take additional investigative steps.

Alternatively, if the employer made absolutely no effort to investigate the applicant, courts have considered this to be a total lack of care. In these situations, the court will usually not play the "what if" game to determine whether an investigation, if conducted, would have revealed sufficient information to have prevented the hiring. A well-documented and adequate investigation of an applicant, together with policies that eliminate incompetent applicants, can help employers avoid liability in negligent hiring cases.

Job applications

The job application is usually the first step an employer uses to gain information about an employee. In an effort to conduct an adequate investigation, an employer should use a form designed to obtain complete, accurate and useful information. (See also Chapter 02: Pre-employment issues.) State laws vary with regard to information that can be obtained from applicants. Check applicable state laws when developing an application form.

Authorization

The application should include authorization to obtain information from all former employers, educational institutions and other people mentioned on the form. Indemnification of prior employers and the prospective employer for liability arising out of such inquiries should also be included in the authorization.

Dishonesty may result in discharge

It is useful to prominently note on the form that failure to disclose information and dishonesty on the application may result in immediate discharge, whenever it may be discovered. This may encourage the applicant to take care in completing the form as well as quell the impulse to misrepresent qualifications and background information.

Unrequested information

An applicant is under no obligation to furnish information that is not specifically requested by the employer – for this reason the form should be carefully drafted to avoid omissions by the employee.

Credit history

The federal Fair Credit Reporting Act (FCRA), regulates, together with any applicable state law, businesses that supply credit reports. The FCRA specifically permits the furnishing of credit reports to prospective employers but requires certain notice be provided to the applicant. Some states provide greater protections to employees by prohibiting an employer from considering an applicant's credit history.

Drug testing

The doctrine of negligent hiring has been used to hold employers liable when their employees, because of intoxication or drug use, injured or assaulted others. Employers have, therefore, initiated drug and alcohol testing programs. Some states prohibit or limit pre-employment drug testing and, in others, employees have claimed that the tests violate their rights to privacy and that employers do not have a right to regulate what they do off the job.

HIV/AIDS testing

Federal law, such as the Americans with Disabilities Act (ADA), may protect people who are HIV positive from discriminatory employment acts. Additionally, state law may protect such individuals.

Negligent retention

Negligent retention is the breach of an employer's duty to be aware that an employee is unfit for the job and to take corrective action through retraining, reassignment or discharge. Negligent hiring is a breach of the employer's duty to investigate an employee's fitness before hiring him or her. The principal difference between negligent hiring and negligent retention is the time at which the employer gained knowledge of the employee's unfitness.

Negligent hiring occurs when, prior to the time the employee is actually hired, the employer knew or should have known of the employee's unfitness. The issue of liability primarily focuses on the adequacy of the employer's pre-employment investigation of the applicant's background.

Negligent retention occurs when, during the course of employment, the employer becomes aware or should have become aware of problems with an employee that indicate unfitness and the employer fails to take further action, such as an investigation, discharge or reassignment.

Employers are being sued because they failed to fire or reassign employees who later caused injuries or committed crimes. Because negligent hiring is similar to negligent retention, often the complaint will allege both claims. Issues and considerations discussed in regard to negligent hiring may also be applicable to negligent retention. Based on the specific facts, however, the court may make a distinction between negligence in hiring and negligence in retention.

Employer defenses

After-acquired evidence of employee wrongdoing

In a 1995 case, the U.S. Supreme Court held that evidence of employee misconduct, which is discovered after a discharge, does not act as a complete prohibition from recovery under the Age Discrimination in Employment Act (ADEA). However, the after-acquired evidence must be taken into consideration when fashioning an appropriate remedy for discriminatory discharge. The Supreme Court found that as a general rule, in cases in which the employer discovers that an employee engaged in misconduct of such severity that the employee would have been discharged, the employee may only recover back pay from the date of the unlawful discharge to the date the employer discovered the misconduct and is not entitled to reinstatement.

This case provides an incentive for employers to conduct aggressive independent investigations to verify information given in resumes and employment applications. Of course, in the case of post-hiring employee misconduct, it will be extremely difficult to prove that such evidence would have been discovered prior to the termination and the resulting litigation, because it is the termination itself and the resulting litigation that normally bring such matters to light. Employers should note that under some decisions, they must prove that they would have fired the employee, not simply that they could have done so.

Workers' compensation exclusivity defense

In some states, workers' compensation provides the exclusive remedy for covered employees who were injured on the job, while other states have created exceptions to this rule.

Further reducing the risk of litigation

- Whenever discharge is being considered and the employer considers giving the employee "one more chance," be certain to evaluate the situation the way a jury might in a negligent retention case.
- In any situation involving an individual with access to the public and potentially dangerous equipment, an injured party may criticize the employer's security procedures, hiring procedures and background screening. At trial, the employer may be accused of not recognizing potential "danger signs" even though those signs may not be noticeable to the average person. Because the risk to the public is greater in these situations, such employers are held to a higher degree of care to investigate and review employees to prevent foreseeable or reasonably foreseeable injuries.
- Employers should recognize that if they are aware of complaints of sexual harassment against an employee but do not take any corrective measures, they may be subject to suit by the person harassed, not only for sexual harassment under Title VII but also state tort theories including negligent retention.

- Because performance evaluations are an indication of an employee's continuing fitness/competence for the job held, employers should realize that in continuing to employ an employee whose performance evaluations suggest that the employee is unfit or incompetent, they are setting themselves up for a negligent retention claim.
- Employers should remember to re-evaluate and perhaps recheck references to ascertain an employee's fitness/competence for the new job if the employee is transferred to another job, particularly one with greater contact with fellow employees, customers and the public.

Union organizing activity

Chapter 17

The composition of the four-member National Labor Relations Board (NLRB) depends on the political party of the president of the United States. Democratic presidents tend to appoint pro labor members and Republican presidents lean toward pro-business members.

The decisions of the NLRB have been very pro-employer since Trump took office. The NLRB has the power to change its regulations without Congressional approval and has utilized this power to their advantage. For instance, they have begun reversing many of the Obama-era decisions that made it easier for unions to organize employees.

Twenty-seven states have "right-to-work" laws restricting unions. A handful of counties and municipalities also have passed their own versions on a local level. The best way for an employer to remain union free; however, is to create and maintain a workplace where employees see unions as irrelevant. An employer's ability to operate union free carries with it the obligation to establish the policies, procedures, practices and a work environment where unions are unnecessary and not "value added" in the eyes of employees.

Consistent with those objectives, every employer should develop a strategic action plan. The following is a suggested template for an "eight-point strategic action plan" to help employers create a work environment designed to make the company less vulnerable to union organizing and establish the necessary policies, procedures and practices to respond effectively to union organizing if and when it occurs.

Eight-point strategic action plan

1. **Make unions unnecessary**
   Because most union organizing is issue driven, it is critical that employers understand their employees' specific issues and concerns and develop effective strategies to resolve problems before employees turn to a labor union for possible solutions. Management at all levels must have a commitment to positive employee relations. An employer should establish an employee relations model built upon recognizing individual achievement and merit and responding to employee issues and concerns before employees look outside the company for resolution of their concerns.

2. **Conduct a comprehensive employee relations audit**
   Employers are encouraged to conduct an internal employee relations audit to assess potential issues and concerns as a first step. A critical aspect of an employee relations audit is to solicit information from employees regarding their concerns and issues by

using focus groups, individual interviews, surveys and/or any other proven method that will gain the needed input from employees. Employers should then use this information to analyze what the company is doing right, as well as areas that need improvement.

Conducting an employee opinion survey is the most effective method of obtaining unbiased input from all employees concerning their feelings about the company and the working climate. The survey should reach 100% of the employees, giving them the opportunity to respond confidentially, without fear of retribution for unfavorable comments. As a vehicle of upward communications, the survey will accomplish the following:

- Provide management with information concerning employees likes and dislikes and garner suggestions from all employees, not just the "squeaking wheels."
- Involve all employees and convey to them that the company recognizes that each of their opinions is important.
- Secure opinions about specific questions regarding personnel policies, wages and benefits, communications, supervision, job security, working conditions and several other critical employee relations areas.
- Ensure anonymity, thereby allaying fears the employees may have about frankly expressing their opinions.
- Overcome supervisory resistance by assuring everyone that the major purpose of the survey is to help them in their job. The fact is that good supervisors are not threatened by surveys because they view them as an opportunity to improve.

Management should then prepare an immediate action plan designed to provide solutions to problems uncovered. The employer should also inform employees about actions the company has or will take, why actions are being delayed and why certain actions are not feasible.

In addition, a comprehensive audit should also examine current policies, procedures and practices to ensure that they are both lawful and necessary to advance the goal of effective employee relations. Pay close attention to the tone and language used in company policies and procedures. Employee handbooks and policy manuals should not only serve to educate employees about company procedures and expectations, they also should be a positive employee relations tool.

3. **Respond to employee issues and concerns**
An effective employee relations audit should identify the major issues and concerns particular to the employer's workforce. Equipped with this information, the employer can then respond to employee issues and concerns. Notably, an employer's ability to solicit employee issues and concerns, as well as the employer's ability to implement changes to respond to those concerns, becomes severely limited once the employer has knowledge of active union organizing. However, if an employer routinely solicits employee issues and concerns, the employer will be in a much better position to prevent/resolve issues that cause employees to seek unionization and implement proactive measures to deal with those issues – sometimes even after organizing begins.

4. **Develop workplace leadership**
Cultivating leadership requires leadership training and accountability:

- **Leadership training**
  Because supervisors and managers are the key to positive employee relations, employers must provide them with the necessary training to develop the requisite skills of effective leadership. Managers and supervisors must be effective communicators. They also must:
  - understand employee rights and employer obligations to ensure compliance with employment laws
  - be able to effectively resolve employee conflicts
  - master the dos and don'ts of positive employee relations.

  Because of the critical role that supervisors and managers play in maintaining union free status, all levels of management should also be trained in union avoidance skills and techniques so they can identify union activity, respond effectively to pro-union arguments and successfully communicate the company's message to employees – without violating the law.

- **Accountability**
  Company leaders should be held accountable for effective employee relations. For instance, failure to deal effectively with employee concerns, employee turnover, charges and complaints should reflect negatively on the supervisors. Conversely, high employee morale and loyalty should reflect positively on them.

- **Adopt a union-free culture**
  Employers should consider developing a concise "position on unions" that describes the rationale for the company's objective to remain union free. Such a written policy can serve several important functions:
  - It states in unequivocal terms that the employer intends to remain union free by creating a workplace where employees see unions as unnecessary.
  - It expresses the company's commitment to positive employee relations – that supervisors and managers are committed to employee issues and concerns.
  - It provides the basis for supervisors and managers to explain the company's position to employees.

  An effective position on unions should:
  - clearly state the company wants to remain union free
  - emphasize the employer's commitment to communication
  - indicate that the company recognizes and rewards individual achievement
  - highlight company efforts to promote dignity and respect.

- **Identify supervisors**
  Supervisors are statutorily excluded from any bargaining unit. Moreover, those key leadership positions serve as the company's most effective tool in developing positive employee relations and provide the first line of defense against

unionization. "Supervisors" are defined under Section 2(11) of the National Labor Relations Act (NLRA) as:

> "... any individual having authority, in the interest of the employer, to hire, transfer, suspend, layoff, recall, promote, discharge, assign, reward or discipline other employees or responsibly to direct them or to adjust their grievances or effectively to recommend such action, if in connection with the foregoing the exercise of such authority is not of a merely routine or clerical nature, but requires the use of independent judgment."

Determining supervisor status for particular individuals can sometimes be difficult. In making this determination, therefore, consider the following:

- What authority does he or she have and what authority has he or she actually exercised?
- Job duties are critical – job titles are irrelevant.
- Do employees consider the individual to be a supervisor?
- Does the individual attend management meetings?
- Does the individual receive management training?
- What is the ratio of supervisors to supervised employees?
- Does the individual receive higher wages than employees?

Because of their regular daily contact with employees, front-line supervisors must exemplify the company's commitment to positive labor relations; they must listen and respond to employee issues and concerns and they must watch for any of the early warning signs of potential union activity.

5. **Develop effective communication mechanisms**

Critical to developing and maintaining positive employee relations is the development of effective workplace communication mechanisms. Elements of workplace communication include:

- Direct communication to employees:
  - clarify company expectations
  - explain policy and benefit changes.
- Input from employees to management:
  - identify employee concerns and issues
  - determine employee priorities
  - get employee input.
- Cross-communication between management:

    - Supervisors and managers must communicate well with one another and have a thorough understanding of policies and procedures in order to communicate effectively with employees.

- Analyze existing communications:

    - Does the communication media adequately and effectively reach all employees?

    - Is the company providing the type of information employees want and need in a way employees understand?

- Develop an effective union free communication strategy.

Employers that want to remain union free should implement a comprehensive communication strategy designed to educate employees about the risks and disadvantages of unionization well before there are signs of union activity. This communication plan becomes even more important in light of the NLRB's efforts through changing regulations to shorten the timeframe between when a petition is filed for an election and the election date.

Accordingly, employers should develop a communication platform designed to inform employees about the company's position on unions beginning at employee orientation and then periodically throughout their tenure of employment. General themes of an effective communications strategy include:

- **Emphasize company strengths**
  Competitive wages and benefits, a positive work environment, good personal relationships with employees, etc.

- **Address issues and concerns before union activity begins**

- **Identify union weaknesses**
  Costs of unionization, union corruption, dangers and risks of collective bargaining, strikes and the potential impact of the union on the work environment.

- **Present the impact of unionization**
  Union weaknesses versus proven company track record and strengths.

6. **Identify potential bargaining unit strategies**
As noted previously, when filing a petition, a union chooses the employee job classifications it wants in a proposed bargaining unit. Understandably, a union typically seeks a unit it believes will enable it to prevail in an election. Notably, unions are statistically more successful when organizing bargaining units of 50 employees or less and significantly less successful when the petitioned-for unit is much larger.

An employer can reduce its vulnerability to union organizing by making sure specific job classifications share a sufficient community of interests with other employees such that it would be more difficult for the union to isolate and target the smaller groups.

Any changes to operations or specific job duties, however, should be done before the employer is aware of any union organizing. Making such changes after organizing begins could be viewed solely as an impermissible attempt to undermine union activity.

7. **Implement "salting defense strategies"**
Salting is an aggressive union-organizing tactic in which a trained, paid union organizer obtains employment with a non-union company and then uses his or her position as an employee to gather information for the union and solicit signatures on union authorization cards. While it may seem unfair, union salting is lawful and employers cannot refuse to hire otherwise qualified candidates because they want to try to unionize the employer nor can the employer terminate an employee once hired merely because the employee intends to solicit support for the union.

   Accordingly, employers should carefully design lawful application procedures and hiring policies.

   Because one of the goals of the salting game is to intimidate the employer into making mistakes, every person involved in the recruiting process should be trained regarding what to expect from potential salts and how to respond lawfully.

8. **Implement effective policies and procedures to protect the workplace**
When confronted with potential union organizing, many employers struggle with the extent to which they can prevent non-employees and employee union organizers from engaging in organizing activity on the company premises. For instance, employers often question:

   - whether non-employees can be denied access to the workplace to discuss the union with workers
   - whether employees can discuss the union on "company time," and it needs to be noted that the NLRB has determined that employees are presumptively permitted to use company email systems during non-working time to engage in protected concerted activity, including union organizing
   - whether employees have a right to wear union buttons and/or pass out literature on company premises
   - whether employees can post pro-union literature on company bulletin boards or can solicit authorization cards from co-workers in the workplace.

   Under most circumstances, employers can prohibit non-employee union agents from entering the workplace.

   However, it would be unlawful for an employer to completely prohibit them. Generally, an employer can implement policies and procedures that restrict certain union related activities for legitimate business reasons. The extent of such restrictions, however, typically depends upon a number of factors, including, but not limited to:

   - the type of activity the employer is trying to restrict (such as handouts, solicitation, postings, email or Internet use)
   - the type of employer (such as manufacturing, healthcare, hospitality, construction or service)
   - the nature of the employer's property rights (such as private property, public property like shopping malls or retail stores or quasi-public property like hospitals, restaurants and hotels).

While the specific content of lawful solicitation/distribution rules varies depending on the circumstances, nondiscriminatory enforcement of all such policies and procedures is essential. Generally, this means that an employer must treat all types of communication the same; the employer cannot selectively enforce policies and procedures to limit or restrict only union-related communication or activities.

Chapter 18

Social media

For purposes of this chapter, social media includes all electronic social networking sites through which applicants and employees may congregate, such as Facebook, Twitter, various blog-hosting sites and LinkedIn. While there are hundreds, if not thousands, of such sites, the law regarding the use of social media in employment is still in its infancy. As there have been very few reported court cases regarding it, this chapter is limited to discussing potential issues that may arise in using social media in employment decisions, rather than providing definitive answers regarding such usage.

Generally, it is easiest to think about the employment issues regarding social media in two timeframes:

1. pre-hire screening
2. post-hire.

Pre-hire screening implications

The use of social media in the pre-hire screening of applicants for employment is fraught with peril. It is especially dangerous during the pre-interview stage, though risks continue to linger even thereafter. It is impossible to anticipate every single issue that might arise from using social media during pre-hire screening. However, the following sections address some of the major concerns.

Privacy

Many social media sites, including Facebook, contain postings that are available to the general public and those that are only available to a select group of persons. For instance, on Facebook, certain portions of a person's "page" are only available for viewing to persons who have been made "friends" of the poster. While it may not raise privacy implications for a potential employer to view the public portions of an applicant's Facebook or other social media page, it could cause privacy issues if the potential employer somehow was able to view the private portions of the page. For instance, if a potential employer coerced one of its employees who were "friends" with the applicant to provide access to the private portions of the applicant's page, it might constitute a legally actionable invasion of privacy.

Discrimination

Persons using social media commonly post pictures of themselves that may reveal their race, sex and national origin. They also often post information about their birth date, religion and marital status. It would not be legally prudent for a company to ask for such information on an employment application. It is equally imprudent for a potential employer to search social media for such information about applicants, especially before an interview has been conducted. Using such information when making employment decisions could result in discrimination claims under Title VII of the Civil Rights Act (Title VII).

Disabilities

Persons using social media frequently post information about their medical conditions and/or disabilities. Under the Americans with Disabilities Act (ADA), companies cannot make inquiries of applicants that are likely to reveal the existence of a disability until the post-hire/pre-employment time period. It likely would be a violation of the ADA for a potential employer to utilize social media to find out such information during an earlier time period.

Sexual orientation

Although private employees are not currently protected at the federal level, public employees are protected. Additionally, many states and even some municipalities, prohibit discrimination based on sexual orientation. Persons using social media frequently either specifically state their sexual orientation or make posts about events in their lives that make their sexual orientation obvious. Potential employers who use social media in the hiring process open themselves up to potential claims that the real reason an applicant was not hired was because the potential employer had learned of the applicant's sexual orientation.

Spare time pursuits

Some states prohibit companies from refusing to hire applicants based upon certain specified spare time pursuits. For instance, some states, especially some that produce tobacco, make it unlawful for a company to refuse to hire someone based upon their tobacco use. Since social media users frequently post comments or pictures regarding such spare time activities, a potential employer may face a lawsuit for refusing to hire someone who it found out had engaged in such protected pursuits through use of social media during the hiring process.

Fake pages

It is not uncommon to find fake social media pages, where someone creates a social media page claiming to be someone else, such as a friend, enemy, co-worker or celebrity. Students in high school and college are especially known for creating such pages as pranks. Since it is difficult, if not impossible to determine whether or not the social media page being viewed is legitimate, companies should be especially leery about using any information learned from them in employment decisions.

It is generally recommended that employers do not investigate social media sites before hiring a candidate. Indeed, some states including Minnesota, are considering barring employers from requiring workers and job candidates to make their social media accounts available for review.

Post-hire implications

As can be expected, some of the pre-hire implications of using social media will also apply to the post-hire time period. Some of the additional major post-hire issues with using social media in employment decisions are discussed herein.

Discrimination

The most common area of concern for employers under Title VII of the Civil Rights Act in the post-hire timeframe is their employees' use of social media to unlawfully harass each other or others. Statements made online can constitute legally actionable harassment just as oral statements can. In fact, since the statements on social media sites are electronically printed, they are even more dangerous.

Protected activities

Under the National Labor Relations Act (NLRA), even non-union employees can engage in "protected concerted activity" regarding certain aspects of employment (such as discussing working conditions). Companies should be aware that employees likewise have a right to do so using social media. Therefore, companies should be careful not to discipline employees for making statements on a social media site that might constitute protected concerted activity under the NLRA.

Whistleblowers

Most states prohibit employers from discharging employees because they report that the employer has engaged in unlawful activity. Depending upon the wording of a state's whistleblower statute, it is possible that an employee's statement in social media that his or her employer is engaging in unlawful activity might be protected.

Defamation

Employees can make defamatory comments in social media about other employers, vendors or customers that might subject the company to potential liability.

Trade secrets

Employees sometimes post confidential trade secret information in social media that belongs to their employers or, sometimes even competitors or vendors, which can create liability for the company.

State laws

Some states have enacted laws prohibiting employers from requesting social media passwords from applicants or employees or demanding access to social media accounts.

Policy basics

Many companies are now implementing social media policies. Some basic tips for doing so are as follows:

- A social media policy should advise employees of what is and is not permissible in their postings. For instance, employers should make it clear that their other policies (such as harassment, equal employment opportunity and the like), also apply to postings on social media. Employees should also be warned not to post information that is defamatory or breaches privacy or trade secrets. However, employers should ensure that any policy is compliant with the National Labor Relations Act (NLRA) and does not broadly prohibit employees from making disparaging comments about the company, from using company logos or disclosing confidential or proprietary information.
- Employers should consider requiring employees to include a disclaimer in their social media postings indicating that the views expressed are theirs alone and do not represent those of the company. This is especially important where the employee has indicated the name of his or her employer.
- Employers should consider including a statement advising employees to respect copyrights when posting on social media. Copyrighted material should only be posted after obtaining permission from the copyright owner.
- Employees should be warned not to link or otherwise refer to the company website without obtaining the advance written permission of the company.
- The company should reserve the right to monitor websites, social networking sites and blogs.
- Employees should be advised that their social media activity cannot interfere with his or her job. In fact, many employers may want to entirely prohibit employees from engaging in social media networking during work time.

Federal recordkeeping requirements

Appendix

A

Various federal and state statutes require employers to keep employee applications and other employment information for a specified period of time. The person charged with the administration of personnel files and applications is responsible for ensuring that the required information is retained in conformity with the following guidelines.

> **Note:**
> Many states also have their own recordkeeping requirements.

FMLA – Family and Medical Leave Act

Type of records	Retention period	Coverage
Payroll records for each employee including full name, identification number, home address, date of birth if under the age of 19, sex, occupation, day and time workweek begins, hours worked each day and week, total daily or weekly earnings, overtime compensation, basis of overtime computation, total additions to or deductions from wages, total wages for each pay period, date of payment and the pay period covered by the payment.	Three years from last date of entry for employers covered by the FLSA	All employers covered by the FLSA (one or more employees). FMLA covers employers with 50 or more employees during 20 or more calendar workweeks in either the current or preceding calendar year.
Individual employment contracts, collective bargaining agreements, plans, trusts, certificates and required notices.	Three years from last effective date	All employers covered by the FLSA (one or more employees).

Type of records	Retention period	Coverage
Sales and purchase records by total dollar volume, weekly, month or quarterly.	Three years	All employers covered by the FLSA (one or more employees).
Supplementary basic records, including worksheets showing daily starting and stopping time of employees, wage rate schedules and work time schedules.	Two years	All employers covered by the FLSA (one or more employees).
Order, shipping and billing records.	Two years	All employers covered by the FLSA (one or more employee).
Records of additions to/deductions from each employee's wages; employee purchase orders; records used in determining amount and computation of addition / reduction.	Two years	All employers covered by the FLSA (one or more employees).
Any certificates of age (if applicable). Employer may be required to keep additional wage and hour records on employees in certain specialized occupations and on employees who may be otherwise exempt from FLSA.	Until termination of employment	All employers covered by the FLSA or child labor laws (one or more employees).

Title VII of the Civil Rights Act ADA – Americans with Disabilities Act

Type of records	Retention period	Coverage
Any personnel or employment records, including application forms that an employer makes or keeps and records related to hiring, promotions, demotions, transfers, layoffs, terminations, rates of pay, selections to training programs and the like.	One year from the time the record is made or the personnel action is taken, whichever is later	Employers covered by Title VII (15 or more employees in each of 20 consecutive calendar weeks of the current or preceding year).

Type of records	Retention period	Coverage
All personnel records relevant to a charge filed with or actions brought by the Equal Employment Opportunity Commission (EEOC).	Until final disposition of the charge or action	Employers covered by Title VII (15 or more employees in each of 20 consecutive calendar weeks of the current or preceding year).
EEO-1 report filed with the EEOC.	While current	Employers covered by Title VII with 100 or more employees.

ADEA – Age Discrimination in Employment Act

Type of records	Retention period	Coverage
Payroll records containing each employee's name, address, date of birth, occupation, rate of pay and compensation earned each week.	Three years	Employers covered by the ADEA (20 or more employees for each working day in each of 20 or more calendar weeks in the current or preceding calendar year).
Any personnel records that an employer makes and that are related to: • job applications and inquiries • promotions, transfers, selections for training, layoffs, recalls, discharges • job orders submitted to agencies or unions for the recruitment of employees' test papers • results of physical exams • any advertisements of notices of job opportunities.	One year 90 days for applicants for temporary jobs	Employers covered by ADEA.
Employee benefit plans and seniority and merit systems.	One year after termination of plan	Employers covered by the ADEA.

EPA - Equal Pay Act

Type of records	Retention period	Coverage
Any records that relate to the payment of wages, evaluations, job wage rates, job descriptions, merit systems, seniority, agreements or other collective bargaining matters that explain the basis of a wage differential to employees of the opposite sex.	Two years	Employers covered by the FLSA (one or more employees).
All records required to be kept by the FLSA.	Three years	Employers covered by the FLSA.

OSH Act - Occupational Safety and Health Act

Type of records	Retention period	Coverage
A log and summary of all recordable occupational injuries and illnesses for each establishment (OSHA Form 200) and a supplementary record (OSHA Form 101). **Note:** Employers also required to report any worker fatality within eight hours and any amputation, loss of an eye or hospitalization of a worker within 24 hours.	Five years	Private sector employers covered by the OSH Act with 11 or more full or part time employees.
Employee exposure records on toxic substances and harmful physical agents (including environmental and biological monitoring information and material safety data sheets).	30 years	All employers covered by the OSH Act.

Type of records	Retention period	Coverage
Employee medical records (including medical histories; examinations and test results; medical opinions and diagnoses; description of treatment and prescriptions; and employee complaints).	Duration of employment plus 30 years	All employers covered by the OSH Act.

IRCA – Immigration Reform and Control Act

Type of records	Retention period	Coverage
Form I-9	Three years after the date of hire; or one year after date the employment is terminated, whichever is later.	Employers employing persons to perform labor or services in return for wages or other pay.

ERISA – Employee Retirement Income Security Act

Type of records	Retention period	Coverage
Records providing basis for all required plan descriptions or reports or necessary to certify any related information, including vouchers, worksheets, receipts and applicable resolutions.	Six years after filing date of documents	Private-sector companies that offer pension plans to employees.
Records pertaining to each employee-participant in the plan for determinations of benefits that are due or may become due.	As long as relevant	Private-sector companies that offer pension plans to employees.

Note:
The IRS also recommends keeping certain employee tax related documents.

Appendix

B

Posting requirements

Employers are required to maintain specified postings in two types of locations:

- the hiring location where applicants are first received
- the work location.

Notices posted in the work location must be in a place where the notice can be readily observed by the employees in the course of their activities, such as bulletin boards near time clocks, in designated department locations or in cafeterias. Employers are required to post unaltered posters. Multiple locations are usually required for separate employee units.

Federal posting requirements

The following postings are required by federal law. Many posters are available via the Internet at:

- https://www.dol.gov/general/topics/posters

1. **Your Rights Under the Fair Labor Standards Act (Federal Minimum Wage) (FLSA)**
   Poster provided by the U.S. Department of Labor Wage and Hour Division. For more information, call:
   - (866) 487-9243
2. **Family and Medical Leave Act (FMLA)**
   Poster provided by the U.S. Department of Labor Wage and Hour Division. For more information, call:
   - (202) 693-0066
3. **Employee Polygraph Protection Act (EPPA)**
   Poster provided by the U.S. Department of Labor Wage and Hour Division. For more information, call:
   - (866) 487-9243
4. **Job Safety and Health Protection**
   Poster provided by the Occupational Safety and Health Administration (OSHA). For more information, call:

◈ (800) 321-6742

5. **Know Your Rights: Workplace Discrimination is Illegal**
   Poster provided by the Equal Employment Opportunity Commission (EEOC). For more information, call:

   ◈ (800) 669-4000

6. **Uniformed Services Employment and Reemployment Rights Act (USERRA)**
   Poster provided by the U.S. Department of Labor (DOL). For more information, visit:

   ◈ https://www.dol.gov/agencies/vets/programs/userra/poster

State-specific posting requirements

State	Required posters
Alabama	• Child labor law • Workplace violence prevention poster • Human trafficking • Workers' compensation notice • Unemployment compensation fraud • Unemployment compensation partial claims notice • Unemployment compensation – Your Job Insurance
Alaska	• Summary of Wage and Hour Act • Emergency information • Safety and health protection • Unemployment insurance • Required notice to separated employees • Workers' compensation • Child labor law
Arizona	• Notification of constructive discharge • Discrimination is prohibited in employment • Notice to employees: You are covered by unemployment insurance • Smoke-free Arizona • Safety and health protection on the job • Workers' compensation • Exposure to bodily fluids • Exposure to MRSA, spinal meningitis or tuberculosis
Arkansas	• Minimum wage/overtime/child labor/wage collection

State	Required posters
Arkansas (continued)	• Unemployment insurance • Right to know (public employees) • Workers' compensation • Job safety and health • Hand washing (restaurants and food handling businesses) • Human trafficking poster (hotels, motels, private clubs with liquor permits and transportation-related businesses)
California	• Notice of inspection by immigration agencies • Wage orders • Minimum wage • Paid sick leave • Payday notice • Safety and health protection on the job • Emergency telephone numbers • Access to medical and exposure records • Operating rules for industrial trucks (for companies using forklifts and other industrial trucks or tow tractors) • Injuries caused by work • Workers' compensation • Whistleblower protections • No smoking • Farm labor contractor statement of pay rates (farm labor contractors) • Prevailing wage • Workplace harassment and discrimination • Transgender rights in the workplace • Pregnancy disability leave (employers with 49 or more employees) • Family care and disability leave (employers with 50 or more employees) • Notice to employees regarding insurance benefits • Unemployment insurance benefits • Voting leave • Human trafficking (farm labor contractors)
Colorado	• Paid leave and whistleblower • Overtime and minimum pay standards

State	Required posters
Colorado (continued)	• Anti-discrimination • Unemployment insurance • Workers compensation • Notice to employer of injury • Pay day notice • Pregnancy accommodations
Connecticut	• Electronic monitoring (if applicable) • Administrative regulations • Prevailing wage law • Section 7 of Public Act 19-1 • Postings specific to mercantile, retail, restaurant and food service, including child labor
Delaware	• • Sexual harassment notice • Consolidated employment laws (including discrimination, minimum wage, payment of wages, workers' compensation, breaks, child labor)
District of Columbia	• DC Family Medical Leave Act (DCFMLA) • Equal Employment Opportunity (EEO) • Accrued sick and safe leave COVID-19 leave under DCFMLA • DC Parental Leave Act • LGBTQ diversity in the workplace • The right to breastfeed • Protecting Pregnant Workers Act • Pregnancy and parental rights in the workplace • Child labor • Minimum wage and overtime • Living wage • Building Services Act • Wage theft notice to hire • Unemployment compensation • Workers' compensation • Occupational safety and health
Florida	• Prohibition of discrimination • Minimum wage

State	Required posters
Florida (continued)	• Reemployment assistance program • Child labor laws • Workers' compensation • Recipients of federal financial assistance
Georgia	• Agribusiness workplace posters • Equal pay • Workers' compensation • Unemployment compensation and insurance • Employer vacation
Hawaii	• Employment discrimination • Minimum wage/Overtime/Payment of wages • Unemployment insurance • Workers' compensation • Job safety and health • Disability compensation • Whistleblower protection • Breastfeeding in the workplace • Dislocated workers/Plant closings • Human trafficking
Idaho	• Equal employment opportunity • Minimum wage • Unemployment compensation • Workers' compensation • Anti-discrimination
Illinois	• Your rights under Illinois employment laws (Wage Payment Collection Act, Child Labor Law, Minimum Wage Law, Equal Pay Act, Victims' Economic Security and Safety Act and the One Day Rest in Seven Act) • Victims' Economic Security and Safety Act • Sexual harassment and job discrimination • Emergency care for choking* • Unemployment insurance benefits • Workers' compensation • Smoke free Illinois • Day and temporary labor services

State	Required posters
Illinois (continued)	• Pregnancy rights • Occupational safety and health • Illinois service member leave • Employee classifications (construction contractors) • Consumer Coverage Disclosure Act
Indiana	• Minimum wage • Job safety and health • Unemployment compensation • Workers' compensation • Teen work hours • Application for wage claim
Iowa	• Equal employment opportunity • Job safety and health • Minimum wage • Unemployment compensation and insurance • Workers' compensation • No smoking • Summary of work-related injuries and illnesses
Kansas	• Equal employment opportunity • Child labor law • Unemployment compensation • Workers' compensation • No smoking
Kentucky	• Equal employment opportunity • Wage discrimination because of sex • Wage and hour laws • Job safety and health • Child labor law • Unemployment insurance • Workers' compensation

State	Required posters
Louisiana	• Age discrimination • Sickle cell trait nondiscrimination • Genetic discrimination • Out of state motor vehicles • Child labor law • Workers' compensation • Earned income credit • National Guard • Payment of wages • Unemployment insurance • Whistleblower protections (public employers) • Pregnancy rights • Equal opportunity (if distributing federal funds)
Maine	• Sexual harassment • Regulation of employment • Child labor laws • Minimum wage • Job safety and health (public sector) • Video display terminal operators' rights • Whistleblower protection act • Employment security act • Workers' compensation • Human trafficking
Maryland	• Employment discrimination • Equal pay • Wage and hour (including notice to tipped employees) • Child labor law • Job safety and health • Health insurance coverage • Unemployment insurance • Workers' compensation • Earned sick and safe leave

State	Required posters
Massachusetts	• Fair employment • Minimum wage/Overtime/Child labor • Earned sick time • Parental leave • Safety and health • Temporary worker right to know • Chemical right-to-know workplace (public employees) • Domestic worker rights • Unemployment compensation and insurance • Workers' compensation • Paid family and medical leave • No smoking
Michigan	• Discrimination prohibited • Minimum wage and overtime • Paid medical leave • Job safety and health • SDS locations (for companies with hazardous chemicals) • Youth employment • Unemployment compensation • Whistleblower protection
Minnesota	• Age discrimination • Minimum wage • Job safety and health • Unemployment compensation • Workers' compensation
Mississippi	• Unemployment compensation • Workers' compensation
Missouri	• Discrimination in employment • Workers' compensation • Unemployment benefits • Minimum wage • Youth employment

State	Required posters
Missouri (continued)	• Discrimination in housing (businesses involved in the sale or rental of housing) • Discrimination in public accommodations (businesses doing business in places open to the public) • Notice to victims of domestic and sexual violence leave time allowed
Montana	• Wage and hour • Unemployment compensation • Workers' compensation • Discrimination is against the law • Clean Indoor Air At • Pregnant employees • Persons with disabilities • Fair housing • Agricultural employers have multiple required posters
Nebraska	• Minimum wage • Discrimination prohibited • Unemployment compensation and insurance
Nevada	• Rules to be observed by employers • Job training and employment programs • Sick leave • Personal protective equipment • Lie detector tests • Domestic violence • Domestic workers • Annual minimum wage bulletin • *Paid leave • Discrimination • Pregnant workers • Unemployment insurance • Emergency phone numbers • Fraud and abuse hotline • Safety and health • Workers' compensation • Alcohol/Drug free workplace policy statement

State	Required posters
New Hampshire	• Equal pay • Protective legislation* • Right to know* • Whistleblower protection act* • Workers' compensation* • Independent contractor or employee * • Minimum wage
New Jersey	• Discrimination • Reporting and recordkeeping requirements under state wage, benefit and tax laws • SAFE Act • Family leave insurance • Earned sick leave • Wage payment • Wage and hour abstract • Child labor laws • Workplace smoking • Schedule of minors' hours • Conscientious Employee Protection Act (whistleblower) • Unemployment and temporary disability benefits • Gender equity • Safety and health (public employees) • Misclassification of independent contractors • Workers' compensation
New Mexico	• Human rights • Job safety and health • Minimum wage • Unemployment insurance • Workers' compensation • Human trafficking
New York	• Veteran's benefits and services • Retaliatory action by employers • Discrimination

State	Required posters
New York (continued)	• Minimum wage • Job safety and health • Public work/prevailing wage rates • Public work project • No smoking • Workers' compensation and disability benefits • Unemployment insurance • Criminal conviction records • Fair play (construction industry) • Mandatory nurse overtime (healthcare industry) • Fringe benefits and hours • Expression of breastmilk • Equal pay • Sexual harassment • Notice of pay • Posting of hours for minors
North Carolina	• Consolidated workplace labor laws • Occupational safety and health protection (including unemployment compensation and workers' compensation insurance) • Workers' compensation notice • Unemployment insurance certificate of coverage
North Dakota	• Minimum wage and work conditions • Unemployment compensation/insurance • Workforce safety and insurance
Ohio	• Minimum wage • Minor labor laws • Workers' compensation • Unemployment compensation • Workplace domestic violence • Fair employment practices • Risk reduction (public employees) • No smoking

State	Required posters
Oklahoma	• Workers' compensation • Minimum wage • Unemployment compensation • Occupational safety and health (public employees) • E-Verify participation • Right to work • Whistleblowers
Oregon	• Paid leave notice • Breaks/Overtime • Family leave • Minimum wage • Job safety and health • Unemployment compensation • Workers' compensation • Equal pay law • Victims of domestic violence, harassment, sexual assault and stalking • Sick time • No smoking • Live entertainment workers (entertainment industry) • Predictive scheduling (retail, hospitality and food service employers with 500+ employees) • Notice to agricultural workers (agriculture industry)
Pennsylvania	• Equal pay • Minimum wage/Overtime • Equal opportunity and fair practices • Right to know (public sector) • Unemployment compensation (also, separate poster for state employees) • Workers' compensation • Child labor • Hours of work for minors • No smoking

State	Required posters
Rhode Island	• Pay Equity Act • Discrimination is illegal (including on basis of pregnancy or criminal history) • Pregnancy discrimination • Minimum wage • Parental and family medical leave (50+ employees) • Right to know • Workers' compensation • Unemployment and temporary disability benefits • Workplace smoking • Sexual harassment • Prevailing wage (government-financed projects) • Child labor
South Carolina	• Discrimination • Labor law abstract • Unemployment compensation • Workers' compensation
South Dakota	• Reemployment assistance • Safety on the job
Tennessee	• Discrimination • Wage regulation/Child labor • No smoking • Job safety and health • Unemployment compensation and insurance • Workers' compensation
Texas	• Payday law • Unemployment compensation • Workers' compensation (four separate) • Notice of ombudsman program • Earned income tax credit • Right to remain silent (public employers) • Hazard communication program (public employers) • Job service complaint system (public employers)

State	Required posters
Utah	• Job safety and health (10+ employees) • Unemployment compensation • Workers' compensation
Vermont	• Child labor • Healthcare whistleblower protection • Safety records • Minimum wage • Parental and family leave • Earned sick leave • Sexual harassment • Employer's liability and workers' compensation • Workers' compensation reinstatement rights • Unemployment compensation • Crime victims • Pregnancy accommodations
Virginia	• Credit for low-income individuals/social services • Unemployment compensation • Workers' compensation • Occupational safety and health protection
Washington	• Notice to employees regarding on-the-job injuries • Your rights as a worker • Job safety and health • Domestic violence resources • Paid family and medical leave • Unemployment benefits • Specialized posters for religious organizations, fishing boat workers and agricultural employers
West Virginia	• Human rights • Parental leave (state governments and county boards of education) • Minimum wage • Nurses overtime and patient safety (hospitals) • Wage payment law • Drug and alcohol-free workplace (state government)

State	Required posters
West Virginia (continued)	• Prohibited workplace harassment (state government) • Whistleblower law (state government) • Unemployment compensation • Workers' compensation • Smoking restrictions • Workplace security (public employers)
Wisconsin	• Fair employment law • Family and medical leave • Bone marrow and organ donation leave (50+ employees) • Plant closing/Layoff (50+ employees) • Minimum wage • Minimum wage, workers with disabilities • Child labor hours and days of work • Protections against use of honesty testing devices • Retaliation protection for healthcare workers • Unemployment compensation and insurance • Healthcare benefits cessation (if applicable) • Public employee health and safety (public employers) • Hazardous chemicals (public employers)
Wyoming	• Unemployment insurance • Attention employees and applicants • Workers' compensation • Workers' rights • Minimum wage • Health and safety protection on the job

Index

M

Wages and Hours – An Employer's Guide

The Department of Labor estimates that nearly 70% of employers are in violation of the Fair Labor and Standards Act (FLSA). With fines and penalties, small errors in wage and hour administration can snowball quickly into embarrassing and expensive situations for your company. When to pay, who to pay, how much to pay – there are so many questions employers have to answer! **Wages and Hours – An Employer's Guide** is written in plain English and includes a detailed table of contents and easy-to-use indexes, so you'll quickly find the information you need to make a decision. In addition to in-depth material concerning the FLSA, this guide is complete with state-by-state charts breaking down state-specific and local regulations. Written by attorneys at Squire Patton Boggs.

Hiring, Firing and Discipline for Employers

This book is designed to help you avoid the many pitfalls that await employers in three of the most treacherous areas of the employment cycle: hiring, firing and discipline. Get an in-depth look at the do's and don'ts and find the answers you need! In addition to the laws you must comply with, you'll also find key tips that will help you manage your employees on a day-to-day basis. Includes chapters on: pre-employment issues, background checks, new hire reporting, employment contracts, interviews, layoffs and MORE! Written by attorneys at Ford & Harrison LLP.

Workplace Safety and Health Compliance Manual

The Occupational Safety and Health Act of 1970 (the OSH Act) has been the principal force of change acting to reduce work-related injuries, deaths and diseases in American workplaces. It has led to the issuance of hundreds of safety and health regulations that affect every type of workplace – from the clerical office, to the industrial plant, to the construction site. This publication makes understanding the OSH Act and the standards/regulations of the Occupational Safety and Health Administration (OSHA) easy, so you'll know what to do, how to do it and a little bit of why. That means you get the answers you need fast, so you can get back to work faster. Written by Ed Foulke, Jr., previously of the Occupational Safety and Health Administration, a lead attorney at Fisher & Phillips LLP.

Employee Benefits – An Employer's Guide

The laws governing employee benefits are very detailed and complex. Benefits take many forms, from holiday pay to complicated pension plans. This guide is intended to provide a well rounded overview of the complex principal laws that apply when an employer provides benefits for its employees. From basic definitions to information on particular types of benefits, this guide includes in-depth explanations, tips for compliance and a breakdown of benefit types to keep your business out of trouble and in compliance. Written by the attorneys at Ogletree Deakins LLP.

A Guide to FMLA and ADA

This guide walks you through the many complicated procedures associated with keeping your business in compliance with the Family and Medical Leave Act (FMLA) and the Americans with Disabilities Act (ADA). As an employer, you are responsible for seeing to the needs of your employees, and this guide helps you navigate the complex situations that arise when an employee requires medical leave or a reasonable accommodation for a disability. Failure to comply with the FMLA and ADA can lead to costly penalties. That's why this plain English publication includes tips and tricks, forms, checklists and more to keep you out of trouble and in compliance with the law. Written by Nancy Holt of Ford & Harrison LLP.

Employment Verification – An Employer's Guide to Immigration, I-9 and E-Verify

This guide walks you through the many complicated procedures associated with verifying the work authorization of your employees and maintaining a business that is in compliance with the Immigration Reform and Control Act (IRCA). Enforcement of these immigration laws has never been greater and this appears to be part of the trend to increase worksite enforcement. But with our informative, plain-English guide, you'll have all the information you need to stay in compliance and out of trouble, saving you money and headaches. It includes tips and tricks, forms, checklists and more! Written by attorneys with Messner Reeves.

Step 1: SELECT YOUR MANUALS

Publication Name	Qty	Price	Total
Wages and Hours – An Employer's Guide		$75	
Hiring, Firing and Discipline for Employers		$75	
Workplace Safety and Health Compliance Manual		$75	
Employee Benefits – An Employer's Guide		$75	
A Guide to ADA and FMLA		$75	
Employment Verification – An Employer's Guide to Immigration and I-9		$75	
		Total:	

FEDBOOKS23

Step 2: PAYMENT AND SHIPPING INFO

☐ Invoice ☐ Check enclosed ☐ Credit Card

Name

Title

Company

Shipping Address (We ship UPS. No P.O. boxes, please.)

City | State | Zip

Phone | Fax

Email

Number of Employees

Card # (Please circle: VISA, MasterCard, AMEX, Discover)

Expiration Date | Security Code

Step 3: PLACE YOUR ORDER

Online Visit www.hrsimple.com/shop/federal

Phone Call toll-free 866-439-2227.

Fax Fax this order form to 312-629-5347.

Mail Mail this order form with check payable to:

American Chamber of Commerce Resources
1033 S. Claremont Ave.
Chicago, IL 60612

100% SATISFACTION GUARANTEE:

If you're not completely satisfied with our publications, simply return them and we will give you a full refund on your purchased items!

Get an in-depth look at our publications online at www.hrsimple.com/solutions